TAKASHI MATSUGI and ALOIS OBERHAUSER (Eds.)

Interactions Between Economy and Ecology

Schriften zu Regional- und Verkehrsproblemen in Industrie- und Entwicklungsländern

Herausgegeben von Theodor Dams und Joachim Klaus

Band 59

Interactions Between Economy and Ecology

edited by

Takashi Matsugi
Alois Oberhauser

Duncker & Humblot · Berlin

Die Deutsche Bibliothek – CIP-Einheitsaufnahme

Interactions between economy and ecology /
ed. by Takashi Matsugi ; Alois Oberhauser. –
Berlin : Duncker und Humblot, 1994
(Schriften zu Regional- und Verkehrsproblemen in Industrie- und Entwicklungsländern ; Bd. 59)
ISBN 3-428-08162-5
NE: Matsugi, Takashi [Hrsg.]; GT

Fotoprint: Berliner Buchdruckerei Union GmbH, Berlin
Printed in Germany

ISSN 0582-0170
ISBN 3-428-08162-5

Gedruckt auf alterungsbeständigem (säurefreiem) Papier
gemäß der ANSI-Norm für Bibliotheken

Editors' Foreword

This publication contains the papers of the 14th Joint Seminar of the Faculties of Economics at the University of Nagoya and the Albert-Ludwigs-Universität, Freiburg. It covers a topic which is of great relevance now and will be of even greater importance in the future: "Interactions between Economy and Ecology". The editors are delighted that this volume, like its predecessors is published in our series.

The following papers cover a variety of aspects of ecological policy, ranging from theoretical basic research, empirical studies, business experiences to legal problems. The interested reader will get a good insight into different points of view of environmental policy.

The Faculty of Economics of the Albert-Ludwigs-Universität wishes to thank the Ministerium für Bildung und Wissenschaft of the Landesregierung Baden-Württemberg, the Rektorat and the Akademisches Auslandsamt, the City of Freiburg and the Regierungspräsidium for substantial financial support of the meeting in Freiburg. Furthermore we are grateful to the European Parliament in Strasbourg/France, the Kehrichtbeseitigungsanlage (refuse disposal plant) in Schaffhausen/Switzerland and the Badische Stahlwerke in Kehl for their aid in carrying out the Seminar and the pertinent study tours. Last but not least the Faculty would also like to thank the Wissenschaftliche Gesellschaft of the Albert-Ludwigs-Universität who made this publication possible by financing the printing.

Freiburg, June 1994

Theodor Dams Joachim Klaus

Table of Contents

Japanese and German Positions in the International Debate on Economical and Ecological Issues

Theodor Dams

1. Common concern and responsibility in the 90s

Both Japan and Germany rank among the richest highly industrialized countries, and both have historical similaritics in their transition from an agrarian to a post-industrial (affluent) society (see: K. Ohkawa and H. Kohama, 1989; W. Hoffmann, 1931; Th. Dams, 1987). But there are at least two great differences in economic development which are closely connected with ecological problems in the past and at present time.

(1) Japanese economical development has started later than in Germany (Prussia) in the last third of the 19th century, mainly after World War II, and resulted in very high growth rates in a relative short period (see: Th. Dams, 1987, p. 12O).

(2) This rapid economic growth has been accompanied by a heavy concentration of population and industry in a geographically very limited area along the coast (4OO km) based on the economic potentials of Tokyo and Osaka - In Germany there is a wider spatial spread of industrial locations, more or less in eight areas from north to south (see: Th. Dams, 1957).

In Japan, the industrial growth in a very short time span as well as the regional density of population and working places had caused severe ecological problems. In Germany environmental damages of the magnitudes observed in Japan do not exist. Nevertheless, the German society is confronted with ecological challenges, too, but of another type and dimension.

Both countries - Japan and Germany - are aware of the international ecological challenges; the Brundtland-Report (1984) has stimulated an intensive discussion on greater common responsibility on world wide level, followed by the Stockholm Initiative on Global Security and Governance (April 1991). The summit of all these efforts was the United Nations Conference on Environment and Development (UNCED, Rio de Janeiro 1992).

The ecological positions of Japan and Germany should be considered in relation to the debate in the framework of the international conferences mentioned above. We should realize that the instrumental inputs on the national level to protect the environment and to take into account the ecological problems are closely linked with and will influence the openness to formulate the goals and aims on the international level. And both countries have tried to timely present their concepts in order to bridge the gap between the national and international objectives. Divergent positions have to be reflected in relation to the impact of solutions on competitiveness in international markets.

2. UNCED - positions and impacts for Japan and Germany

The adoption of the Rio-Charter and the Agenda 21 by Japan and Germany is a common basis for a critical consideration of the orientation of politics concerned in both countries.

The "Earth Summit" (UNCED, 1992) has been joined by Governments officials, representatives of Non-Governmental Organizations (NGO's), private business people and members of the research institutions; all of these groups mentioned above have carefully prepared working papers; sometimes these groups have organized special meetings (NGO's, Industrial Federations, etc.) in order to lobby efficiently.

Japan and Germany have presented reports covering their national policy as well as the international objectives linked with the UNCED. Private enterprises (MNCs) have elaborated special documents for this purpose. Last but not least, the Non-Governmental Organizations have demonstrated their strong engagement by presenting the close relationship between poverty and ecological damage in Developing Countries and the production-consumption structures of affluent societies.

The results and recommendations of the Rio-Conference have been signed by Japan and Germany. Both countries have noticed that they will follow the guidelines of the Memorandum of this conference, which should be more than "moral suasion".

A short description of the common positions of Japan and Germany leads to the following conclusions: For the first time, the Rio-Declaration has formulated the principle of "the appropriate inclusion of others" (a wording formulated by R.A. Dahl and Ch.E. Lindblom, 1953). What is the notion of "appropriate inclusion of others" in the ecological context? The following objectives have been formulated: accounting for the need of following generations in the present use of natural resources; an awareness of the right of development in Third World Countries; alleviating the absolute poverty in Developing Countries by a higher transfer of official aid (ODA) coming from industrialized countries; etc.

Furthermore, the ecological responsibility of the industrial countries has been sincerely expressed by the fact that 80% of the global environmental damages are caused by the "rich nations of the North". As a challenge for economists, the principle of external negative effects' internalization into the account of micro-economic units (private households and industrial enterprises), who are causing external negative costs should be carefully followed. They should also reflect on solutions to protect the environment by adopting ex-ante measures which combine the inclusion of social costs in the private accountancy more effectively.

The Rio-Declaration has put forward its main objective to sign in 1995 the "Earth Charter" which will have the binding character of international law. The "Agenda 21" sets out the programme of action for the near future, but covering the time span for more than one decade. Nearly all sectors, branches of activities and political duties are mentioned - an 800 page volume! This document has been elaborated by the "North" and the "South". Nevertheless, the distribution of duties are quite different on the international level regarding the two parts of the world.

For Japan and Germany the following points of "Agenda 21" have particular impact: (1) The new approach for development policy (anti-absolute poverty concept which integrates the elements of combating man-made-disasters; disaster preparedness; the combination of humanitarian aid, natural disaster reduction and economic cooperation). (2) The protection of the atmosphere (the World-Climate-Convention connected with the objective to reduce CO_2-emissions and so-called greenhouse gases).

The "Agenda 21" "... call(s) for industry to increase energy efficiency, to develop cleaner technologies and production processes, to improve pollution abatement technologies, to replace chlorofluorocarbons and other ozone-depleting substances ...".

To summarize the impact of this internationally agreed paper and the different positions of the two countries concerned:

(1) The bilateral and multilateral Official Development Aid (ODA) favour towards the LFC's should be critically reflected by using "Agenda 21" criteria. The "catch-word" nowadays is the notion of "sustainable development" which has been the centre of the discussions of Rio and which will determine the new project design of developing politics. For the last few

years the German Government has been implementing a special screening for development projects and programmes in LDC's by taking into account ex-ante the potential ecological impact (UVP = "Umweltverträglichkeits-prüfung" with the categories I - IV).

(2) The anti-poverty-approach gives priority to ODA grants and loans. The NGO's work is mainly linked with this objective and the participation of people is the main element of this strategy. An analysis of Japan's Development Policy illustrates that a different orientation has taken place which is more influenced by supporting the interests of the industry by ODA activities. Japan is the highest absolute ODA spender, and therefore there will be scope for a reorientation based on the "Agenda 21" criteria.

(3) In the so called "Climate-Convention" Japan is vigourously attempted to find international solutions as soon as possible. This position can be logically understood: Japan is a geographical composition of islands. Due to the fact that there is a close relationship between the deterioration of the global climate and the vulnerability to natural disasters (mainly the increase of the sea level caused by damage to the global climate, but also natural hazards such as hurricanes, cyclones etc.), Japan will influence a world wide policy to decrease the air pollution and the emission of CO_2. In this context a German Parliamentary Commission has elaborated a very impressive document (Enquête-Komission, "Klimaänderung gefährdet globale Entwicklung" 1992, p. 1O9). One of the results of this investigation is that an increase in the sea level of 5Ocm will have a very negative ecological and socio-economic impact and will lead to a severe threat for millions of people in coastal regions. In particular the report mentions flooding in coastal areas, erosion of the coast line, an increasing impact of cyclones etc.

Germany (as well as the EC) have adopted the objective to reduce CO_2 emissions. The European Community will stabilize the actual CO_2 emission level by the year 2OOO; Germany will decrease the present CO_2 emission by 25-3O % by the year 2OO5. The climate Convention of Rio (1992) has presented criteria of a lower degree. Japan, who has attained good results in the past (saving energy and decreasing CO_2 emission) will not accept a percentage decrease based on the actual situation, but is more interested in the recognition of the present results of lower emissions and starting with marginal reductions. This position is explained by the fact that quite a lot of countries have higher emissions and should therefore accelerate the procedure of decreasing. The different positions of countries are closely linked with their competitiveness in international markets.

For Germany the objective of reducing the CO_2 emissions has to be considered within the framework of the EC. Nevertheless, there are divergent opinions as far as the volume of CO_2 emissions are concerned. The Germans have formulated a more ambitious aim to reduce CO_2 emissions (see above) and it will be very difficult to reach this goal in the time set, e.g. 22,7% of the total CO_2 emission is produced by transport vehicles. According to an analysis by the PROGNOS-Institute in Basle, this objective can only be reached by implementing 24 different measures in the transport sector concerned. The implementation of all these measures seems unacceptable for the different groups and under these circumstances the political decision process will be very difficult in a democratic and pluralistic system. Furthermore, a huge amount of investment has to be made for the construction of public transport facilities.

Japan has adopted efficient measures as well for the construction of infrastructure, for the development of automobiles with lower emissions as well for the supply of alternative transport facilities.

3. Some reflections on theoretical foundations

To quote once more the "Agenda 21": "Global and local environmental issues are interrelated". For economists this statement is not a surprising explanation. But, the interdependencies cover more levels than suggested in the Rio-Report.

In order to acquire a better understanding of the national positions in relation to the ecological problems we need a classification of the external effects. Figure 1 illustrates "Causing and Affected Parties in the National and International Context" (see: Th. Dams, 1991). The relationship between "Those Affected" and "Those Causing" is systematically analyzed, using the four entities in GNP Accounting, namely "Enterprises", "Private Households", "State/Government" and "Foreign Countries".

The blank rectangles represent interdependencies in non-market relations within an economy and society. External effects which link foreign countries, are the lightly shaded squares. Finally there is an area in which neither national entities nor individual countries are directly responsible (dark space). In the latter case both have the opportunity to lower their production costs by "exporting" external diseconomies. (e.g. polluted air and water) to international public territories (oceans, atmosphere etc.) or to invest abroad in order to escape national regulations in the field of environmental policy. - Foreign countries and territories not claimed by any state are more or less outside of the realms of any national economic and social accounting. Nevertheless, neighboring countries take a stand against production activities of individual states which negatively influence the living conditions or seriously weaken their own international competitive position. Solutions are less tangible for far reaching countries areas (oceans, the atmosphere etc.) where no country or respective entity can be held accountable for damages or negative impacts of such external diseconomies. Based on these general reflections, the topics "Economy" and "Ecology" cover problems in national and international relations; and Figure 1 is an efficient framework to illustrate different positions of Japan and Germany:

(1) The internal ecological problems (Private Households; Enterprises and State/Government);
(2) The international ecological problems:
    a) Companies, households and governments can pass on a part of their costs to "neighbouring" countries;
    b) Countries "export" their pollution to unclaimed areas;
    c) Foreign private direct investments transfer production units to other countries including the ecological problems of the home market.

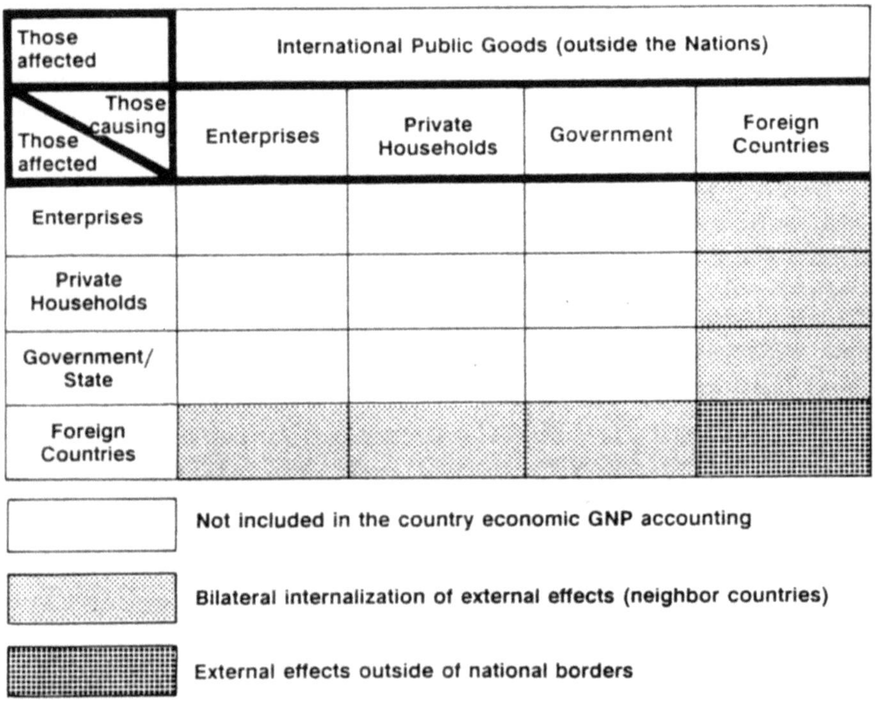

Figure 1: Causing and Affected Parties in the National and International Context

The paper follows this classification and outline in a more general way, it is not possible to present all empirical figures available for the two countries (see Th. Dams, Loccum 1992).

Taking into account the quotation "Global and local environmental issues are interrelated" ("Agenda 21") we can work with the above mentioned distinction in order to compare the positions of Japan and Germany.

Internally produced garbage is a very good example: in Japan per capita household garbage is one third higher than in Germany (448 Kg in comparison to 35O Kg). However when one considers recycling or removal the conclusions may be somewhat altered: two third is incinerated (for electrical power generation) in Japan, only one fifth in Germany. On the other hand, three quarters are stored at refuse disposal sites in Germany, one third in Japan.

Another example of a different situation is that Japan doesn´t have ecological problems with neighbouring countries due to the fact that the national territory is a group of islands; it is very well known that Japan has evacuated polluted water into the coastal areas of the sea. In Europe, for example, the discharge of polluted waste water into the Rhine river causes environmental problems in Switzerland, Germany, France and the Netherlands. Therefore there exists a challenge to neighbouring countries to find adequate solutions to avoid a negative impact in the regions concerned.

Furthermore, foreign private direct investments can be closely connected with environmental damage. Since some time Japan has been transferring "dirty industries" to other countries (e.g. the Philippines, Indonesia). This solved "home-made-ecological problems" relatively quickly at a time in which government and enterprises were encountering great difficulties caused by public discussion of severe health damages.

In Germany, for the transfer of industrial productions to foreign countries the ecological costs hasn't played a role (see IFO Investigation).

4. Some internal ecological problems

At the present time, Japan is considered to be a very good example of successful environment protection. Some years ago B. Gunnarson formulated the slogan (1974): "The ecological Harikiri of Japan - the fatal end of economic growth". Some years later a German official visitor explained his vision with the following sentence: "Japan is the Mecca for progressive ecologists" (H. Weidner, 199O). A Japanese representative of a very well known industrial unit has formulated the phrase: "Japan - the ecological miracle" (Y. Nishijima).

What has happened in Japan in a relative short time span taking into account the contradictory remarks of B. Gunnarson (1974) and Y. Hishijima (1993)?

In 1955-58 an ecological deterioration took place (soil contamination, polluted sea water, air pollution etc. which caused severe health problems and a great number of victims. The cities of Yokkaichi (SO_2 impact), Minamata (Mercury contamination) and Jintsugawa (Cadmium contamination) were recognised as areas of heavily concentrated ecological damages (see Figure 2). In this situation the Japanese Government undertook special measures with a very high efficiency. Japan immediately introduced an "extensive, specially regulated compensation system for diseases considered to have resulted from environmental pollution". H. Weidner considers that Japan is the only country in the world to have developed this way. The Pollution Related Health Damage Compensation Law of 1973 was immediately applied starting 1974. In 1988 an amendment of this law was passed, and after a relatively short period it was possible to fundamentally revise its legal basis (H. Weidner, 1988). Firstly, firms which are causing the health problems have to pay an emission levy directly (8O% of a specific fund are collected from stationary sources emitting a specified amount of flue gas). 2O% is collected indirectly through an automobile weight tax paid by owners of mobile sources of pollution (H. Weidner). Secondly, rehabilitation programs for target groups of ecological victims are covered by public expenditures.

The new "Endowment Plan" has taken into account that ecological damage has sharply decreased. Therefore the fund will be lowered to 5O billion Yen. 4O billion Yen will be raised from operators of smoke-emitting factories and 1O billion Yen from the automobile industry. H. Weidner has concluded with reference to this period: "The long history of an important instrument in Japanese environmental policy, the first of this kind in the world, had come to an end. It is now of great interest to see whether the Central Council's explicit recommendations to foster a general preventive environmental policy will be followed by politicians and industrialists."

In other papers this question of a new orientation in the near future will be covered by Japanese authors.

	Disease	Designated Area	Number of Official Certified Patients
Specific Disease	Minamata Disease	Agano River basin Minimata Bay coastal zone	377 616
	Itai-Itai Disease	Jintsu River downstream area	81
	Chronic arsenic poisoning	Toroku District in Miyazaki Prefecture	5
	Subtotal		1,079
Nonspecific Disease	Chronic bronchitis, bronchial asthma, pulmonary emphysema, asthmatic bronchitis and their complications	Tsurumi coast of Yokohama City	398
		Daishi, Tajima and Central part of Kawasaki City	1,449
		Central part of Fuji City	451
		Southern part of Nagoya City	1,564
		Northern and Central part of Tokai City	617
		Yokkaichi coastal area	1,008
		Nishiyodogawa of Osaka City	3,089
		Southern part of Toyonaka City	197
		Western part of Sakai City	322
		Eastern and Southern part of Amagasaki City	3,290
		Dokkai Bay coastal zone of Kita-kyushu City	617
		Central part of Ohmuta City	105
	Subtotal		13,107
	Total		14,186

Source: Environment Agency, 1974.

Figure 2: Areas and Patients Designated for Relief in Japan (March 1974)

In Germany, a different environmental policy has been followed (see the contributions presented at the seminar and demonstrating the "German or/and EC-Approach"). Therefore we here only present some facts for general information. The expenditures for environmental protection have been calculated in Japan to be 1.84% (198O) and 1.O2% (1991) of GNP; in Germany the comparative figures are 1.45% (198O) and 1.74% (1991).

The different trends are caused by the divergent situations described above. In Japan most of environmental investment is paid for by government (88%), in Germany it is only one third.

In the internal market of the European Communities it seems important to compare the subsidies among the member states: in France 62% and in the Netherlands 78% of the environmental investments are covered by government. These figures do have an impact on internal (EC) and international competitiveness. No doubt we must consider that the statistical data is sometimes weak and incomparable, a lot of scientific work still has to be done in this field. Nevertheless, the problem as such is visible.

In Germany 57% of energy inputs are linked to coal production (a higher level than in Japan). The Government has imposed very strong regulations for electric power plants as far as air pollution is concerned (G. Voss, 1992: "Weltweit die strengste Regelung für die Rauchgasreinigung"). From 1982-1992 SO_2 emissions have sharply decreased by 88%, SO_x by 73% (all these investments together had a price increase impact of 3 Dpfg/KWh). The differences in approach are visible: the ex-post reduction of pollution in Japan and the ex-ante measures in Germany.

The different environmental aspects of household refuse problems have been touched earlier. Once more, we do have two different "philosophies". In Japan the incineration of refuse is an energy resource, the emission of furane and dioxin does not play an important role in using efficient technologies applied in the burning process - as has been explained by Japanese technicians. The CO_2 emission does has not have to be taken into account (the oil input for the same quantity of electrical energy would produce more or less the same volume of CO_2).

The so called "Duales System" (Dual System) and the "Grüner Punkt" (Green Spot) is carefully observed by Japanese visitors coming to Germany, especially to Freiburg. This problem has not been solved efficiently until now.

5. The responsibility in relation to world wide problems

The different or common positions in the international debate have been described in chapter 2. Japanese Government is highly engaged to curb global warming by reducing the output of carbon dioxide. As the EC has done, Japan has promised that, by the end of the century, the emission of CO_2 per person will be held to the 1990 level. The sharp decline of CO_2 emissions in the 197Os was closely linked with the rise of oil prices, but the reduction in oil prices in the 198Os has produced more carbon dioxide emissions, mainly caused by petrol guzzling cars, and by the trend to buy bigger cars. Furthermore, energy consumption is rising: 5% from 1987 to 1988, and 2.7% in 1991. The Prime Minister Kiichi Miyazawa intends to present a proposal for a law which will cover international environmental issues. Some contradictory positions will have to be overcome: green taxes, carbon taxes, mixtures of subsidies for energy conservation, and penalties on companies using energies wastefully. The final decision has not yet been taken. But, international competitiveness will have to be reflected if subsidies are paid (The Economist, 19.9.1992, p.68).

Furthermore, in Japan as well as Germany, both countries have in mind to combine world-wide responsibility with the enlargement of new markets in favour for their own industries. The environment industry is a growing export sector, Germany is leader in water-treatment equipment, Japan in air pollution equipment, Germany is ranked lower for waste management and environmental services (see: OECD Observer August/September 1992).

The Economic Planning Agency, Government of Japan, has presented a document entitled "The Five-Year Economic Plan: Sharing a Better Quality of Life Around the Globe" (June 1992). The word "Harmony" is frequently used in this paper ("in harmony with the environment", p. 53). The paper includes some proposals on how to unite individual aims with overall social goals (a very well known approach in welfare economics and, as economists are aware, a theoretical reflection with serious limitations).

At the same time Keidanren, the Japanese "BDI", is trying to support this outline by "moral suasion". In other cases this organisation is taking some very practically minded action. The talks with China about the "fast-developing countries´ energy policy: China's filthy coal-fired plants, which Japan has the technology to clean, shower acid rain on Japan's forests." (The Economist, 1992).

6. A common foundation for environmental reconsideration?

It seems to be very difficult to compare environmental economic issues on a bilateral level (Japan - Germany) due to the fact that the principal considerations should be integrated in the cultural context. In a relative short time span a radical change of values has occurred in both societies, in Japan and Germany. Furthermore, new conflict solving procedures have been developed. We can learn a lot from Japan with respect to the so called "Mediation-Method" (H.J. Fietkau and H. Weidner, 1992), a bargaining process between different groups of society engaged in environmental questions with divergent options. Peaceful conflict solving ("versöhnliche Streitbeilegung") is a common procedure in Japan in the field of environment problems - and not to go immediately to the judicial courts! The first attempts have been undertaken in Germany, too (see: Loccum. Workshop, May 1992, Problemlösung und Konfliktregulierung im Umweltbereich durch Verhandlungs- und Vermittlungsverfahren). "Environment Auditing" has been recently discussed in relation to the EC-Commission's proposal (see: H. Karl; G. Meurin, Zeitschrift für Angewandte Umweltforschung, 1992).

These new procedures have to be considered in relation to an effort to bring together ethical and economical values. Let us conclude the paper with some reflections related to this problem.

(1) The German Unification has put forward the opportunity to revise and reformulate the German Constitution (Grundgesetz). One of the most intensively discussed points is whether to include the protection of Environment. Until now, the first proposal has been rejected, but the discussion is still open. The inclusion of this goal will have a considerable impact: the permanent consideration that all legislation and judicial measures are in good governance with this part of the Constitution!

(2) A strong discussion has started to declare "nature" as a "legal claim" (Rechtsgut) with a "subject quality". (German) Philosophers have presented remarkable contributions in favour of such a solution. Hans Jonas (Responsibility as a principle: Prinzip Verantwortung) has explained this view; as has R. Spaemann, Munich. In Japan, Shintoism could be a source of support to this kind of philosophical reflection with the same objective 250 years ago, Shosan Suzuki and Baigan Ishida (EDO-Period) elaborated some philosophical contributions which are very close related to the opinions mentioned above. As Japanese people have told me, both are quoted by environmentalists. Last but not least, I must mention the Final Commemorative Lecture of our famous colleague of the famous Nagoya University, Prof. Takashi Fujii (6. May 1992) in this context: Co-Living with the Environment "Management of the Earth System". I have to quote: "Can Man Live Together With

the Earth?" No doubt, in Fujii's view man and earth must be equally positioned!

(3) Some of these ideas and options are reflected by using the term "Sustainable Development". A term which has not yet be "operationally" formulated!

I do hope that we will find some time in these days to integrate these basic questions into our economic world and that we will discuss the main topics of how to bring together economy and ecology in a common framework which could be acceptable for both sides.

References

Dahl, R.A. and *Lindblom, C.E.:* Politics, Economics and Welfare, New York 1953.

Dams, Th.: Industrieansiedlung in ländlichen Entwicklungsräumen. Daten und Überlegungen zur regionalen Wirtschaftspolitik, Bonn 1957.

Dams, Th.: On the Connection between Economy and Ecology in International Economic Relations. See: *Dams, Th./Matsugi, T.* (Ed.): Protectionism or Liberalism in International Economic Relations? Berlin 1991.

Dams, Th.: Die Internationalisierung Japans. Ökologie und Ökonomie: Bemerkungen zu Positionen Japans und der BRD. See: *Pascha, W./Seifert/W.Striegnitz* (Ed.): Die Internationalisierung Japans im Spannungsfeld zwischen ökonomischer und sozialer Dynamik, Rehburg-Loccum 1993.

Deutscher Bundestag: Klimaänderung gefährdet globale Entwicklung. Enquête-Kommission, Bonn 1992.

EC-Commission: Richtlinienvorschlag für eine Kohlendioxyd- und Energiesteuer, Brüssel 1992.

Fietkau, H.J./Weidner, H.: Mediationsverfahren in der Bundesreblik Deutschland. See: Das Parlament, Bonn 1984.

Fujii, T.: Ecology and Development. The Ecology of Man and the Ecology of Greenery in the Earth System. See: Planning Administration, Tokyo 1993.

Gunnarson, B.: Japans ökologischer Harakiri oder das tödliche Ende des Wachstums, Hamburg 1974.

Hoffmann, W.: Stadien und Typen der Industrialisierung, Jena 1931.

Kaidandren: Global and Environment Charta, Tokyo 1991 (Position des japanischen Industrieverbandes).

Karl, H./Meurin, G.: The "Environment - Auditing". See: Zeitschrift für Angewandte Umweltforschung, Bonn 1992.

Loccum-Ev. Akademie: Problemlösung und Konfliktregulierung im Umweltbereich durch Verhandlungs- und Vermittlungsverfahren, Workshop, May 1992.

Nishijima, Y.: Including Environment in Internal Economics for Sustainable Development. Manuscript, Yokohama 1992.

OECD: Environmental Change and S&T Institutions, Paris 1992.

Ohkawa, K./Kohama, H.: Lectures on Developing Economies. Japan's Experience and its Relevance, Tokyo 1989.

Stiftung Entwicklung und Frieden: Nach dem Erdgipfel. Rio-Declaration and Agenda 21. SEF, Bonn 1993.

Stockholm Initiative: On Global Security and Goverance. The Charter of the United Nations. SEF, Bonn 1991.

Voss, G.: Indikator Umweltschutz und Indikator Energieversorgung. See: IW-Trends, Köln 1992.

Weidner, H.: Erfolge und Grenzen technokratischer Umweltpolitik. See: Das Parlament, Bonn 1984.

Recent Studies on Environmental Problems in Japan
- A Survey -

Takashi Matsugi

1. Introduction

It was quite common to observe that environmental problems appeared in the process of economic development in all countries in the world. In Japan damage from industrial pollution started to affect human health already in the Meiji period. A famous case was the poisoning from toxic metals in Ashio copper mines, as is described in Environment Agency[1].

In the time of rapid economic growth, the Japanese economy had to pay the price for it and parts of the land, especially industrialized areas, were heavily polluted. Some examples were Yokkaichi Asthma and Minamata Disease. After these experiences, anti-pollution measures were taken and the polluter pays principle (PPP) was established under the anti-pollution legislation in 1967. This is the Basic law for Environmental Pollution Control which defines the scope of environmental pollution to be addressed by government and clarifies the responsibilities of the national government, local governments and business enterprises. At that time, "bads" were not items circulated in the market and the neo-classical market theory failed in solving environmental problems. In the Pigovian welfare economics, taxes and subsidies could be alternative policy measures, but when faced with actually increasing pollutants, direct regulations were preferred for urgency to these suggested policy measures, for otherwise human lives could have been exposed to a very serious danger. In the welfare economics, such terms as externality and social costs were used to explain theoretical relations between economic variables, without solving actual pollution problems. The measurement of these terms was a task left to the following generation.

---

[1] Environment Agency (1993): Quality of the Environment in Japan 1992, Printing Bureau, Ministry of Finance.

Apart from traditional economics, new schools appeared from viewpoints like regionalism and institutionalism. It was argued around that time, for example, that pollution would threaten the regional ecological balance on the one hand and that capitalism as an economic system would exploit natural resources and devastate the world life environment on the other.

The first oil crisis in 1973 changed relative prices between crude oils and other inputs and had a considerable impact on the research and development of energy saving technologies, which directly or indirectly contributed to mitigate pollution. One of the most remarkable effects has been the technical progress in desulphurization, which makes industries clear the regulations on sulphur emission with reasonable additional costs.

Referring to the above mentioned historical development of environmental problems in Japan, a survey will be made in the following to describe recent theoretical and empirical contributions made by Japanese researchers.

2. Theoretical studies

The number of publications in the field of environmental studies is increasing, not only in Germany, but also in Japan and other countries. It is worthwhile, therefore, to make a current survey of these studies to distinguish similarities and differences among positions of authors.

Ueda and co-authors[2] present the idea that recent studies on environmental problems in Japan can be classified into five groups according to their philosophies and analytical tools. (1) The first group consists of regionalists and/or ecologists. (2) The second group emphasizes the importance of resources to sustain global development. (3) The third group includes economists who rely on the external diseconomy approach. (4) The fourth group prefers the concept of social costs as a key word to study environmental issues. (5) The fifth group insists that capitalists are responsible for pollution from the view point of political economics.

We find that this classification does not limit the number of groups and so it is not clear-cut. The more clear-cut criterion is a dichotomy which classifies objects into two sets. The one represents the market approach which should include the groups (2), (3) and (4) mentioned above, to which price-theoretical concepts and analysis can be applied. The other represents

---

[2] *Ueda, K./Ochiai, H./Kitabatake Y./Teranishi, S.* (1991): Kankyou Keizaigaku (Environmental Economics), Yuuhikaku.

the non-market approach which should include the groups (1) and (5), in which emphasis is put on value judgement and institutional elements.

2.1. The market approach

The market approach stands in principle for the traditional Pigovian welfare economics. One of the remarkable results was obtained by Shibata[3] who used the new concept of "adjusted indifference curves" and presented a bargaining model like the Edgeworth's box diagram to analyze external diseconomy cases. Arayama[4] considers the Pigovian model as a partial equilibrium type and attempts to extend it to a general equilibrium one analyzing CO_2 levies and emission rights.

Another remarkable result was obtained by Uzawa[5] who presented a theoretical foundation for the computation of the imputed price for greenhouse gas and for land forest. He maximizes the discounted present value of future utility indices which are defined as a function in final consumption of goods allocated to the members of the economy. This model is extended by Okumura[6] to analyze a two country case.

Ochiai[7] considers the conditions for sustainable economic development and the optimal development policy, based on contributions by Kato[8] and Kitabatake[9]. He assumes that the environment can reproduce itself, but economic development consumes a part of the environment. After defining the reproduction function of the environment, he maximizes the discounted present value of the utility arising from economic development and then derives the shadow value of the environment from this model. It is proposed

---

[3] *Shibata, H.* (1971): A Bargaining Model of the Pure Theory of Public Expenditures, Journal of Political Economy, Vol. 79, No. 1.

[4] Compare the contribution of *Arayama, Y.* in this volume.

[5] *Uzawa, H.* (1991): Global Warming Initiatives: The Pacific Rim, in: *Dornbusch, R.* and *Poterba, J. M.* (eds.): Global Warming, The MIT Press.

[6] Compare the contribution of *Okumura, R.* in this volume.

[7] *Ochiai, H.* (1988): Sizen Kankyou no Saisei to Kaihatsuzei (Renewal of Natural Environment and Development Tax), in: Keizaigaku Ronso, Vol. 40, No. 1.

[8] *Kato, H.* (1989): "Jizokuteki Kaihatu" Gainen no Keisei to Kongo no Hatten ni Tsuite (On the Concept of "Sustainable Development"), in: Kankyo Kagaku Kaishi, Vol. 2, No. 1.

[9] *Kitabatake, Y.* (1989): Optimal Exploitation and Enhancement of Environmental Resources, in: Journal of Environmental Economics and Management, Vol. 16.

that this value can be adopted as the tax rate on the use of the environment for economic development.

Apart from these theoretical studies, attempts are being made to evaluate the Environmentally adjusted net Domestic Product (EDP). The United Nations suggested in 1993 that the Standard National Accounts should be revised to include effects of economic activities on the environment. The purpose is firstly to estimate systematically the effects of economic activities such as production, consumption and investment on those environmental elements as animals, plants, air, water, soil etc. The second purpose is to include those "bads" in the National Accounts which have been neglected because we have no prices for them. According to Hamada[10], it is assumed that the environment has such functions as to supply resources, to clean up pollution and to afford amenities. The EDP will be estimated by evaluating possible costs to sustain these functions at a certain defined level.

2.2. The non-market approach

It is obvious that pollutants are "bads", but there is no way to estimate how bad they are in economic terms, because no prices are available for them in the market. In spite of this fact, it was urgent to save those people who were badly affected by pollution. Polluters were then accused from the viewpoint of human rights and evidence was collected and made accessable to the public to initiate anti-pollution movements. Shouji and Miyamoto[11] was one of the earliest publications that reported damage suffered by those who lived and worked in heavily polluted areas without official protection measures at that time.

Tsuru[12] was a pioneer who criticized the political structure of capitalism in which legislation and regulations in favor of capitalists as in Japan in the time of rapid economic growth could not control spreading pollution. This criticism, supported by Miyamoto[13], made the central government feel responsible for pollution control and take the necessary policy measures in

---

[10] *Hamada, K.* (1992): EDP ni tsuite no Ichi Kousatsu (A Consideration of Environmentally adjusted net Domestic Product), in: National Economic Accounts Quarterly, No. 95, Economic Planning Agency.

[11] *Shouji, M./Miyamoto, K.* (1964): Osorubeki Kougai (Dreadful Pollution), Iwanami Shoten.

[12] *Tsuru, S.* (ed.) (1968): Gendai Shihon-Shugi to Kougai (Modern Capitalism and Pollution), Iwanami Shoten.

[13] *Miyamoto, K.* (1975): Nihon no Kankyou Mondai (Environmental Problems in Japan), Yuuhikaku.

1960s and 1970s. At the same time Tamanoi[14], from the standpoint of regionalism and also ecological consciousness, accused local governments of being apt to neglect their responsibilities to control polluters at the local level. It should be noted that these procedures gave rise to the Japanese character of environmental policy to rely more on direct regulations than on the market mechanism.

3. Empirical studies

Concerning empirical studies on environmental problems, OECD[15] refers to Ban[16] as one of the important contributions in this field. He presented a newly developed macroeconometric model consisting of the energy sector and energy using sectors. Then he estimated demand functions by sector to get information on the effects of energy prices on the demand for energy in the period after the oil crisis in 1973. He finds that an increase in the real energy price has played an important role in improving the energy efficiency of the Japanese economy since the first oil shock. High energy prices usually slow down the growth of an economy. However, they also stimulate at the same time the substitution of other inputs for energy and induce the development of energy saving technologies, for it is observed that energy and capital are substitutes in major industries in Japan.

By using the estimated results, he investigates the possibility of keeping the level of CO_2 emission in the year 2000 within the 1990 level. To achieve this target, it would be necessary to introduce a carbon tax of more than thirty percent on fossil fuels. The imposition of this tax would lead to a reduction in GNP of 28 trillion yen totalled for the period from 1991 to 2000. It is concluded that this welfare loss will be smaller than that of an alternative policy to regulate CO_2 emission by giving emission rights to industries and households.

---

[14] *Tamanoi, Y.* (1978): Economy to Ecology (Economy and Ecology), Misuzu Shobou.

[15] OECD (1991): Environment Committee Meeting at Ministerial Level Backgrand Paper No. 1 - No. 5.

[16] *Ban, K.* (1991): Energy Conservation and Economic Performance in Japan - An Econometric Approach to CO_2 Emissions-, Discussion Paper No. 112, Faculty of Econ., Osaka University.

Concerning the substitutability between energy and other inputs, Nemoto[17] estimated production functions by sector including energy as one of inputs and obtained the results that energy and capital were substitutable in most cases, while energy and labor were complementary.

Nishijima[18] and Yanagioka[19] made attempts to evaluate environmental costs in case of desulphurization and other technologies adopted in Japanese industries. They find that commodity prices will rise by roughly seven percent, when these estimated environmental costs are imposed on prices. Based on the evaluation, they propose to internalize these environmental costs so that the nation should take the burden of maintaining environmental quality for themselves and contribute to the global sustainable development.

Matsuoka and others[20] try simulation to show how the location of cities in a certain area affects the total volume of CO_2 emissions by considering traffic systems in cities. Based on the simulated result, they propose how to reduce CO_2 emission by replanning city location and changing the traffic system.

On the micro-economic level, firms are concerned with environmental problems and have invested heavily in facilities to reduce pollutants as well as in research and development activities to improve technologies. Kishida[21] made a case study to find how Japanese firms tried to cope with environmental problems. Taking the tendency of globalization into consideration, he investigated the shift from pollution control to environmental management on the part of Japanese firms. Yoshida[22] is interested in the inherent problems of environmental technology transfer from the viewpoint of the organization theory. As an example of non-profit institutions, the organization of International Center for Environmental Technology Transfer (ICETT) in Yokkaichi is studied. It is found that it is necessary to keep the balance between a physical and an organizational aspect in such an institution as ICETT.

---

[17] *Nemoto, J.* (1984): Energy to Hi-energy Seisan Youso no Aida no Daitai Kanousei ni tuite (On Substitutability between Energy and Non-Energy Inputs - An Econometric Analysis Using Multiple CES Production Function), Economic Studies Quarterly.

[18] Compare the contribution of *Nishijima, Y.* in this volume.

[19] Compare the contribution of *Yanagioka, H.* in this volume.

[20] *Matsuoka, Y./Morita, T./Arimura, R.* (1992): Toshi Kouzoi oyobi Toshi Haichi to Chikyuu Ondanka (City Structure and City Location in Relation to Global Warming), in: Kikan Konkyou Kenkyuu.

[21] Compare the contribution of *Kishida, T.* in this volume.

[22] Compare the contribution of *Takeshi, Y.* in this volume.

4. Concluding remarks

In June 1992, the United Nations Conference on Environment and Development (Earth Summit) was held in Brazil with a view to reaching international agreement on substantial measures to realize the sustainable economic development of the world. In spite of the efforts made in the Conference, discrepancies still remain among industrialized and developing countries concerning the choice between preservation and development.

There is no doubt that developing countries are faced with serious environmental problems of their own, arising from agricultural production, industrialization and urbanization, as is shown in Fujisaki[23] and Matsugi[24]. But it is necessary for developing countries to get eliminate absolute poverty. In this connection, Gore[25] makes reasonable proposals including demographic transition, environmental technology transfer and a Global Marshall Plan. However there still seems to be a long way to go before reaching worldwide agreements.

What is necessary today is to provide more information which helps to us solve environmental problems, not only national but also of global nature. In the field of economics, attempts should be made to build a model which consists of more stock variables than in those proposed up to date.

---

[23] *Fujisaki, N.* (1992) Hatten Tojoukoku no Kankyou Mondai (Environmental Problems in Developing Countries), Asia Keizai Shuppankai

[24] *Matsugi, T.* (1992): Philippines no Kankyou Mondai to Kankyou Seisaku (Environmental Problems and Policies in the Philippines), in: Economic Science Quarterly, Nagoya University.

[25] *Gore, A.* (1992): Earth in the Balance, Houghton Mifflin Company.

References

Arayama, Y. (1994): General Equilibrium Analysis of CO_2 Levies and Emission Rights. A contributed paper to the 14th joint seminar Freiburg/Nagoya - published in this volume.

Ban, K. (1991): Energy Conservation and Economic Performance in Japan - An Econometric Approach to CO_2 Emissions-, Discussion Paper No. 112, Faculty of Econ., Osaka University.

Baumol, W. J./Oates, W. E. (1988): The Theory of Environmental Policy, 2nd ed., Cambridge University Press.

Environment Agency (1993): Quality of the Environment in Japan 1992, Printing Bureau, Ministry of Finance.

Fujisaki, N. (1992) Hatten Tojoukoku no Kankyou Mondai (Environmental Problems in Developing Countries), Asia Keizai Shuppankai.

Gore, A. (1992): Earth in the Balance, Houghton Mifflin Company.

Hamada, K. (1992): EDP ni tsuite no Ichi Kousatsu (A Consideration of Environmentally adjusted net Domestic Product), in: National Economic Accounts Quarterly, No. 95, Economic Planning Agency.

Hattori, S. (1992): Senshinkoku no Kankyou Mondai to Nougyou (Environmental Problems and Agriculture in Developed Countries), Fumin Kyoukai.

Hobller, P./Dean, A./Hayafuji M. (1992): New Issues, New Results: The OECD's Second Survey of the Macroeconomic Costs of Reducing CO_2 Emissions, OECD Economics Department Working Papers No. 123.

Hisamune, T./Kumazawa K. (eds) (1991): Kankyou Hozengata Nougyou to Sekai no Keizai (Environment Preserving Agriculture and the World Economy), Noubunkyou.

Ishi, H. (1988): Chikyuu Kankyou Houkokusho (Global Environment Repoert), Iwanami Shoten.

Japanese Cooperatives (1992): Kankyou Hozen to Kyoudoukumiai (Environmental Preservation and Cooperatives), Ienohikari Kyoikai.

Kada, R. (1990): Kankyou Hozen to Jizokuteki Nougyou (Environment Preservation and Sustainable Agriculture), Ienohikari Kyoikai.

Kapp, K. W. (1950): The Social Costs of Private Enterprise, Harvard University Press.

Kato, H. (1989): "Jizokuteki Kaihatu" Gainen no Keisei to Kongo no Hatten ni Tsuite (On the Concept of "Sustainable Development"), in: Kankyo Kagaku Kaishi, Vol. 2, No. 1.

Kato, H. (1991): Kankyou Rinrigaku no Susume (Introduction to Environmental Ethics), Maruzen.

Kishida, T. (1994): Organizations for Environmental Management. A contributed paper to the 14th joint seminar Freiburg/Nagoya - published in this volume.

Kishimoto, T. (1986): Koukyo Keizaigaku (Public Economics), Yuuhikaku.

Kitabatake, Y. (1989): Optimal Exploitation and Enhancement of Environmental Resources, in: Journal of Environmental Economics and Management, Vol. 16.

Kudo, K. (1980): Kankyou no Keizeigaku (Economics of Environmen), in: Keizaigaku Daiziten, Touyou Keizai Sinpousha.

Kumagai, H. (1978): Kousei Keizaigaku (Welfare Economics), Soubunsha.

Leontief, W. (1970): Environmental Repercussions and the Economic Structure: An Input-Output Approach, Proceedings of International Symposium on Environmental Disruption, Tokyo.

Matsugi, T. (1992): Philippines no Kankyou Mondai to Kankyou Seisaku (Environmental Problems and Policies in the Philippines), in: Economic Science Quarterly, Nagoya University.

Matsuoka, Y./Morita, T./Arimura, R. (1992): Toshi Kouzoi oyobi Toshi Haichi to Chikyuu Ondanka (City Structure and City Location in Relation to Global Warming), in: Kikan Konkyou Kenkyuu.

Ministry for Foreign Affaires (1992): Kankyou to Kaihatsu-Nihon no Keiken to Torikumi (Kokuren Kankyou Kaigi eno Nihon no Houkokusho), Ookurashou Insatsukyoku.

Ministry for Foreign Affaires (1991): Chikyuu Kankyou Mondai Sengenshu (Collected Statements on Global Environmental Problems), Ookurasyou Insatsukyoku.

Ministry for the Environment (1990): Chikyuu Kankyou no Seiji Keizaigaku (Political Economics of the Global Environment) Daiamondo-sha.

Ministry for the Environment (1990): Kankyou Hakusho (Annual Report of the Environment), Ookurashou Insatsakyoku.

Mishan, E. J. (1969): Growth: The Price We Pay, Staple Press.

Miyamoto, K. (1975): Nihon no Kankyou Mondai (Environmental Problems in Japan), Yuuhikaku.

Miyamoto, K. (1987): Nihon no Kankyou Seisaku (Japanese Environmental Policy), Ohtsuki Shoten.

Miyamoto, K. (1989): Kankyou Keizaigaku (Environmental Economics), Iwanami Shoten.

Motoyama, Y. (1990): Kankyou Hakai to Kokusai Keizai (Environmental Destruction and International Economy), Yuuhikaku.

Murota, T. (1979): Energy to Entropy no Keizaigaku (Economics of Energy and Entropy), Touyou Keizai, Shinpou-sha.

Nemoto, J. (1984): Energy to Hi-energy Seisan Youso no Aida no Daitai Kanousei ni tuite (On Substitutability between Energy and Non-Energy Inputs - An Econometric Analysis Using Multiple CES Production Function), Economic Studies Quarterly.

Nihon Keizai Shinbun, Inc. (1990): Terasu de Yomu Chikyuu Kankyou Tokuhon (On Global Environment for Reading on the Terace), Nihonkeizai Sinbunsha.

Nishijima, Y. (1994): Internalization of Environmental Costs for Sustainable Development. Learning from the History of Fighting Sulfur Dioxide in Japan. A contributed paper to the 14th joint seminar Freiburg/Nagoya - published in this volume.

National Reseach Council (1989): Alternative Agriculture, National Academy Press.

Ochiai, H. (1988): Sizen Kankyou no Saisei to Kaihatsuzei (Renewal of Natural Environment and Development Tax), in: Keizaigaku Ronso, Vol. 40, No. 1.

OECD (1991): Environment Committee Meeting at Ministerial Level Backgrand Paper No. 1 - No. 5.

Okumura, R. (1994): A Dynamic Analysis of Global Warming. A contributed paper to the 14th joint seminar Freiburg/Nagoya - published in this volume.

Pethig, R. (ed.) (1992): Conflicts and Cooperation in Managing Environmental Resources, Berlin, Heidelberg, New York.

Pigou, A. C. (1920): The Economics of Welfare, 1st ed.

Shibata, H. (1971): A Bargaining Model of the Pure Theory of Public Expenditures, Journal of Political Economy, Vol. 79, No. 1.

Shibata, H. (1972): Pareto Optimality Trade and Pigovian Corrective Tax, Economica (N. S.), Vol. 14, No. 154.

Shibata, H. (1974): Pareto Optimality and Gains from Trades: A Further Elucidation, Economica, (N.S.) Vol. 39, No. 161.

Shibata, H. (1983): Fiscal Measures Against Pollution: Are Effluent Taxes and Abatement Subsidies Equivalent?, in: Dieter Biehl, Karl W. Roskamp and Wolfgang Stolper (eds.): Public Finance and Economic Growth, Detroit: Wayne State University Press.

Shibata, H./Winrich, S. (1993): Control of Pollution When Offended Defend Themselves, Economica (N.S.), Vol. 50, Nr. 200.

Shibata, H./Shibata, A. (1988): Koukyou Keizaigaku (Public Economics), Touyou Keizai Shinpou-sha.

Shouji, M./Miyamoto, K. (1964): Osorubeki Kougai (Dreadful Pollution), Iwanami Shoten.

Takeshi, Y. (1994): Transfer of Environmental Technology - Transfer Technology and Roles of Non-profit Institutions. A contributed paper to the 14th joint seminar Freiburg/ Nagoya - published in this volume.

Tamanoi, Y. (1978): Economy to Ecology (Economy and Ecology), Misuzu Shobou.

Teranishi, S. (1983): Kougai Kankyou Mondai eno Ichi Shikaku (A View on Pollution and Environmental Problems), in: Hitotsubashi Ronsou, Vol. 90, No. 4.

Teranishi, S. (1984): Gendai Haikibutu Mondai no Keizaigaku Joron (Economic Introduction to Recent Waste Problems), in: Hitotsubashi Ronsou, Vol. 98, No. 2.

Teranishi, S. (1992): Chikyuu Kankyou Mondai no Seiji Keizaigaku (Political Economics of Global Environmental Problems), Touyou Keizai Shimpo-sha.

Tsuru, S. (ed.) (1968): Gendai Shihon-Shugi to Kougai (Modern Capitalism and Pollution), Iwanami Shoten.

Tsuru, S. (1972): Kougai no Seiji Keizaigaku (Political Economics of Pollution), Iwanami Shoten.

Uchishima, Z. (1990): Chikyuu Kankyou no Kiki-Kenkyuu no Genjou to Kadai (Crisis of Global Environment-Present State of Research and Problems to Solve), Iwanami Shoten.

Ueda, K. (1991): Junkangata Shakai eno Mosaku: Rinen, System, Yuudou (An Essay on the Recycle Society: Concept, System and Initiative), in: Kankyo Kenkyu, June, 1991.

Ueda, K./Ochiai, H./Kitabatake, Y./Teranishi, S. (1991): Kankyou Keizaigaku (Environmental Economics), Yuuhikaku.

Uzawa, H. (1974): Jidousha no Shakaiteki Hiyou (Social Costs of Automobiles), Iwanami Shoten.

Uzawa, H. (1991): Global Warming Initiatives: The Pacific Rim, in: Dornbusch, R. and Poterba, J. M. (eds.): Global Warming, The MIT Press.

Worldwatch Institute (1987): State of the World, W. W. Norton & Company, Inc.

Yamada, T. (1987): Koukyo Keizaigaku (Public Economics) Nihon Keizai Shinbun-sha.

Yanagioka, H. (1994): Evaluation of Environmental Costs in Japan. A contributed paper to the 14th joint seminar Freiburg/Nagoya - published in this volume.

The Importance of Environmental Policy for International Competitiveness[1]

Gerold Blümle

A. Introduction

Can the decentralized coordination of market economies embrace the necessity of environmental conservation in the long term, or is this aim endangered by the conflict between personal economic interest and environmental conservation? These questions are the subject of controversial discussion[2]. Of course left-wing ecologist technocrats know the answer and that the solution lies inevitably in a system which Watrin admonishingly called "eco-dictatorship"[3]. The experience gained in technologically planned economic systems does not seem to have led to convincing achievements in environmental conservation, as we have learnt from the states of the former Eastern Bloc. According to the German Federal Minister Töpfer's programme "Ecological Construction", immediate action in the new federal states will require at least 36 to 46 billion DM[4].

Furthermore the confidence in politicians' far-sightedness in Western democracies, who set standards for the economy with regard to the future, begins to sway on observing professional populist politicians with ever shortening time horizons moving from election to election. As the examples show, Eastern as well as Western politicians with an interest in public living standards, seem to give priority to short-term domestic competitiveness of their system or party.

---

[1] I am grateful to Mr. Manfred Stein for valuable comments.

[2] See *Blümle* (1984), p. 56-79

[3] *Watrin* (1980/1), p. 7 f.

[4] IWD (1991), p. 2

Thus politicians' time perspectives hardly exceed those of employers[5]. The USA's conduct during the Rio summit concerning the problem of CO_2-discharge provides an example, and sadly not a shining one. The expression of "ecological dumping"[6] has also been recently coined, meaning the strategical use of national ecological standards in foreign trade policy. For politicians the polit-economic aims of foreign trade policy conflict with the ecological policy and how the priorities are set in times of increasing unemployment does not require long discussion.

Liberal economists believe that the solution of the problem lies, as von Hayek called it, "in competition as a process of discovery" and in prices as the most efficient information system. One can agree that the competence in problem solving and the speed of adaptation of this system has proved to be extraordinarily good. However the skeptic will wonder whether it is not a circular argument to say that through competition we are better off and to define the outcome of competition as "better". The opinion that, analogous to the process of selection in biological evolution, also in economic competition the better will survive, seems to me very questionable when one tries to shirk the answer what is "better" with reference to the non-normativity of science. In Germany the competition process for goods proceeds according to the principle of the constructive censure resolution. Just as the former chancellor is voted out, so is the former good, which is then replaced by the new one. Time will show whether the new chancellor, or the new good, really was the better choice and it is questionable whether the former chancellor or the former good will still be available in case of a bad choice. In other words the process of competition may not be reversible[7]. If it is not, and if it neglects the costs of pollution, whose consequences are only perceived at a later date, then future developments would seem to be associated with considerable risks. This all the more since competition is related to goods and as the indisputable aim of economic development should be *securing the future of humankind.*

At the same time the employers in their reactions to environmental policy declarations on the one hand and their methods of waste disposal on the other hand, give the public the impression that their international competitiveness is gravely endangered by the costs of environmental conservation.

---

[5] See *Hansen* (1988)

[6] *Rauscher* (1992)

[7] See *Blümle* (1984), p. 63

Given the international mobility of capital we have to ask whether for their locational choice employers prefer countries which have comparatively low standards for environmental conservation and therefore low costs in the international competition. The figures for Germany's direct investment, which shows rising net capital exports since 1984, seems to be an indication that the industrial location Germany is in jeopardy. However on examining the countries where German direct investments are made, almost nothing indicates that the respective environmental policy had been decisive for the choice of the location. On the other hand we should consider how far the national requirements of environmental policy jeopardize the competitiveness of a national economy or whether a long-term oriented policy could not, in the long run, channel the innovative forces of market coordination, which might lead to economic and at the same time ecological success. It is the aim of this article to show that in environmental conservation it is also of great importance to differentiate between short and long run perspectives and that in international comparison long-term orientation of the environmental policy might even be advantageous in view of foreign trade policy.

After some remarks concerning the historical development of ecology, which will show that the contemporary problems are not recent, the question of costs for environmental conservation will be treated in international correlation. Their relevance in comparison to labour costs will then be qualified. Thereafter I will examine the conception of measuring competitiveness and sketch what the competitiveness of German economy is about. Finally I will apply the theory of the dynamic external economy to the above mentioned questions and draw conclusions for a long-term oriented environmental policy.

B. Principal topic

1. Historical development of ecology

Going back to the ancient times before Christ, already in 450 BC the Persian king Artaxerxes I tried to reduce the deforestation of cedars in Lebanon[8]. The picture of a tropical virgin island was paradise for Dante in his "Divine Comedy". The problems of environmental conservation posed themselves already at the time when the economic exploitation of these landscapes began at the beginning of colonialism[9]. Under the influence of

---

[8] See *Grove* (1992), p. 78 (p. 76-81)

[9] Ibid p. 77

the physiocrats and Jean-Jacques Rousseau, measures to conserve the environment, i.e. to stop deforestation, were taken on Mauritius already in the 18th century during the French occupation. On Mauritius, in a regulation dated 1769, correlations between deforestation and climate were described. In 1791 measures were taken to reduce water pollution caused by indigo factories and sugar mills[10]. Already in 1765 British environmental conservation measures prescribed the setting-up of national parks[11]. In 1791 a forest law protected the woods on Saint Vincent, Antilles, on account of the climate. The German explorer Alexander von Humboldt (1769 to 1859) strongly influenced the development of ecology. The extinction of animals such as the aurochs in Poland (1627) and the dodo on Mauritius (1670) preoccupied people very much and led to apocalyptic predictions of the extinction of mankind following climatic changes[12]. These apocalyptic predictions reached a peak in the mid-19th century and it seems that economic interest was always been an obstacle to environmental conservation measures[13]. Grove ends his article on the development of ecology with the remark "our contemporary understanding of the global threat goes back to ideas which date already more than one hundred years back. It is regrettable that so much time had to elapse before the warnings of the natural scientists were gradually taken seriously."[14]

It has to be considered that, as stated above, the emergence of ecology took place before the "Wealth of Nations" was published, i.e. at the beginning of the industrial revolution. In view of the extent of man's influence today on the environment, it would surely be thoughtless to say that what has been good for such a long time will also be good in the future. But with the consequences of pollution, also the possibilities to control them improved. On the other hand pollution cannot be restricted to particular countries, it must be looked upon as a multilateral problem. This encourages free-rider behaviour by politicians, as can be witnessed at international conferences, who attempt to profit from measures taken by other countries or to use eco-dumping as an instrument for foreign trade policy. A prisoners' dilemma accordingly leads to the conclusion that international environmental policy is

---

[10] See *Grove* (1992), p. 78

[11] Ibid p. 79

[12] Ibid p. 80

[13] Ibid p. 80

[14] Ibid p. 81

worse than national[15]. In my opinion we can expect even less from environmental policy on an international level than from national policy.

Thus we have to ask even more urgently: will a competitive economy have the foresight to facilitate an environmentally beneficial development or, in other words, is a competitive economy more likely to facilitate such a development than the dirigiste policy of an eco-dictatorship?

It appears important in this context to shift the principle of competition to a higher level. It is well known that open economies grow faster than closed ones. International competition thus seems to increase the international ability to solve problems. If in international competition, countries which lead the way in environmental policy, have in the long run only advantages, we could view the future optimistically. If these hopes are legitimate - and I am convinced that they are - ex ante harmonization of environmental policy in the European Communities would not to be desirable. We would then have harmonization on the lowest level rather than competition between different national environmental conservation measures. Instead, applying a stricter environmental policy, international competition could lead to long-term economic success and thus other countries would be provided with incentives to catch up in their environmental policy[16].

In the following, however, I would like first to discuss the importance of environmental costs.

2. *The importance of environmental costs*

Environmental costs[17] in the sense of costs for conservation measures[18] are like depreciation in so far as they diminish the cutback of "environmental assets". They only become net investments into the "environmental assets" when the quality of the environment has improved beyond the starting

---

[15] See concerning this opinion: *Frey* (1985), p. 123-127

[16] See *Knödgen* (1981), p. 39 f. for general aspects also: *Berthold* (1992), p. 78.

[17] See also the definition of "costs of use of the environment" as disadvantages, which result from the utilization of specified environmental elements as resources for production and consumption at any point of the system. *Klaus* (1989), p. 63. Based on this, Klaus develops a complex model of an environmental bill of costs. *Klaus* (1989), p. 64 f. (with further bibliography).

[18] Costs for environmental conservation measures are defined as investments and running costs of the public and private sector.

point[19]. Environmental costs are composed of capital expenditure and the operation costs of the producing and the state sector. They belong to those aspects of environmental conservation which are widely ignored in public and even by relevant politicians[20]. Even the "basis for recording 'environmental costs'" is still to be clarified[21]. That explains the danger of exploding costs due to "excessive conservation expectations". To avoid these, the "vicious circle of ideology, actionism and ignorance [...] especially concerning the environmental costs" must be broken[22].

In 1988 the ten most important Western industrialized countries (USA, Canada, Japan, FRG, France, Great Britain, Sweden, The Netherlands, Denmark and Italy) spent approximately 171,5 billion DM on conservation measures, to which the expenditures of the producing sector must be added. However the (estimated) costs are comparatively low in comparison with the (estimated) costs for environmental damage. On examining the methods used for cost estimates and valuation processes, we can identify contrary tendencies of incorrect estimates. That is why omitted activities, respectively price-induced distribution effects are not taken into consideration, whereas willingness to pay analyses mostly overestimate the costs of environmental damage[23].

The development and implementation of conservation measures incurs costs which rise progressively with rising standards[24]. An efficient use of the available funds can only be guaranteed by cost-benefit analysis. It should be clear that measures in highly polluted areas will, as a rule, be more efficient than in areas which have a considerably lower concentration of the harmful substance in question[25]. The law of diminishing utility also applies in this context. Concerning the lack of consideration of the highly variable dimi-

---

[19] See *Simonis* (1987), p. 117

[20] This was demonstrated by the discussions at the Wirtschaftspolitisches Kolloquium of the Adolf-Weber-Stiftung end of october 1989 in Frankfurt, Klemmer (1990), p. 46

[21] *Klemmer* (1990), p. 47

[22] *Klemmer* (1990), p. 46

[23] On the problems of damage estimation, see Rat von Sachverständigen für Umweltfragen (1987), p. 80 f.

[24] For a survey of the sectors where environmental costs arise, see *Heinzelmann* (1991), p.36

[25] Concerning the costs, the distribution problem should also be discussed in the case of area-specific argumentation. The example of a national diversification in public demand for environmentally beneficial goods shows for the FRG, that there was a high predominance of expenditures for acquisition in the counties and districts (joint authorities), which effected in 1987 approx. 79% (94%) of the total investments and approx. 68% (81%) of the running material costs for environmental conservation. Cf. *Sprenger* (1990), p. 52 f.

nishing emission costs depending on the specific installation, Klemmer mentions "overall economic costliness", in particular as "exchange (in the FRG) between different companies is generally forbidden."[26] Environmental conservation measures are therefore more expensive than they would have to be to achieve the same effect[27]. Overall economic losses of welfare emerge. It is therefore important to pay particular attention to efficiency of instruments used in environmental policy, before applying them.

Technical progress helps to diminish the consumption of non-renewable resources in production and consumption and the costs of environmental conservation[28]. A central problem is that the selection of instruments for environmental policy creates innovative incentives. When, for example, legal requirements predominate, there is a danger of "innovation cut-backs"[29], i.e. a "boomerang effect" caused by excessive requirements[30]. Bonus called it the "silent engineers cartel"[31]. Instead of legal requirements which are obviously easier to put through because they appear to give highest priority to environmental concerns, instruments should be applied which should correspond to marketable permits in their effects. Marketable permits not only have the advantage of a higher cost efficiency, incurring less costs under the same environmental standards, but they also have the highest innovative efficiency[32] under market conditions. Increasing international competition should then ensure the particular innovative efficiency of marketable permits and furthermore, as will be discussed later, is particularly important for competitiveness.

The expenditures of the public and private sector for environmental measures constitute an important part of the gross national product (GNP) in the industrialized countries. As it is shown in table 1 the contribution was, as a rule, above 1% in the last decade.

---

[26] *Klemmer* (1991), p. 137

[27] *See Klemmer* (1990), p. 48 f.

[28] The use of technical progress to protect the environment is explained in *Kemper* (1989), p. 161 f.

[29] See *Klemmer* (1991), p. 138

[30] *Klemmer* (1990), p. 25

[31] *Bonus* 1984, p. 107 f.

[32] See e.g.: *Hartwig* (1992), p. 157 f.

Table 1: Expenditures for environmental conservation[1] in percentage of GNP[2] (selected industrialized countries)

	1980	1986	1990
Canada	2,04	1,59	1,33
USA	1,62	1,47	1,37
Japan	1,80	1,34	1,33
West Germany	1,45	1,53	1,62
Denmark	1,52	0,98	0,88
Finland	1,30	1,16	1,05
France	0,87	0,88	0,95
Great Britain	1,54	1,24	0,94
The Netherlands	1,10	1,25	1,47
Norway	1,10	0,81	0,63
Austria	1,12	1,50	1,88
Sweden	1,09	0,92	0,86

[1] Public and private expenditures; US$ in prices and exchange rates of 1980
[2] US$ in prices and exchange rates of 1980

Source: Voss (1991), p. B-7

The high level of expenditures for environmental conservation must affect employment. It is widely feared that conservation measures threaten jobs and the international competitiveness[33]. Concerning employment, conservation costs are judged in relation with the higher investments for environmental conservation. Capital lockup and depreciation increase and result in higher capital costs. If these costs can not be passed on by increasing prices, revenue must decrease. As a consequence, production will be reduced and/or

[33] For the discussion on this point, see *Wicke/Schulz, E./Schulz, W.* (1987), p. 91 f.

production will be transferred abroad with corresponding negative effects on domestic employment. If it is possible to shift the increase in costs to price increase, the ensuing sales decline will also cut employment potential.

Some authors come, however, to the conclusion that increased environmental conservation has positive effects on the employment situation[34]. Their prevailing argument is the additional effect on the demand of public and publicly induced conservation investments[35]. On analyzing the balance, both demand and supply oriented analysis emphasize positive, if not always very strong effects on employment. However considerable methodical problems strongly restrict the relevance of these results[36].

Concerning the international cost differences between companies, it should be pointed out that there are internationally considerable sectoral and microeconomic differences both between the levels and the structure of environmental conservation expenditures. These are due to company, production and technology specific factors, as well as diverging national environmental policies[37]. It seems probable that cost differences between domestic and foreign companies are highly elastic to differences between the national requirements on environmental conservation[38]. Mostly the internationally varying financial burden of companies is considered to depend mainly upon the way the burden is shared: the principle of common burden or the polluter-pays principle[39]. However this implies for one that the financing of the common burden principle has no effects on the microeconomic costs, and for another that both principles have similar efficiency effects. This seems unlikely. If we assume that the microeconomic differences in the application of both principles are not significant, then the above mentioned percentage of GNP seems to provide a suitable measurement for the average microeconomic burden caused by environmental conservation costs. If we consider that the differences of burden in West Germany were always within 1% of its competitors (tab. 1), then the importance of a loss of international com-

---

[34] See *Wicke/Schulz, E./Schulz, W.* (1987) as well as Köhler (1985)

[35] To the qualification of these scenarios (ecology jeopardizes or creates jobs) see *Koll* (1989), p. 46 f., as well as *Maier-Rigaud* (1989), p. 58.

[36] See Sachverständigenrat für Umweltfragen (1987), p. 89 f. (with further bibliography).

[37] See *Knödgen* (1981), p. 30

[38] *Knödgen* (1981), p. 30. For an international comparison of noise emission standards (1975) see ibid. p. 31

[39] Environmental standards give the impression that the polluter-pays principle applies, but public subventions can also give them the character of common burden.

petitiveness through rising environmental conservation expenditures must be qualified.

3. *The importance of labour costs*

The question arises as to how conservation costs compare with the most important cost factor, labour costs; in particular the fact that "the labour costs of a country [...] more than all the other cost factors decide the international price and market competitiveness."[40] International competitiveness is based on priced and non-priced factors[41]. In priced factors labour costs as well as environmental conservation costs are included. However, it should be pointed out that these expense categories overlap. This becomes clear when jobs are created by companies with the aim of improving ecology in the companies themselves. Competitiveness is, however, determined by economic reality. International comparison thus asks for a qualification of labour costs related to productivity, i.e. unit wage costs[42]. Unit wage costs are defined as labour costs per unit of output. They are composed of labour costs per hour related to productivity during one hour, i.e. output per hour[43].

When calculating net value added one has to be very careful "at which prices it is valued and with which exchange rates made internationally comparable."[44] International comparisons of unit wage costs are to an extent comparisons of labour's share in national income because the comparison of labour costs and net value added is made at ruling prices and exchange rates[45]. It is therefore the ratio of nominal labour costs to nominal net value added, each of which are converted at the ruling exchange rate.

"The ratio of labour's share in national income is only a figure relating to the functional distribution of income, which does not per se say much about the production conditions in a country. Ex post, it shows how the net value added of one year was divided between labour and capital."[46]

---

[40] *Kroker* (1990), p. D-1

[41] See *Salowsky* (1992), p. 2 as well as chapter IV

[42] See *Kroker* (1990), p. D-2

[43] See *Hooper/Larin* (1989), p. 336

[44] *Kroker* (1990), p. D-3 f.

[45] See hereto the international comparison of the salary ratio in the processing industry in 1980 and 1987 for seven selected industrialized countries in: *Kroker* (1990), p. D-4 f.

[46] *Kroker* (1990), p. D-5

Only the definition of the unit wage costs in real terms on a common currency basis as the relation between nominal labour costs to real net value, i.e. production at stable prices, allows a useful interpretation.

Real unit wage cost data in local currency can be converted into the currency of account at current exchange rates. From the point of view of the currency of account (or rather the national currency) the exchange rate should be used as a quotation of prices (quotation of quantities)[47]. Exchange rate changes have a direct effect on relative unit wage costs in the countries concerned. In contrast to labour's share in national income, shifts in the relative position of labour costs which result from exchange rate changes, are expressed by unit wage costs[48]. The difference lies in the assessment of real output on the calculation of international unit wage costs in a common currency. This is the starting-point for Hooper and Larin's criticism[49]. They summarize: "In the past three decades a considerable literature has been devoted to getting around this valuation problem in the international comparison of real outputs, by developing purchasing power parity exchange rates to translate outputs into common currency units."[50] In the following table 2 Hooper/Larin calculate unit wage costs for 1960, 1965 and 1970 to 1987 as a quotient of labour costs per hour at current exchange rates in US$ and output per hour in 1980 prices and US$ for nine important industrialized countries.

These data show that the FRG was among the three countries with the highest unit wage costs since 1971 and, with the exception of 1984 and 1985, was always at least in second place. Considering national differences and the temporal fluctuations in values, it is apparent that the costs of environmental conservation are of very little importance in comparison with the unit wage costs.

---

[47] On this and the problems of converting to real net value added, see *Hooper/Larin* (1989), p. 336 f.

[48] See *Kroker* (1990), p. D-7. Kroker separates the effect of the exchange rate with a comparison of the unit wage costs based on the national currency and on the D-Mark, Ibid., p. D-8.

[49] See *Hooper/Larin* (1989), p. 336 f.

[50] *Hooper/Larin* (1989), p. 337

Table 2: Unit wage costs in 9 important industrialized countries[1]

	1960	1965	1970	1975	1980	1981	1982	1983	1984	1985	1986	1987
Canada	29,2	24,6	31,8	47,9	62,6	65,7	75,3	75,5	70,2	67,3	68,1	72,2
USA	28,9	27,7	35,0	46,3	65,7	70,8	74,4	73,1	71,7	71,2	70,0	69,0
Japan	13,8	16,9	18,8	42,8	56,2	59,7	51,9	53,0	51,1	49,4	71,1	81,8
FRG	18,8	23,3	29,5	62,8	101,1	84,5	81,3	76,5	68,0	66,3	92,6	115,1
France	21,3	23,6	23,5	49,1	76,4	66,5	60,8	58,5	54,0	54,3	72,0	83,9
Italy	15,4	18,7	20,9	44,0	59,0	51,1	48,6	47,4	42,1	42,1	56,5	67,4
Netherlands	17,0	24,0	27,1	62,7	87,0	69,6	67,3	61,1	50,8	49,1	69,4	85,3
Belgium	21,6	28,0	30,3	65,2	97,0	78,0	61,7	53,8	49,1	49,5	65,7	77,9
Great Britain	22,1	25,3	27,3	51,5	107,4	99,0	88,5	76,4	67,4	67,7	79,9	90,4

[1] Hooper/Larin (1989), p. 347

4. Aspects of international competitiveness

Internationally differing ecological standards induce internationally varying financial strains on companies. Effects on international competitiveness are inevitable[51]. Depending on the national environmental policy, different effects on the international competitiveness are to be expected[52]. Knödgen gives the following reasons for actual effects on the international competition:

- ecologically induced changes in the market share of domestic suppliers
- export success of the domestic ecological industry and
- ecologically induced relocations of industry[53].

The international competitiveness of a company is normally equated with the ability to sell its own products on the market at appropriate conditions[54]. This is also called "ability to sell"[55]. Sell calls it the ability "to keep one´s share of the market against international competitors without public protection (tariff protection, subventions, etc.)."[56] "A company will stay in the market when it is capable of keeping its share of the market and obtain a price higher than the costs of production including opportunity costs of the owned capital."[57] Thus we obtain the international competitiveness of a sector as its average dynamic market position without the sectoral protection.

The "structure-conduct-performance-paradigm"[58] of industrial organisation also provides a starting point to examine the companies' competitiveness. Market structure, company conduct and market performance are the basis for building up input and output oriented indicators of competitiveness[59].

---

[51] See *Jarre's* (1978) basic article about "Ökonomische Interdependenzen zwischen Umweltschutz und Wettbewerb".

[52] See *Knödgen* (1981), p. 33 f.

[53] Ibid p. 35 f.

[54] A meaningful definition of competitiveness as purely supply-oriented "market presence", which can also be presented formally as the vectors of the whole range of production, is provided by *Maggi* (1987), p. 367 f. A comprehensive list of the judgement criteria for the international competitiveness of companies can be found in: *Schmidt* (1990), p. 102.

[55] See *Orlowski* (1982), p. 11 f.

[56] *Sell* (1991), p. 183

[57] Ibid p. 183

[58] See *Gabler* (1988), p. 2520 f. (industrial economy)

[59] See *Pichler/Clement* (1990), p. 490 f.

Indispensable to a measurement concept of international competitiveness of a nation is the clarification of its terms. However this is not without its difficulties. The Scientific Board of Experts of the Federal Ministry of Commerce and Trade concedes that "the concept of international competitiveness is not always meaningful."[60] It is agreed that international competitiveness is the ability of all companies of an economy to sell their products and make profits in the long run. The danger of this aggregated derivation of international competitiveness of a nation from the microeconomic perspective is that it overlooks the causes of domestic economic structures and conditions of production[61]. The forward-looking dynamic aspect of competitiveness requires the consideration of mutual dependencies between domestic structural changes and the foreign trade position. "Competitiveness can be understood as a potential foreign trade position characterized by domestic economic determinants [...], which are to be judged together with changes of the structure of the world trade."[62] The Council of Experts for the Evaluation of Economic Development does justice to this broader understanding of the term with its restricted definition, "Competitiveness in a dynamic economy is the ability to develop new special products and to find new technological solutions which lead to rising income at a high level of employment."[63] The domestic economic aspect is expressed in the concern for income and employment[64]. Thus the question is "whether 'dynamic competition' in an economy is sufficient to create sufficient profitable employment and to achieve satisfactory growth with increasing material welfare."[65] Foreign trade equilibrium is therefore only a short-term aspect of international competitiveness. In measuring international competitiveness, it should be observed that this is a long-term dynamic phenomenon. The large number of different influential factors in the short run and the equalisation mechanism in the long run mean that the current account balance does not provide information about the international competitiveness of an economy. The exchange rate is also not a suitable indicator of competitiveness, as it is determined less by locational advantages than by decisions on capital assets.

---

[60] Wissenschaftlicher Beirat beim Bundesministerium für Wirtschaft (1984), Ziffer 6 according to *Vollmer* (1986), p. 203

[61] The influence of the production and trade structure of a country on its international competitiveness is pointed out by *Orlowski* (1982), p. 83.

[62] *Jürgensen* (1976), p. 468

[63] Sachverständigenrat zur Begutachtung der gesamtwirtschaftlichen Entwicklung (1981), Ziffer 459 according to *Vollmer* (1986), p. 202

[64] See also *Berthold* (1992), p. 9-10 and the therein mentioned bibliography.

[65] *Vollmer* (1986), p. 213

Price and cost comparisons also fail to offer the necessary long-term perspective for the competitiveness of a country. Even analysis of market and trade shares (in this context the so-called Constant-Market-Share-Analysis, CMS, should be mentioned) do not lead us anywhere[66]. Orlowski emphasizes that "all indicators which include the common influence of prices and of non-price supply factors... are useless when one has to assume that the exchange rate tends towards the long-term equilibrium exchange rate."[67]

Ultimately, static ex-post analysis, which does not consider the dynamics of the actual competitive process, seems to prevail in the different measurement concepts[68]. However the efficiency of national competition is decisive in the long run. Berthold emphasizes the significance of "home-made" factors. He considers the regulations on factor markets and the burden of fiscal charges to be the decisive negative restriction on adaptive capacity, which is crucial for the international competitiveness[69]. If an intensified environmental policy increases this fiscal pressure, then the conflict between international competitiveness and environmental conservation would still be justified, if, as we have seen, the costs of environmental conservation are of minor importance compared to other costs.

5. Environmental costs and competitiveness

It is interesting that in a survey of the Federal Association of German Industry of 416 companies, 61% stated that they carry out voluntarily expenditure for environmental conservation which exceed those legally required[70]. The loss of competitiveness caused by the costs for environmental conservation can therefore not be that serious. Concerning the ecological technologies, the FRG lies ahead of the USA (22%) and Japan (12%)[71] with a share of 29% of the foreign applications for patents. It is interesting that the three countries with the most patents pending are those where the expenditures for environmental conservation were clearly highest in 1980, 1986 and

---

[66] See *Vollmer* (1986), p. 207 f. Sell also thinks that it is too simple to use market share analysis to judge international competitiveness, *Sell* 1991, p. 190. After intensive testing of market share analysis, Orlowski also comes to the conclusion that it is not suited to testing international competitiveness in an equilibrium. *Orlowski* (1982), p. 41 f. esp. p. 61

[67] *Orlowski* (1982), p. 62. The emphasis corresponds to the original.

[68] See *Blattner*, N. 1987, p. 391-414 as well as *Vollmer* (1986), p. 199-215

[69] *Berthold* (1992), p. 58-65

[70] IWD (1990), p. 2

[71] IWD (1990a), p. 2

1990 (1990 in billion US$: USA 49.645; Japan 16.450; FRG 14.965 and France 7.022)[72]. The share of public expenditure was extremely high, and private very low in Japan, whereas in USA (58,6%), Austria (61,7%) and in FRG (59,0%) the share of private expenditures was very high[73]. This fact seems to be an important indicator in a world where international competitiveness is particularly conditioned by the ability to innovate.

When examining the share of foreign trade among the individual states of the Federal Republic of Germany, one gets the impression that this foreign trade takes place between countries which are economically similar rather than between those which differ economically. Even if one admits that the border between inter-industrial and intra-industrial trade, and thus their extent depends on the depth of the disaggregation of goods, many do agree that foreign trade between developed economies is mainly intra-industrial and that therefore the value of the theory of comparative advantage is of little empirical importance. In a world where in developed economies returns of scale in production, product differentiation and monopolistic competition are of decisive importance, the requirements for the value of these approaches seem to be no longer fulfilled - apart from the increasing inadequateness of the static method[74].

Kravis[75] tried to test the Heckscher/Ohlin theorem. If a country specializes in labour-intensive export goods, then labour should be abundant and the export industry will employ these workers, who will thus be less well paid. In reality wages were especially high in these sectors. Kravis concluded that the predictions of the Heckscher/Ohlin theorem is not valid for highly developed economies. Decisive for export are namely the availability of human capital, inventions and different technologies, which does not comply with the assumption of homogeneity on which the theorem is based. Crucial for foreign trade, and at the same time for the international competitiveness, is therefore the availability of qualified production factors and technical know-how. According to the "availability approach" we must answer the question, as to why availability differs[76].

---

[72] IW-Trends (1991), p. B4

[73] Ibid. p. B5

[74] See the works of: *Lorenz* (1967) and *Blattner* (1971)

[75] *Kravis* (1956), p. 143-155

[76] If the permanent availability of factors such as raw materials and climate are decisive for production, then foreign trade can, in accordance with Ricardo, be explained by different production functions.

In judging foreign trade it is essential to make the distinction between goods for which price competition is central and those for which quality and know-how are essential. For technologically more sophisticated goods, price competition is no longer so important, whereas the significance of quality competition increases. According to a survey in the United Kingdom, only 5% of the companies bought foreign machines because of a more competitive price, 30% bought them because of their technical superiority, 21% because there was no British alternative, 20% because of the better terms of delivery and finally 8% because of the preparedness to supply special models. A similar survey held among successful US-exporters showed that only 28% of the decisions were motivated by the price. In 25% of the cases the better technology, in 12% the after-sales service and finally in 10% the design was decisive for success[77]. In this context one should also mention Kravis and Posner's[78] theory of the "technological gap trade."[79] Lorenz interprets Kravis' "availability approach" development theoretically in Schumpeter's sense and speaks of monopolistic availabilities[80]. The dynamics of growth and thus also of foreign trade show themselves in a sequence of temporary monopolies with a continuous obligation to innovate. Hufbauer[81] even points out that high wage costs necessitate innovation, which leads to the fact that only countries with high wages play a predominant role in foreign trade with high-technology goods and he speaks of a "pecking order"[82] of international trade. Thus we can interpret the above mentioned empirical result. When countries with higher expenditures for environmental conservation are countries where higher environmental costs arise because of higher environmental standards, then the greater success in patent application can be interpreted, according to Hufbauer's theory, as being caused by these higher costs. Essential for the neo-technology approach is, apart from the rules of patent protection and the availability of human capital, the absorption capacity of the domestic market.

In this context Linder's[83] theory becomes significant, in which demand plays the most important role. According to this hypothesis, potential export

---

[77] *Winters* (1985), p. 208

[78] *Posner* (1961), p. 323-341

[79] See e.g. *Bender* (1992), p. 453.

[80] *Lorenz* (1967), p. 86

[81] *Hufbauer* (1966), p. 30-32

[82] "The technological gap account thus implies a 'pecking order' of trade". *Hufbauer* (1966), p. 32

[83] *Linder* (1961)

goods are those for which there is a domestic market. This is based on the following hypotheses.

1. It is unlikely that producers will develop a good, which will be unsuccessful on the domestic market.
2. It is possible that foreigners are unable to develop a good, which is exclusively for the foreign market.
3. It is doubtful, whether such a product can be launched on the foreign market without prohibitive costs.
4. Incentives for innovations come more often from users than from the "drawing board". Communication with users (proximity and understanding) therefore becomes especially important[84].

Preferences and per capita income are decisive for domestic demand. Thus Linder's theory contrasts to some extent the factor endowment approach. Countries with a high per capita income mostly have a high level of capital equipment. In particular Linder forecasts trade between countries with similar per capita income and thus similar factor equipment.

How does real trade develop? The same forces which create domestic trade also create foreign trade[85]. "Trade creating forces" are monopolistic competition and product differentiation, technological superiority, organizational leads in the application of factors, entrepreneurial efficiency and returns of scale. With the growing standard of living (per capita income) preferences express themselves in a more diversified manner. Barker[86] explained in that way, why the imports have an import elasticity > 1. With a growing standard of living, consumers increasingly ask for sets of goods' characteristics and not for the goods themselves. Demand forces increasing differentiation. With increasing returns of scale the differentiation of goods eventually leads to foreign trade via market expansion[87]. As an example of Linder's approach related to environmental conservation, one can refer to the fact that in Denmark wind power plants were developed for the domestic market and in the meantime have became an export success[88]. To make progress in domestic environmental conservation measures would, in the long run, increase the international competitiveness by creating a corresponding domestic market. In comparison to Linder's general hypothesis, some ad-

---

[84] *Winters* (1985), p. 43 (refers to works of *Rothwell* 1980)

[85] *Linder* (1961), p. 102

[86] *Barker* (1977), p. 153 - 172 quoted from *Gandolfo* (1987), S. 272 - 273

[87] Pratten came to the conclusion that in 9 of 27 industries the minimum efficient scale (MES) makes up half of the capacity of the market in the UK. See *Winters* (1985), p. 47

[88] *Hilscher* (1983), p. 5-11

ditional aspects have to be indicated in this context, which support my conclusion that advancing to a stricter environmental policy strengthens international competitiveness in the long run.

1. The international demand for ecological products (generally also energy-saving) and methods will inevitably increase.
2. Increasing ecological consciousness in the private sector will, with growing living standards, increase the demand for ecologically beneficial goods and production methods.
3. In this context it may be important for international marketing when customers know that goods come from a country with high environmental standards[89]. This can also be a locational advantage for a country with higher environmental standards.
4. Growing ecological consciousness in the private sector will lead to the "quality" of the environment becoming increasingly significant to locational decisions, due to the ecological dependency of mobile labour supply, especially highly qualified labour.
5. It can be pointed out that possibly better environmental quality, for example of water and air, can be a locational advantage through cost reductions in production.

C. Consequences for environmental policy

There is no question that high environmental standards diminish international competitiveness and the advantages of location in the short run. An entrepreneur facing strong international price competition will not accept arguments related to the relative costs for environmental conservation in comparison to the unit wage costs. But international competition is increasingly non-price competition and it is therefore clear that a country with high wages, such as the Federal Republic of Germany, is no longer a suitable location for goods' production where only price competition is relevant. Environmental policy will not be orientated to cost efficiency aspects as an essential long-term aspect, even if it is sensible to attain environmental standards at the lowest possible cost. Innovations are decisive in international competition in view of a market whose long-term expansion can hardly be doubted. Environmental policy must be particularly concerned with the deployment of efficient innovatory instruments and should not lag behind the international development due to short-term cost orientation. It should

---

[89] It is claimed that the German automobile industry rejects a speed limit on motorways because the internationally reputation of German cars is based on the fact that there are no speed limits in Germany.

rather create incentives for the development of ecologically beneficial goods and methods by introducing harsher standards to the domestic economy via a corresponding domestic market. Let us hope that in solving these essential tasks for our future, international competition between national environmental policies will not be impeded by protectionism and international solutions of the lowest common denominator.

References

Barker, J. (1977): International Trade and Economic Growth: An Alternative to the Neoclassical Approach, Journal of Economics 1977, 1, Cambridge, p. 153 - 172

Bender, Dieter (1992): Außenhandel, in: Vahlens Kompendium der Wirtschaftstheorie und Wirtschaftspolitik, Vol. 1, 5th ed.

Berthold, Norbert (1992): Wettbewerbsfähigkeit der deutschen Wirtschaft - Gefahr im Verzug?, Berlin

Blattner, Nikolaus (1971): Die Rolle des Wettbewerbs im Aussenhandel, Zürich

Blattner, Nikolaus (1987): Voraussetzungen der schweizerischen Wettbewerbsfähigkeit: Möglichkeiten und Grenzen der empirischen Analyse, in: Schweizerische Zeitschrift für Volkswirtschaft und Statistik, 123 (1987), 3., p. 391-414

Blümle, Gerold (1984): Der Fortschrittsglaube der Ökonomen, Gefahr oder Hoffnung, in: *Blümle, G.* (ed.): Fortschritt und Schöpfungsglaube oder Die Machbarkeit des Glücks, Freiburg, p. 56-79

Board of Experts for Environmental Problems (1987): Umweltgutachten, Stuttgart u. Mainz

Bonus, Holger (1984): Marktwirtschaftliche Konzepte im Umweltschutz: Auswertungen amerikanischer Erfahrungen im Auftrag des Landes Baden-Württemberg, Stuttgart

Frey, Bruno S. (1985): Internationale Politische Ökonomie, Munich

Gabler (1988): Wirtschaftslexikon, Vol. 3

Gandolfo, Giancarlo (1987): International Economics I, The Pure Theory of International Trade, Berlin u.a.

Grove, R.H. (1992): Die Anfänge des Umweltbewußtseins, in: Spektrum der Wissenschaft, September 1992, p. 76-81

Hartwig, Karl-Hans (1992): Umweltökonomik, in: *Bender, D., u.a.* (ed.): Vahlens Kompendium der Wirtschaftstheorie und Wirtschaftspolitik, Vol. 2, 5th ed., Munich

Hansen, Thomas (1988): Marktversagen versus Politikerversagen: Ein Beitrag zur Theorie der optimalen intertemporalen Allokation erschöpfbarer Ressourcen unter dem Aspekt des Planungshorizonts, Freiburg

Heinzelmann, Regula (1991): Umweltschutz: Herausforderung und Chance, Frankfurt a.M.

Hilscher, G. (1983): Dänische Windturbinen verkaufen sich gut, in: Sonnenenergie 5/1983

Hooper, Peter/Larin, Kathryn A. (1989): International Comparisons of Labor Costs in Manufacturing, in: The Review of Income and Wealth, 35 (1989), 4., p. 335-355

Hufbauer, Gary C. (1966): Synthetic Materials and the Theory of International Trade, London

IWD (1990): Informationsdienst des Instituts der Deutschen Wirtschaft, Vol.16, Issue 9, Cologne

IWD (1990a): Informationsdienst des Instituts der Deutschen Wirtschaft, Vol.16, Issue 49, Cologne

IWD (1991): Informationsdienst des Instituts der Deutschen Wirtschaft, Vol. 17, Issue 9, Cologne

IW-Trends (1991): Institut der Deutschen Wirtschaft (ed.), 18 (1991), 4., Cologne

Jarre, Jan (1978): Ökonomische Interdependenzen zwischen Umweltschutz und Wettbewerb, in: Zeitschrift für Umweltpolitik, 1/1978

Jürgensen, Harald (1976): Über einige Kategorien einer Messung der internationalen Wettbewerbsfähigkeit von Industrienationen, in: Wirtschaftspolitik, Wissenschaft und politische Aufgabe, Festschrift zum 65.Geburtstag von Karl Schiller, Bern u. Stuttgart, S.467-482

Kemper, Manfred (1989): Das Umweltproblem in der Marktwirtschaft, Volkswirtschaftliche Schriften, Issue 390, Berlin

Klaus, Joachim (1989): Kosten der Umweltnutzung, in: Umweltschutz und Marktwirtschaft aus der Sicht unterschiedlicher Disziplinen, *Jörg Klawitter/Reiner Kümmel* (ed.), Würzburg

Klemmer, Paul (1990): Umweltschutz und Wirtschaftlichkeit: Grenzen der Belastbarkeit der Unternehmen, Berlin

Klemmer, Paul (1991): Gesamtwirtschaftliche Effekte ökonomischer Instrumente des Umweltchutzes, in: Umweltschutz: Herausforderungen und Chancen für die Wirtschaft, Beihefte der Konjunkturpolitik, Issue 38, Berlin, S.135-152

Knödgen, Gabriele (1981): Umweltschutz und internationaler Wettbewerb, in: ifo-Schnelldienst, Vol. 34, 1981, Issue 1-2, p. 29-46

Köhler, Axel (1985): Arbeitslose für den Umweltschutz, in: Zeitschrift für Umweltpolitik, 8/1985, p. 29-44

Koll, Willi (1989): Umweltschutz, Marktwirtschaft und Beschäftigung, in: Umweltschutz und Marktwirtschaft aus der Sicht unterschiedlicher Disziplinen, *Jörg Klawitter/Reiner Kümmel* (ed.), Würzburg

Kroker, Rolf (1990): Lohnstückkosten im Verarbeitenden Gewerbe, ein internationaler Vergleich, in: IW-Trends, 17(1990), 1., Köln, p. D-1 ff.

Kravis, Irving B. (1956): Availability and Other Influences on the Commodity Composition of Trade, in: Journal of Political Economy, Vol. 64, 1956, p. 143-155

Linder, Staffan Burenstam (1961): An Essay on Trade and Transformation, New York, Stock holm, Göteborg, Uppsala

Lorenz, Detlef (1967): Dynamische Theorie der internationalen Arbeitsteilung, Berlin

Maggi, Rico (1987): Die Analyse der Wettbewerbsfähigkeit wirtschaftlicher Strukturen, in: Schweizerische Zeitschrift für Volkswirtschaft, 123 (1987), 3., p. 367-389

Maier-Rigaud, Gerhard (1989): Die ökonomische Knechtschaft der Ökologie, in: Umweltschutz und Marktwirtschaft aus der Sicht unterschiedlicher Disziplinen, *Jörg Klawitter/Reiner Kümmel* (ed.), Würzburg

Orlowski, Dieter (1982): Die internationale Wettbewerbsfähigkeit einer Volkswirtschaft. Konzeptionelle Grundlagen und empirische Messung einer wirtschaftspolitischen Zielgröße, Göttingen

Pichler, Eva/Clement, Werner (1990): Konkurrenz und Wettbewerbsfähigkeit, Wirtschaftswissenschaftliches Studium, 19 (1990), 10., p. 490-496

Posner, Michael V. (1961): International Trade and Technological Change, in: Oxford Economic Papers, Vol. 13, 1961, p. 323-341

Rauscher, Michael (1992): On Ecological Dumping, Paper presented on the occasion of the annual meeting of Verein für Sozialpolitik 1992 in Oldenburg

Rothwell, R. (1980): Innovation in Textile Machinery, in: Technical Innovation and British Economic Performance, *Pavitt, K.* (ed.), London

Sachverständigenrat zur Begutachtung der gesamtwirtschaftlichen Entwicklung (1981):Investieren für mehr Beschäftigung, Jahresgutachten 1981/1982, Mainz u. Stuttgart

Salowsky, Heinz (1992): Industrielle Arbeitskosten im internationalen Vergleich 1970-1991, in: IW-Trends, 19 (1992), 1., Köln

Schmidt, Ingo (1990): Wettbewerbspolitik und Kartellrecht: Eine Einführung, Stuttgart, 3rd ed., Stuttgart

Sell, Axel (1991): Einführung in die internationalen Wirtschaftsbeziehungen, Berlin u. New York

Simonis, Udo Ernst (1987): Umwelt und Volkswirtschaftliche Gesamtrechnung: Eine konzeptionelle Perspektive, in: Statistische Umweltberichterstattung: Ergebnisse des 2. Wiesbadener Gesprächs am 12./13. November 1986, Statistisches Bundesamt (ed.), Schriftenreihe Forum der Bundesstatistik, Bd. 7, Stuttgart, p. 48-60

Sprenger, Rolf Ulrich (1991): EG-Binnenmarkt und Umweltschutz, in: Umweltschutz: Herausforderungen und Chancen für die Wirtschaft, Beiheft der Konjunkturpolitik, 38/1991

Vollmer, Rudolf (1986): Die internationale Wettbewerbsfähigkeit - Kritische Analyse eines heute viel verwendeten Begriffs, in: *Kuhn, H.* (ed.): Probleme der Stabilitätspolitik, Göttingen, p. 199-215

Voss, Gerhard (1991): Umweltschutz im internationalen Vergleich, in: IW-Trends, (18)1991, 4., Köln, p. B-1 ff.

Watrin, Christian (1980/1): Bestimmt die Wirtschaft unvermeidlich alles ?, Radius 1980/1

Wicke, Lutz/Schulz, Erika/Schulz, Werner (1987): Entlastung des Arbeitsmarktes durch Umweltschutz?, in: Mitteilungen aus der Arbeits- und Berufsforschung, 20 (1987), 1., Stuttgart, p. 89-98

Winters, Alan L. (1985): International Economics, 3rd edition, London

Wissenschaftlicher Beirat beim Bundesministerium für Wirtschaft (1987): Gutachten von Dezember 1984 bis Dezember 1986, Göttingen

Evaluation of Environmental Costs in Japan

Hiroshi Yanagioka

1. Approach to environmental issues

Generally, there are two typical approaches to solving environmental problems. One is *cleaner production* and the other is often called to be *end-of-pipe solution*. This classification is very much familiar to any process engineers who routinely practice process problems with varying inputs and outputs. It is clear in environmental issues that technology that pollutes and/or destructs corresponds to *process*, and cleaner production and end-of-pipe treatment refer to input and output. The Japanese approach to environmental issues has often been criticized by environmental activists in the U.S. and Europe. One such example is that Japan seems to view sustainable development less as a moral crusade than as a massive *commercial opportunity*. This may be related to a typical Japanese way of action where the output side is focused upon rather than the input side. On the other hand, the U.S. and Europe clearly regard it as orthodox that environmental problems need to be tackled at their roots through measures that involve social systems. Even in Japan, this attitude is observed among those who have become aware of environmental issues in recent years. Nevertheless, it is also true that Japan has achieved economic success and has alleviated industrial pollution through application of technology. Thus, if the effectiveness and limits of this approach can be ascertained, it can become vital in resolving environmental problems around the globe in the coming years. To realize this, we need to clarify the costs of environmental technologies to determine whether it can be accommodated by society, and to present how environmental technologies can be linked to social systems.

2. Costs of environmental technologies

The combustion process represents a technical field directly related to the environment. Through this process enormous amounts of pollutants are released into the atmosphere, as reflected by the amount of fuels consumed in Figure 1 and the amount of sulphur dioxide (SO_2) and nitrogen oxides (NO_2) emissions in Figure 2. These compounds present the prime cause for acid rain and photo-chemical smog. The combustion also produces soot or dust, which is finally released from the flue gas stack as fine particles.

The following are examples of environment-related technologies in relation to fuels. Their outline and estimated costs are also given:

2.1. Hydrodesulphurization technology

Under this technology, the sulphur content of petroleum feedstocks, e.g. gas oil and heavy residue oil, is reduced by a catalytic process in which the oil is reacted with hydrogen under a high temperature and pressure to obtain hydrogen sulphide.

Table 1: Example of hydrodesulphurization plants

1 Scale: 30,000 BPSD (approx. 200 M3/h)
2 Feed stock: Atmospheric residual oil of Arabian heavy crude oil (4.2% sulphur content), US$ 97/ton
3 Product oil: Low sulphur oil (0.3% sulphur content)
4 Plant construction cost: US$ 179,000,000 (about 24 billion Yen)
5 Utility: Fuel oil 9,200 Kg/h
Electricity 10,500 kW
Coolant 2,740 tons/h
6 Processing costs:

(1) Operating costs		
- Labor cost for maintenance and operation		US$ 3.49/ton
- Catalyst/chemical cost		US$ 3.58/ton
- Utility cost		US$ 8.47/ton
- Insurance/taxes		US$ 2.33/ton
	(Subtotal)	US$ (17.87)/ton
(2) Depreciation of construction cost		US$ 23.79/ton
	Total	US$ 41.66/ton

Under this process, the total cost per ton will increase by about 40%.

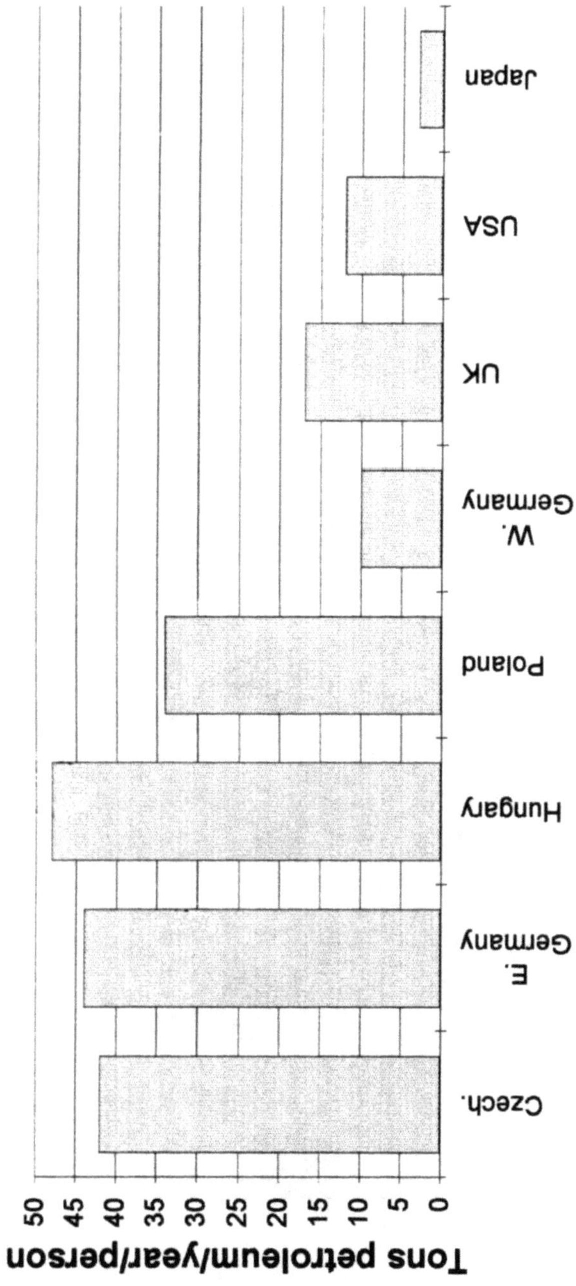

Figure 1: Energy consumption per person

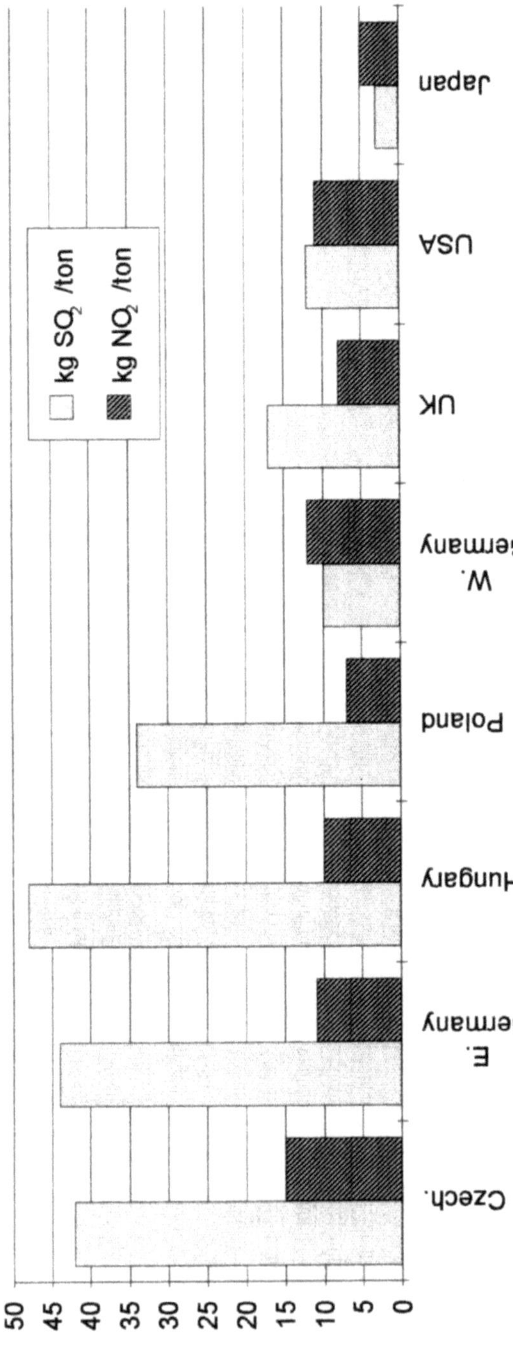

Figure 2: SO_2 and NO_2 emissions to the atmosphere per unit of energy (equivalent to fuel oil)

2.2. Flue gas desulphurization technology

Under this technology, the exhaust gas is treated with an aqueous solution or appropriate reactants to extract sulphur dioxide and to form by-products for other uses. Possible by-products include gypsum, sulphuric acid, sodium sulphite, and sulphur.

Table 2: Example of exhaust gas desulphurizers with gypsum by-product

1 Scale: 300 MW, 1,000,000 Nm^3/H
2 Fuel: Heavy oil (102 tons/h)
3 Processed flue gas: Desulphurization of SO_2 content from 2,000 ppm to 200 ppm
4 Plant construction cost: 5.39 billion Yen
5 Utility: Limestone 7,940 Kg/h
Electricity 3,250 kW
Water 43 Tons/h
6 Processing costs:

(1) Operating costs		
- Labor cost for maintenance and operation		0.10 Yen/KWH
- Cost of limestone		0.09 Yen/KWH
- Utility cost		0.17 Yen/KWH
- Insurance/taxes		0.05 Yen/KWH
	(Subtotal)	(0.41) Yen/KWH
(2) Depreciation of construction cost		0.48 Yen/KWH
	Total	0.89 Yen/KWH
		2,600 Yen/ton

2.3. Flue gas denitrification technology

Under this technology, the exhaust gas is treated with appropriate reactants, and the nitrogen monoxide content is reduced through a catalytic process. If the exhaust gas is reduced to nitrogen, it is released into the atmosphere. If it is changed to other substances, by-products are collected for other uses. Ammonium nitrate can be collected as a by-product.

Table 3: Example of SCR exhaust gas denitrification plants

1 Scale: 300 MW, 1,000,000 Nm^3/H
2 Fuel: Heavy oil (102 tons/h)
3 Processed exhaust: Denitrofication of NO_2 content from 200 ppm to 40 ppm
4 Plant construction cost: 1.59 billion Yen
5 Utility: Catalyst 360 m^3/3-years
Electricity 470 kW
Ammonia 137 Kg/h
6 Processing costs:

(1) Operating costs		
- Labor cost for maintenance and operation		0.02 Yen/KWH
- Cost of ammonia and electricity		0.05 Yen/KWH
- Cost of catalyst		0.16 Yen/KWH
- Insurance/taxes		0.01 Yen/KWH
	(Subtotal)	(0.24) Yen/KWH
(2) Depreciation of construction cost		0.08 Yen/KWH
	Total	0.32 Yen/KWH 930 Yen/ton

2.4. Flue gas dust collector

Dust collection from flue gas has been conducted using gas scrubbers and multi-cyclones. Recently large sized electrostatic precipitators and bag filters have been increasingly used with such advantages of high removal efficiency and ease of handling collected ashes notwithstanding their apparent high installed costs.

Accordingly, if all of the flue gas treating processes described above, namely dust removal, denitrofication and desulphurization were applied to a boiler plant, the cost would be a total of 3,940 Yen/ton of fuel or approximately 10% of the price of fuel oil. In terms of an increase in electricity cost, a total of 1.35 Yen/kWH would be added to the generating cost of electricity, which will be verified in the following chapter in view of added electricity cost due to environmental facilities in power plants.

Table 4: Example of electrostatic precipitators

1 Scale: 300 MW, 1,000,000 Nm^3/H
2 Fuel: Heavy oil 102 tons/h
3 Processed exhaust: Removal of particulate content from 500 mg/Nm^3 to 70 mg/Nm^3
4 Plant construction cost: 1.28 billion Yen
5 Utility: Electricity 940 kW
6 Processing costs:

(1) Operating costs		
- Labor cost for maintenance and operation		0.01 Yen/KWH
- Cost of electricity		0.03 Yen/KWH
- Insurance/taxes		0.01 Yen/KWH
	(Subtotal)	(0.05) Yen/KWH
(2) Depreciation of construction cost		0.09 Yen/KWH
	Total	0.14 Yen/KWH 410 Yen/ton

2.5. Incineration

This represents one of the oldest technologies available. Through incineration, the volume of the material can be reduced and its molecular weight can be lowered, making it easier to handle. However, preventative measures, such as those that have been mentioned previously, generally need to be implemented to alleviate environmental pollution created by this processing.

Table 5: Example of refuse incineration plants

(A) Municipal refuse incineration facility
1 Scale: 200 tons/day, designed for a population of 200,000
2 Plant construction cost: 7.46 billion Yen
3 Processing costs:

(1) Operating cost		4,000 Yen/ton
(2) Depreciation of construction cost		12,000 Yen/ton
	Total	16,000 Yen/ton

(B) Star Dust '80 Project (Yokohama City)

1 Scale: 30 tons/day, separation of refuses by type, use as fertilizers, experimental facility for thermal decomposition of plastics
2 Plant construction cost: 15 billion Yen
3 Processing costs:

(1) Operating cost		80,000 Yen/ton
(2) Depreciation of construction cost		160,000 Yen/ton
	Total	240,000 Yen/ton

2.6. Water treatment

Water treatment, which mainly consists of biological waste water treatment, sedimentation, and filtration, is another technology that has existed for a very long time. It also serves to link the environment directly with human activities. Recently, chemical reaction has been newly adopted to neutralize waste water, reflecting a change toward high-tech treatments that use special chemicals and membranes. The results of recent developments in bio-technology are also being added to enhance nature's biological waste water purification, which is often said to produce pure water if the waste water goes a couple of meters downstream.

Table 6: Example of municipal waste water treatment facility

1 Scale: 10,000 m^3/day, designed for a population of 100,000
2 Plant construction cost: 12 billion Yen
3 Processing costs:

(1) Operating cost		120 Yen/m^3
(2) Depreciation of construction cost		190 Yen/m^3
	Total	310 Yen/m^3

Table 7: Example of industrial waste water treatment facility

1 Scale: 900 m^3/day, industrial and sanitary waste water
2 Plant construction cost: 2 billion Yen
3 Processing costs:

(1) Operating cost		130 Yen/m^3
(2) Depreciation of construction cost		450 Yen/m^3
	Total	580 Yen/m^3

Table 8: Example of small scale waste water treatment facility (e.g. for restaurants)

1	Scale: 20 m^3/day, for family restaurants	
2	Plant construction cost: 8 million Yen	
3	Processing costs:	
	(1) Operating cost Electricity used 0.7 kW	160 Yen/m^3
	(2) Depreciation of construction cost	180 Yen/m^3
	Total	340 Yen/m^3

3. Conditions for accepting environmental technologies

In developing countries, the environment is just as important as in Japan, but in reality, production and energy per se are said to have to be placed priority. Even in Japan, if the cost of environmental technologies is excessive, the mere existence of the technologies will be jeopardized. Consequently, a discussion of the relative costs of the major environmental technologies follows.

Currently, the IEA forbids new construction of thermal power plants using heavy oil as fuel in OECD nations. But also behind this is the high production cost of low sulphur oil used mainly for fuel, as explained in the previous section.

Yet, the price of this type of oil actually traded is not as high as it costs. This is probably due to the fact that refineries are able to set prices for each type of oil from a comprehensive standpoint. Thus, the price difference between high and low sulphur oil seems to be set to allow low sulphur oil to compete with the processing cost of flue gas desulphurization, which is about several thousand Yen per ton.

When coal is used as fuel, on the other hand, it is economically difficult to lower the sulphur content of coal itself. Plants using this as fuel, hence, need to depend on flue gas desulphurization technology. Consequently, let us look at the details of the construction cost of environment-related facilities for a 300 megawatt coal fired power plant, such as the one described in the preceding chapter. The actual cost of these facilities in coal fired power plants is significantly greater than the heart or machinery parts of the plant as it is for other facilities, and requires about twice the cost of the machinery. The machinery parts themselves cost more than two times main components cost which combine BTG, namely the boiler, turbine, and generator. Among the environment-related facilities, typically, the flue gas and waste water treatment facilities require about 20% of the total cost of the power plant.

Next, let us look at how the cost of these environment-related facilities is reflected in the price of electricity. In order to achieve this, it is necessary to uncover the items that make up the price of electricity, which is determined by the cost and warranted appropriate profit. The following table indicates the recent financial situation of nine electrical power companies. The table has been developed by referring to the financial statements made public by the companies.

Table 9: Overview of electrical power industry

1) Operating revenues		
1 Lighting	4.1625 trillion Yen	30.5 %
2 Electric power	9.2940	68.1 %
3 Others	.1911	1.4 %
Total	13.6476 trillion Yen	100.0 %
2) Operating expenses		
1 Labour	1.1860 trillion Yen	9.2 %
2 Fuel	4.2155	32.7 %
3 Maintenance	1.1731	9.1 %
4 Depreciation	1.6501	12.8 %
5 Interest payments	1.5341	11.9 %
6 Power purchased	1.1344	8.8 %
7 Public taxes	.7219	5.6 %
8 Others	1.2762	9.9 %
Total	12.8913 trillion Yen	100.0 %
3) Operating profit	.7563 trillion Yen	
4) Electricity	500.9 billion KWH	

According to this table, the average unit price of electricity is about 20.2 Yen/kWH. Assuming that the maintenance cost, depreciation cost, and interest payments are together equivalent to the cost for machinery of the power plant, we see that the electricity price attributed to this machinery equals 20.2 x (9.1+12.8+11.9)/100 = 6.82 Yen/kWH. Then, since environment-related facilities cover 20% of the power plant's total machineries, the environment-related cost per unit of electricity is 6.82 x 0.2 = 1.24 Yen/kWH. In other words, the environment-related cost per unit of electricity cost is estimated to be about 1.24/20.2 x 100 = 6.1%.

By accepting this cost, we would be able to use fuel such as coal to obtain electricity without causing great environmental problems. Furthermore, if an average family uses 420 kWH per month, the environmental cost of electricity incurred by each household will amount to about 6,200 Yen per year.

Next, let us focus on the problem of water from the view point of ordinary citizens. Today, a typical family in the Yokohama area uses about 30 m^3 of water supply per month. Each person uses about 250 liters per day. The charge for water supply is about 120 Yen/m^3, and for sewerage is about 82 Yen/m^3. The charge for sewerage given here is lower than the cost for treating water stated in the previous section, which is about 310 Yen/m^3, because residential taxes supposedly subsidize the excess cost.

Consequently, a family spends (120+82) x 30 = 6,060 Yen every month for using clear water and clean sewerage. If the income of the household is assumed to be 8 million Yen per year, the proportion of the expenditure is 0.606 x 12/800 x 100 = 0.9%. This figure seems reasonable, considering that measures are implemented for preserving the environment and maintaining hygienic conditions.

How about the problem of municipal waste disposal? If each person produces one kilogram of refuse per day and if separation of different types of waste is not conducted as in Yokohama and all refuse is incinerated, 1 x 365 x 4 = 1.46 tons of refuse will need to be collected by garbage trucks per year for each household. The cost for this is 1.46 x 16,000 = 23,000 Yen, which occupies 4% of the residential tax. It is not a minuscule amount, but it seems to be an acceptable rate.

Then, why are technologically ideal projects, such as the Star Dust Project, abandoned without being implemented? The cost of such projects amounts to 1.46 x 240,000 = 350,000 Yen per year for each household, which is over 60% of the residential tax. This figure is clearly not acceptable.

4. Environmental coefficient and burden ratio

The analysis of the costs of environmental technologies indicates that environmental technologies are put to use only when the cost of such technologies is relatively small compared to the cost of living or the cost of production technologies that require them. The denominators differ from case to case, but the rates as defined are well below 10%, namely: 6% for electricity, 1% for water, and 4% for refuse disposal.

Let us call this percentage the "environmental coefficient." In instances when the environmental coefficient is small, it is indicated that technological approaches to alleviate environmental problems are possible. Today, environmental awareness is booming, only a few people are likely to claim that this coefficient should be zero. Nevertheless, a survey of the people's preferences needs to be conducted timely to ascertain the limit of this burden. After all, we still need to make value judgments with regards to the environment.

The efforts exerted by engineers play an important role in lowering the cost of environmental technologies to reduce the coefficient. Yet, it is noteworthy that this coefficient does not only depend on the cost of the technologies. The cost of the environmental technologies does not necessarily burden either the consumer or the producer. In the case of electricity the consumer takes almost all the cost incurred by the technologies as analyzed in the previous section. Some parts are left unclear for low sulphur fuel oil, but this environmental cost seems to be shared across other petroleum products with significant proportions. About two-thirds of sewerage cost are covered by taxes, and the cost of household waste disposal is paid by local governments, in other words, by local taxes.

I believe the reason behind Japan's strong interest in solving environmental problems through technological means lies in the confidence that Japan has become successful by betting on technological advancement and in the fact that its affluent society has been able to accommodate the burden of the cost of these technologies. The ratio of burden will be influenced by the general disposition of society and its experiences, depending on the characteristics of the environmental problems. It, nevertheless, needs to be optimized in the coming years. If the cost of environmental technologies and its burden become excessive for society, measures for environmental protection need to be shifted to the input side approach or basic Western European approach such as efficient use of resources, energy conservation, "soft path " and frugality. Both this approach and the Japanese approach, generally referred to as the output side approach, should be considered together in pursuit for optimum measures for future environmental preservation.

References

UN Energy Statistics Year Book (1986)

UNECE Environmental Statistics (1987)

Reynolds B.E., et al.: "VRDS/RFCC Provides Efficient Conversion of Vacuum Bottoms into Gasoline" presented at JPI conference Tokyo (1990)

Marchello J.M., et al.: "Gas Cleaning for Air Quality Control" Marcel Dekker, Inc., New York (1975)

Isao Yoshimura: "Refuse and City Life" Iwanami Publishing (1984)

Annual Reports to Share Holders from Tokyo Electric Power Co. and other power companies (1991)

Environmental Policy in the European Community
- A Critical Perspective -

Hans-Hermann Francke
Knut Blind

A. The Problem

The Maastricht Treaties not only aim to integrate the future monetary and fiscal policies of the European Community Members, they also formulate important guidelines for a harmonization of European environmental policy. Although from a fundamental theoretical point of view similar problems arise as with the creation of a European monetary union and integrated fiscal policy, the attempts at environmental harmonization have, until now, attracted little public attention. It may be - given the generally perceived lack of environmental initiatives - that even tentative attempts are more favourably received, without being critically examined. Furthermore international environmental policy is relatively rarely discussed, and its complexity creates barriers to public discussion.

In the following some critical comments on the concept and expected efficiency will be made against the background of currently planned aims and measures of EEC environmental policy. Central to these reflections are the harmonization problems of European environmental policy. In particular it will be considered whether centralised or decentralised environmental policy is the superior concept, and respectively, whether the envisaged regulations of the EEC will continue to permit decentralised environmental policy, or not[1]. For this purpose a short survey of the current contractually fixed aims and measures of EEC environmental policy will be first presented. This is then followed by the critical theoretical treatment. Finally a case study on the introduction of the catalytic converter for cars demonstrates the problems which future centralised European regulation could create for decentralised

---

[1] See *Siebert* 1990.

environmental progress. A detailed appendix lists the Community rules which are currently applicable.

B. The current state of environment policy in the European Community

I. Aims and principles

1. In the Treaty of Rome the theme "environment" was not included by the founding Member States of the European Communities. In 1972 the heads of state and of government of the Member States discussed questions related to environmental protection for the first time at a summit meeting. The first of now five programmes of environmental action[2] was already adopted in the following year. These Communities' environmental programmes last several years and include guidelines and actions, which are to be achieved within the framework of the Communities' environmental policy. Similar programmes were decided in 1977, 1983, 1987 and also in 1993. Starting in 1975 an item for environmental protection appeared in the budget and in 1981 the responsible departments for environmental questions and consumer protection were set up.

A binding target system for Community environmental policy (Title VII) was included in the EC Treaty with the coming into force of the Single European Act in 1987[3]. This was however significantly adapted and extended in the signing of the Treaty for European Union in Maastricht in 1992.

According to Art. 130r, 1 EC Treaty the Community's environmental policy pursues the following aims:

- conservation, protection and improvement of the quality of the environment;
- protection of human health;
- prudent and rational use of natural resources;
- support of international measures towards overcoming regional or global environmental problems.

2. According to Art. 130r, 2 EC Treaty targets should be set at a high level of protection, but consider regional conditions. In this way the reduction of environmental policy to the smallest common denominator should be prevented and greater attention given to the most advanced national demands.

---

[2] See *Krämer* 1991, p. 841-49 and *Klemmer* 1992, p. 15f.

[3] OJ L 169 1987, p. 1ff.

A second principle, the *precautionary approach*, relates to the wish that environmental policy should not react merely passively, but above all be active in preventing environmental damage. The background behind this principle lies in the limited regenerative ability of the environment, so that a critical tolerance level should not be exceeded in the first place. In addition the precautionary approach is based on the recognition that human intervention in the natural world can always have negative effects which should be reduced to a minimum. A concrete result of this basic premiss is the introduction of environmental compatibility tests, in which activities affecting the environment are tested for their negative effects.

Subordinate to the precautionary approach is the *polluter pays principle* (PPP). As environmental damage is generally present when applied, thus enabling the identification of a polluter, the PPP is considered to be a reactive environmental policy. Environmental policy can however be preventively pursued using the PPP if property rights for the originally free environmental goods are defined (Coase), or a price (Pigou tax) for their damage is charged. Thus by using the price mechanism or the costs incurred, the consumption of environmental goods can be rationed. The instruments related to the PPP range from a general ban of certain environmentally damaging substances or the observance of certain pollution limits to emission taxes.

Environmental protection receives inter-sectoral significance in the Maastricht Treaty (in so-called *cross-section clause*), because its concerns are to become a part of other EC policies. The aim of this rather vaguely formulated basic principle is to prevent developments in other policy areas which are inconsistent with the requirements of environmental protection.

Furthermore, the *subsidiarity principle*[4] also applies to environmental considerations (Art. 3 b EC Treaty). This means that the EC will only act on matters concerning environmental protection if this has been expressly authorized and is necessary to achieve its aims, or if the aspired targets can not be met on the national level. As environmental policy has been explicitly prescribed as an area of Community activity (Art. 3 k EC Treaty), there remains, at least from a narrow legalistic view, little space for the application of the subsidiarity principle. However EC action in accordance to Art. 130 s EC Treaty is generally only possible with a qualified majority decision. For the enactment of regulations related to tax, regional planning, water and energy management a unanimous decision is required. Furthermore according to the general safeguard provision (Art. 130 t EC Treaty), it is possible

---

[4] See *Bongaerts* 1992, p. 12ff.

for the single Member States to maintain or adopt reinforcing protective measures, if the commonly decided measures of protection are considered insufficient for individual national needs.

However national independent initiatives are only possible, if they are compatible in all aspects with the Treaty for European Union. In this respect decentralised national decisions have been set narrow limits within the regulatory framework of the Maastricht Treaty. As the economic and social development of the Community should take place "in a balanced way", national or regional decisions on environmental policy are in principle only admissible, if the Commission considers them to be compatible with the Treaty.

II. Instruments and programmes

1. According to Art. 189 of the Maastricht Treaty the Community disposes of the following legal instruments to implement its environmental policy. (The most important policy decisions are listed in the appendix.)

- *Regulations* are generally applied and are binding for all citizens of the Members States of the EC.
- Most significant for environmental policy are the *directives*, of which already over two hundred have been passed. These are binding upon each Member State as to the result to be achieved, however it is left to the national authorities to choose the form and methods of incorporation into national legal and administrative regulations. This allows the Member States a certain scope for action in implementing the defined objectives. The weakness of directives is that some are only hesitantly adopted, or even not at all, and that such inactivity often remains unpunished, despite a possible condemnation by the European Court.
- Furthermore there also exists an option to pass *decisions*, which are only compulsory for certain addressees (Member States, specific individuals or institutions). These make a more differentiated approach possible.
- In contrast, *recommendations* and *statements* tend to have a more voluntary character.

2. In addition, environmental support programmes[5] are issued, through which concrete environmental protection projects are financed or subsidised. These attained a total of over one billion ECU in 1991. Apart from the current expenditure carried out in the category "environment", these include

---

[5] See OJ C 245 1992, p. 4ff.

research support in the environmental sector and the support funds of the various structural funds. An additional cohesion fund will be established by the the end of 1993. This will also finance projects in the fields of environment and transport.

Despite the considerable size of these programmes, their expansion has not directly led to qualitative environmental policy improvements. This is because the support programmes suffer from a series of efficiency reducing factors[6]. Due to the spread of environmental problems over a great many different areas of responsibility, such as transport, energy or agriculture, the co-ordination of these various sectoral economic policies is necessary. However, until now, the Community has not done sufficient justice to, or even totally neglected this requirement. The result was that projects, for example, financed by the structural funds were in significant aspects not in accordance with environmental targets. Apart from inadequate inter-sectoral co-ordination, deficiencies also arose in the allocation of special environmental projects. This was the result of incorrectly made advertisements, allotted monies being diverted to other uses, and neither a continuous control of projects, nor a final efficiency review being carried out. Only very recently have efforts been made by the European Court of Auditors to limit these deficiencies.

C. Critical remarks concerning efficiency

I. International environmental problems viewed from the theory of public goods

1. From an economic viewpoint environmental problems arise - as do other public bads - because in a general sense a market failure has occured. The public finance theory usually explains market failure in terms of either inadequately defined or definable property rights or else informational assymetries. Both lead to external effects or inefficient (market) bargaining solutions. Accordingly, efficient solutions to environmental problems are either designed to eliminate the cause of market failure, or else - if this is too expensive or impracticable - to lead to government intervention. In the latter compensating budgetary activities (taxes and/or expenditure programmes) and/or conditions in the form of regulations or bans are decided. This applies in principle equally to both national and international environmental policy. However the related implementation problems are much more difficult to solve. Firstly the respective national preferences for environmental

[6] See OJ C 245 1992, p. 14ff.

goods differ. Secondly the introduction of internationally uniform standards is not appropriate to the problem, because regional particularities or protection requirements are insufficiently considered.

Additional difficulties for international environmental policy arise if, as in the EC, the participating States have in principle agreed to mutual free trade, for which competitive conditions should be created. The national framework of, for example, production and product design standards, as well as the tax system, should then not internationally discriminate[7]. Thus the need to globally harmonize this framework is derived. The supporters of this policy then generally further strengthen their claim with the threat of environmental dumping which will otherwise occur. As will be shown, however, harmonization policy in fact tends to be counterproductive, because it hinders the otherwise existing opportunities of decentralised environmental policy.

2. The following matrix serves to clarify these problems. It helps to frame the fundamental starting points and policy options of internationally conceived environmental policy[8].

Negative external (environmental) effects

internationally relevant	nationally internalizable	
	yes	no
no	1) decentralized national tax or bargaining solution	2) decentralized national standard solution
yes	3) central international tax or bargaining solution	4) central international standard solution

[7] See *Wicke* 1991, p. 595ff.

[8] *Siebert* 1990, p. 4-17, suggests a different categorization of the environmental problems and additional solution approaches.

It is assumed that the type of environmental problem also determines the possible efficient policy alternatives. The environmental problem is defined by two criteria:

- Firstly it depends whether the environmental problem results because the negative external effects to be eliminated can be internalized or not. If they can in principle be internalized, then economically orientated policy instruments, e.g. taxes or bargaining solutions can be implemented. If however, internalization is not possible, or too costly due to high transaction costs, then only bans are available, in other words, regulation will be adopted.
- Secondly it is important for international environmental policy to consider whether the external environmental effects are internationally relevant or not. A centralized international environmental policy measure is only justified in this case, independent of whether internalization or a regulation solution is envisaged. If the environmental problem is not internationally relevant, then decentralized or national solutions should be sought.

Thus the four fields of the matrix classify the various types of environmental problem according to the different appropriate (national and/or international) responsibilities and instruments.

Field 1 defines the category of environmental problems resulting from negative external effects and which are only nationally relevant, e.g. the pollution of national waters and soil by residents, which could be efficiently solved, if an appropriate market internalization were possible. The environmental responsibility here lies with national or regional decision makers, who become - independent of international harmonization efforts - as it were, on the spot or decentrally active.

On the other hand field 2 defines those environmental problems which are also only nationally relevant, but appear to be inaccessable to market orientated policy measures, such as taxes or bargaining solutions, because the necessary internalization of externalities due to excessive information or transaction costs can not be achieved. In this case regulation is necessary, in other words bans and/or the fixing of standards, which must be nationally or regionally decided. In order that problems are tackled efficiently and are politically acceptable, they should be independent of international regulation.

In contrast to the first two categories, fields 3 and 4 cover the group of environmental problems which are internationally relevant because the causal externalities have effects beyond national borders. Typical examples are air and water pollution, which extend across frontiers. As far as pollution is concerned where the polluter and injured party can be nationally clearly identified (field 3), then bargaining solutions can be successfully pursued, as, for example, attempts to protect international waters show. Only if market environmental policy instruments can not be applied, because the polluters and those affected by international relevant pollution can not be identified at reasonable cost, then centralized, international regulation solutions must be sought. These however have the basic disadvantage, that their efficiency is suboptimal and the necessary international acceptance is difficult to achieve. The example of the introduction of the catalytic converter for cars presented below is typical.

II. The restrictions on decentralized environmental policy resulting from internationally harmonized solutions

1. If one attempts to classify the frequency of environmental problems using the above matrix, it appears that those in the upper lines dominate, which are predominantly of nationally limited importance. It may be that internationally relevant pollution will become increasingly important in the future. However at the moment the largest part of the total damage and dangers can be locally classified. Thus the task is to weigh up whether the inclusion of national environmental policy in an internationally centralized framework of regulation promotes decentralized efficiency or not. In other words, does international harmonization of the environmental scope of action extend or restrict the total existing possibilities of efficient solutions?

The above systematization appears initially to give a clear answer: the policy potential in field 4 should be enlarged in the EC. Because regulation solutions rely upon higher - usually state - institutions for their enforcement and surveillance, the establishment of EC responsibility creates the possibility of finding solutions even in an international setting, which would be otherwise difficult to enforce. However it must be assumed here, that the internationally agreed regulations will generally be weak, because they rely upon the broad consent of the affected Member States. The common level of approval will therefore be relatively low.

In this context the difficulty often arises that the "soft" international regulation solutions become a substitute for "harder" national regulations and thus prevent effective decentralized environmental policy. This crowding-out effect can also arise because national suppliers refer to damage to their international competitiveness. National political decision-makers may also avoid unpleasant decisions by refering to international jurisdiction.

Similar dangers of the undesirable substitution of national with centralized international competence or policy instruments exist between the problem areas assigned to fields 3 and 4. Above all this would be particularly large if the target of international tax harmonization were pursued more intensively than up to now. National tax solutions to internalize external environmental effects would then be excluded, so that the German successes in introducing the catalytic converter for cars, which will be presented below, would not have been possible.

But it is not only national tax solutions, but also international bargaining solutions which can be hampered by the establishment of centralized environmental EC institutions, because the two significant obstacles[9] for successful bargaining solutions are strengthened by the existence of superior international institutions. On the one hand the psychological difficulties in recognising the property rights of a polluter will tend to rise, so that those negatively affected tend, even more strongly, to call upon international institutions as arbitrators and thus renounce the most efficient path of a bargaining solution. On the other hand the strategic behavior which often disturbs bargaining solutions is strengthened if agreements are to be reached within larger international borders.

2. Against this background, a judgement of the possibilities of efficient environmental policy created by the introduction of centralized EC institutions tends to be negative, if one takes the view of a country in which efficient environmental policy has already gained considerable general acceptance. The distinctly enlarged policy potential in the area of international regulatory solutions (field 4) is compared to the limitations (field 1) and substitution effects (field 2) of environmental opportunities on a decentralized or national level. As national problems are more frequent than international ones, the probability of potential problem solving is in total smaller.

Nevertheless it should be positively emphasized that the institutional agreements reached in the EC have until now been in favour of allowing efficient national solutions. Putting this intention into concrete terms will however become more difficult as the tax policy instruments are centrally harmonized. The following example of the introduction of the catalytic converter for cars should demonstrate this problem.

---

[9] See *Kirchgässner* 1992, p. 60ff.

D. The introduction of catalytic converters for cars as an example of the difficulties in implementing decentralised environmental policy in the EC

I. History[10]

1. In the sixties it had already been recognised in the USA and Japan that rapid growth in car traffic had made it necessary to adopt measures to reduce car emissions. Thereupon limit regulations were introduced for car emissions und successively reinforced until the mid-seventies, when in 1975 the equiping of cars with catalytic converters became compulsory in order to fulfil the strict standards.

At the beginning of the seventies the first, rather half-hearted efforts were undertaken in the European Community, using limit guidelines, to bring about a reduction in the emissions of harmful chemicals (above all CO and HC) from cars. The first decisive EC-wide exhaust regulation which set regulations for nitrogen oxides (NO_x), was above all instigated by Germany and came into force in 1984. More severe limits, which would have forced the introduction of catalytic converters were defeated by the unanimous-vote rule in the Council of Ministers, because Greece and Denmark considered the negotiated regulation to be inadequate. Only after majority decisions had been admitted in the Council of Ministers was it possible, through the Single European Act in 1987, for all Member States to set fixed limits, making the installment of a computer controlled catalytic converter indispensable for luxury class cars from 1989 and from the beginning of 1993 for newly registered small cars.

However despite considerable efforts, Germany could neither introduce catalytic converter technology at a national level more rapidly, nor implement stricter limits on national territory. Therefore other methods had to be pursued, in order to do justice to the urgency and the German public's desire for reduced traffic emissions.

The first step in 1985 was to reduce the tax on oil for unlead fuel by 2 Pf./l., and raise the price for leaded fuel by 2 Pf./l. This differentiation in the tax scale[11] was increased and is now 11 Pf./l. Furthermore, supported by the general safeguard provision (Art. 130 t EC Treaty), the government was able to prohibit leaded normal fuel completely by February 1988.

---

[10] See *Neu* 1990, p. 22ff, and *Krämer* 1991, p. 849ff.

[11] See *Kalleicher* 1991, p. 137ff.

The aim of this tax policy was to increase the market share of catalytic converted cars. These oil tax policy measures, which raised the relative and absolute running costs of vehicles requiring leaded fuel, were accompanied by a differentiation in the vehicle tax[12] starting in 1985, which granted a fixed-term tax exemption for vehicles, whose harmful exhaust had been reduced. This preferential treatment was intended to financially compensate the one-off additional expenses of a catalytic converted car or the upgrading of a car to reduce its harmful exhaust.

The success of this policy can be judged above all by the number of new vehicle registrations (with Otto motors) with computer controlled catalytic converters[13]. These numbered only six percent of the total in 1985, but the percentage rose to 76 percent by 1989 and had almost reached 100 percent by 1992[14]. However the readiness of drivers to upgrade their non-converted cars was not increased as much by the tax benefit as had been hoped. Thus in 1990 only one fifth of total vehicles were equipped with a computer controlled catalytic converter[15].

The technical possibilities now exist to implement a reliable and inexpensive control of vehicle emissions. Since the beginning of the nineties the Federal government has therefore been attempting to transform the vehicle tax into a pollution tax, and to take the emission levels of the various fuels into consideration when fixing the tax rates[16].

2. At the beginning of European environmental policy the control costs of emission inspection were very high, and as harmonization[17] was considered more important, it was decided that the emission of harmful substances from vehicles should be regulated with the help of EC-wide product standards. Thus limits for the various exhaust fumes were fixed. These were differentiated by vehicle size group and had to be observed at vehicle registration. In contrast to differentiated emission tax rates, the different national product standards impair the efficient functioning of the internal market, because they represent nontariff barriers and lead to market segmentation[18]. Admittedly a decision by the European Court relating to the Danish

---

[12] See *Kalleicher* 1991, p. 173ff.

[13] See *Grüner* 1990, p. 413.

[14] In May 1992, the share has already reached 97%. See "Umwelt" No. 5 1992, p. 195.

[15] See "Umwelt" No. 12, 1990, p. 586.

[16] See *Kalleicher* 1991, p. 233ff.

[17] See *Sprenger* 1991, p. 39ff.

[18] See Task Force 1990, p. 204.

regulation of returnable bottles gave the interests of environmental policy priority over the requirements of the internal market. However given the volume of intra-industrial trade in European cars, national independent initiatives in environmental protection in the form of strict product standards would severely disturb the functioning of the internal market and are therefore not enforceable. Differing national preferences for environmental goods can be taken into account by making higher charges for polluting fuels. In the future however, this option may be discontinued, because it is aimed to harmonize consumption taxes across the EC. Minimum EC tax rates for the various types of fuel have been applied since October 1992, and these are exceeded in Germany by up to 50%. However the dropping of border controls and the dismantling of competition distortions will lead to demands in the future for totally uniform EC tax rates.

II. Some conclusions for the future development of European environmental policy

1. Firstly, the "history" of the catalytic converter offers some important conclusions.

- The requirements of the European internal market do not allow single Member States to realize their national concepts of an adequate environmental policy by introducing their own standards, which may be stricter than those of the Community. It has been shown that the general safeguard provision (Art. 130 t) is generally subordinate to the requirements of the internal market.
- The only remaining option accorded by Art. 130 t is to adopt stronger protective measures when setting national consumption taxes. Although these are not permitted to fall below a EC minimum rate. However they have not been fixed at a definite percentage rate, so that higher preferences for clean air can be reflected in above average taxes for fossil fuels. As these consumption tax rates are eliminated as a parameter of national environmental policy in the process of increased EC harmonization, the national authorities will loose their last influential competence in the shaping of environmental policy. They will then only be able to choose the form and the means in adopting the EC directives in national laws, regulations and administration provisions.

2. Against this background the question of the justification of increasingly centralized environmental policy harmonization can only be positively affirmed with difficulty. The standard arguments for an integrated environmental policy appear unconvincing because they make unrealistic assumptions.

Firstly it is not certain that increasing harmonization within the Community will lead to similar preferences. Attitudes to the environment in the various nations are influenced by tradition and mentality and thus differ. These can surely only be influenced over a very long period of time. Secondly, the national preferences for environmental goods are very different today, and furthermore are influenced in some cases by considerable income differences. The acceptance of stricter environmental regulations is decisively dependent upon this fact. However without the slowly changing acceptance of citizens, environmental laws can not be effectively carried through and enforced.

Appendix

Important environmental directives, regulations and decisions of the European Communities" (at end 1992)[19]

1. General, programmes
2. Nuclear safety and nuclear waste
3. Prevention of water pollution and water management
4. Control of air pollution
5. Noise
6. Chemicals, industrial risks and biotechnologie
7. Environment and natural resources
   a) Administration and rational use of the environment and of natural resources
   b) Protection of fauna and flora
   c) Waste treatment and clean technology
8. International co-operation

1. General, programmes

Year	Regulations, directives and decisions
1975	Founding of a European foundation for improving the conditions of life and work *(OJ L 139 1975 p. 1)*
1975	Resolution concerning the adaptation of directives or other Community rules for the protection and improvement of the environment to technical progress *(OJ C 168 1975 p. 5)*
1976	Introduction of a common procedure for the establishment and updating of a inventory list of the sources of information in the field of environmental protection in the Communities *(OJ L 031 1976 p. 8)*
1985	Directive concerning environmental compatibility tests for certain public and private projects *(OJ L 175 1985 p. 40)*
1986	Resolution on the strengthening of Community measures of environmental protection *(OJ C 003 1987 p. 3)*

[19] See Fundstellennachweis 1992 of the common law.

1989 Decision over two specific programmes for research and technological development in the field of environment: STEP and EPOCH (1989-1992) *(OJ L 359 1989 p. 9)*
1990 Regulation for the establishment of a European environmental agency and a European environmental information and observation network *(OJ L 120 1990 p. 1)*
1991 Directive on the standardization and appropriate form of reports on the implementation of certain environmental protection directives *(OJ L 377 1991 p. 48)*
1991 Regulation of an advisory committee for the protection of the environment in the Mediterranean area (MEDSPA) *(OJ L 063 1991 p. 1)*
1991 Regulation of an advisory committee for the protection of the environment in the coastal area and waters of the Irish Sea, the North Sea and the Channel, the Baltic and the North-East Atlantic (NORSPA) *(OJ L 370 1991 p. 28)*
1992 Regulation concerning a Community System for the awarding of an environmental symbol *(OJ L 099 1992 p. 1)*
1992 Regulation for the creation of a financing instrument for the environment (LIFE) *(OJ L 206 1992 p. 1)*

2. Nuclear safety and nuclear waste

Year	Regulations, directives and decisions
1959	Directive for establishment of basic safety standards for the health protection of the general public and workers against the dangers of ionizing radiation (modified in 1962) *(OJ L 011 1959 p. 221) (OJ L 057 1962 p. 1633)*
1975	Adoption of a programme for the management and storage of radioactive waste *(OJ L 178 1975 p. 28)*
1976	Directive for establishment of (revised) basic safety standards for the health protection of the general public and workers against the dangers of ionizing radiation (modified in 1979, 1980 and 1984) *(OJ L 187 1976 p. 1) (OJ L 083 1979 p. 18) (OJ L 246 1980 p. 1) (OJ L 265 1984 p. 4)*
1980	Resolution on the appointment of a Consultative Ad-hoc-committee for the reprocessing irradiated nuclear fuels *(OJ L 052 1980 p. 9)*
1980	Resolution for the implementation of an advisory committee in the field of radioactive waste *(OJ C 051 1980 p. 1)*

1980 Resolution on the reprocessing irradiated nuclear fuels *(OJ C 051 1980 p. 4)*

1987 Decision concerning Community agreements for the exchange of information in the case of radiological emergency situations *(OJ L 371 1987 p. 76)*

1989 Approval of a specific research and technological development programme for Euratom for the disposal of atomic waste (1990-1994) *(OJ L 395 1989 p. 28)*

1989 Directive concerning the information of the population concerning relevant rules of conduct and health protection measures to be adopted in a radiological emergency situation *(OJ L 357 1989 p. 31)*

1990 Directive concerning the protection external workers who are exposed to danger from ionizing radiation in action in a controlled area *(OJ L 349 1990 p. 21)*

1992 Directive on the supervision and control of the bringing of radioactive waste from one Member State to another in and outside the Community *(OJ L 035 1992 p. 24)*

3. Prevention of water pollution and water management

Year	Regulations, directives and decisions
1975	Directive concerning the quality required of surface water intended for the abstraction of drinking water in the Member States (modified in 1979, 1990 and 1991) *(OJ L 194 1975 p. 34) (OJ L 271 1979 p. 44) (OJ L 353 1990 p. 59) (OJ L 377 1991 p. 48)*
1975	Directive concerning the quality of bathing water (modified in 1990 and 1991) *(OJ L 031 1976 p. 1) (OJ L 353 1990 p. 59) (OJ L 377 1991 p. 48)*
1976	Directive concerning the pollution caused by certain dangerous substances discharged into the aquatic environment of the Community (modified in 1990 and 1991) *(OJ L 129 1976 p. 23) (OJ L 353 1990 p. 599) (OJ L 377 1991 p. 48)*
1977	Decision establishing a common procdure for the exchange of information on the quality of surface fresh water in the Community (modified in 1981, 1984 and 1986) *(OJ L 334 1977 p. 29) (OJ L 319 1991 p. 17) (OJ L 237 1984 p. 15) (OJ L 335 1986 p. 44)*
1978	Resolution on the setting up of an advisory committee on the control and reduction of pollution caused by hydrocarbons at sea *(OJ C 162 1978 p. 1)*

1979 Directive concerning the methods of measurement and frequencies of sampling and analysis of surface water intended for the abstraction of drinking water in the Member States (modified in 1981, 1990 and 1991) *(OJ L 271 1979 p. 44) (OJ L 319 1981 p. 16) (OJ L 353 1990 p. 59) (OJ L 377 1991 p. 48)*

1979 Directive concerning the quality required of shellfish waters (modified in 1991) *(OJ L 281 1979 p. 47) (OJ L 377 1991 p. 48)*

1979 Directive on the protection of ground water against pollution caused by certain dangerous substances (modified in 1990 and 1991) *(OJ L 020 1980 p. 43) (OJ L 353 1990 p. 59) (OJ L 377 1991 p. 48)*

1980 Appointment of an advisory committee on the control and reduction of pollution caused by hydrocarbons at sea (modified in 1985 and 1987) *(OJ L 188 1980 p. 11) (OJ L 089 1985 p. 64) (OJ L 057 1987 p. 57)*

1980 Directive relating to the quality of water intended for human consumption (modified in 1981, 1990 and 1991) *(OJ L 229 1980 p. 11) (OJ L 319 1981 p. 19) (OJ L 353 1990 p. 59) (OJ L 377 1991 p. 48)*

1982 Directive on limits and quality objectives for mercury discharges by the chloralkali electrolysis industry (modified in 1990 and 1991) *(OJ L 081 1982 p. 29) (OJ L 353 1990 p. 59) (OJ L 377 1991 p. 48)*

1983 Directive on limits and quality objectives for cadmium discharges (modified in 1990 and 1991) *(OJ L 291 1983 p. 1) (OJ L 353 1990 p. 59) (OJ L 377 1991 p. 48)*

1983 Resolution on the control of water pollution by dangerous substances *(OJ C 046 1983 p. 17)*

1984 Directive on limits and quality objectives for HCH discharges (modified in 1990 and 1991) *(OJ L 274 1984 p. 11) (OJ L 353 1990 p. 59) (OJ L 377 1991 p. 48)*

1984 Resolution for new forms of co-operation in the water supply sector *(OJ C 272 1984 p. 2)*

1986 Decision to establish a Community information system for the control and reduction of marine pollution by oil and other hazardous substances (modified in 1988) *(OJ L 077 1986 p. 33) (OJ L 158 1988 p. 32)*

1986 Directive on limits and quality objectives for discharges of certain dangerous substances (modified in 1988, 1990 and 1991) *(OJ L 181 1986 p. 16) (OJ L 158 1988 p. 35) (OJ L 219 1990 p. 49) (OJ L 353 1990 p. 59) (OJ L 377 1991 p. 48)*

1990 Directive on the interim measures applicable in Germany for certain Community regulations concerning environmental protection *(OJ L 353 1990 p. 59)*

1991	Directive on the protection of waters from nitrate pollution from agricultural sources *(OJ L 375 1991 p. 1)*

4. Control of air pollution

Year	Regulations, directives and decisions
1970	Directive on the approximation of the laws of the Member States relating to measures to be taken against air pollution by gases from positive-ignition engines of motor vehicles (revised 1974, 1977, 1978, 1983, 1988, 1989 and 1991) *(OJ L 076 1970 p. 1) (OJ L 159 1974 p. 61) (OJ L 032 1977 p. 32) (OJ L 223 1978 p. 48) (OJ L 197 1983 p. 1) (OJ L 036 1988 p. 1) (OJ L 214 1988 p. 1) (OJ L 226 1989 p. 1) (OJ L 238 1989 p. 43) (OJ L 242 1991 p. 1)*
1972	Directive on the approximation of the laws of the Member States relating to measures to be taken against the emission of pollutants from diesel engines for use in vehicles (revised 1989) *(OJ L 190 1972 p. 1) (OJ L 238 1989 p. 43)*
1975	Directive on the approximation of the laws of the Member States relating to the sulphur content of certain liquid fuels (revised 1987, 1990 and 1991) *(OJ L 307 1975 p. 22) (OJ L 091 1987 p. 19) (OJ L 353 1990 p. 79) (OJ L 377 1991 p. 48)*
1977	Directive on the approximation of the laws of the Member States relating to the measures to be taken against the emission of pollutants from diesel engines for use in wheeled agricultural or forestry tractors (revised 1982) *(OJ L 220 1977 p. 38) (OJ L 378 1982 p. 45)*
1980	Directive on air quality limit values and guide values for sulphur dioxide and suspended particulates (revised 1981, 1989, 1990 and 1991) *(OJ L 229 1980 p. 30) (OJ L 319 1981 p. 18) (OJ L 201 1989 p. 53) (OJ L 353 1990 p. 59) (OJ L 377 1991 p. 48)*
1980	Resolution on cross-border air pollution for sulphur dioxide and suspended particulates *(OJ C 222 1980 p. 1)*
1982	Decision to introduce a mutual exchange of information and data from the measuring networks and individual stations for the registration of air pollution in den Member States *(OJ L 210 1982 p. 1)*
1982	Directive concerning a limit value for lead concentration in the air (revised 1990 and 1991) *(OJ L 378 1982 p. 15) (OJ L 353 1990 p. 59) (OJ L 377 1991 p. 48)*
1984	Directive on the combating of air pollution from industrial plants (revised 1991) *(OJ L 188 1984 p. 20) (OJ L 377 1991 p. 48)*

1985 Directive on air quality limit values and guide values for nitrogen dioxide (revised 1985, 1990 and 1991) *(OJ L 087 1985 p. 1) (OJ L 372 1985 p. 36) (OJ L 353 1990 p. 59) (OJ L 377 1991 p. 48)*

1985 Directive concerning the approximation of the laws of the Member States relating to the lead content of petrol (revised 1985 and 1987) *(OJ L 096 1985 p. 25) (OJ L 372 1985 p. 37) (OJ L 225 1987 p. 33)*

1987 Directive concerning the prevention and reduction of environmental pollution by asbestos (revised 1990 and 1991) *(OJ L 085 1987 p. 40) (OJ L 353 1990 p. 59) (OJ L 377 1991 p. 48)*

1987 Directive concerning the approximation of the laws of the Member States relating to measures to be taken against the emission of pollutants from diesel engines for use in vehicles (revised 1991) *(OJ L 036 1988 p. 33) (OJ L 295 1991 p. 1)*

1988 Directive to limit harmful chemical emission from power plants into the air (revised 1990) *(OJ L 336 1988 p. 1) (OJ L 353 1990 p. 59)*

1988 Resolution to limit the use of chlorofluorocarbon and halon *(OJ C 285 1988 p. 1)*

1989 Directive concerning the prevention and reduction of air pollution by new or existing incineration systems for settlement waste *(OJ L 163 1989 p. 32) (OJ L 203 1989 p. 50)*

1991 Regulation concerning substances which lead to a reduction of the ozone layer (revised 1992) *(OJ L 067 1991 p. 1) (OJ L 405 1992 p. 41)*

1992 Resolution of the Commission allocation of import quotas for halon, Tetrachlorcarbon, 1.1.1-Trichlorethan and other fully halogenized chlorofluorocarbon *(OJ L 035 1992 p. 31)*

5. Noise

Year	Regulations, directives and decisions
1970	Directive concerning the approximation of the laws of the Member States relating to the permissible sound level and the exhaust system of motor vehicles (revised 1973, 1977, 1981, 1984 and 1989) *(OJ L 042 1970 p. 16) (OJ L 321 1973 p. 33) (OJ L 066 1977 p. 33) (OJ L 131 1981 p. 6) (OJ L 196 1984 p. 47) (OJ L 238 1984 p. 31) (OJ L 238 1989 p. 43)*
1978	Directive concerning the approximation of the laws of the Member States relating to the permissible sound level and the exhaust system of motorcycles (revised 1987 and 1989) *(OJ L 349 1978 p. 21) (OJ L 024 1987 p. 42) (OJ L 098 1989 p. 1)*

1978 Directive concerning the approximation of the laws of the Member States relating to the permissible sound level and the exhaust system of of construction plant and equipment (revised 1981 and 1985) *(OJ L 033 1979 p. 15) (OJ L 233 1985 p. 9)*

1979 Directive on the limitation of noise emissions from subsonic aircraft (revised 1983) *(OJ L 018 1980 p. 26) (OJ L 117 1983 p. 15)*

1984 Directive concerning the approximation of the laws of the Member States relating to the permissible sound level of motor compressors (revised 1985) *(OJ L 300 1984 p. 123) (OJ L 233 1985 p. 11)*

1984 Directive concerning the approximation of the laws of the Member States relating to the permissible sound level of tower revolving cranes (revised 1987) *(OJ L 300 1984 p. 130) (OJ L 220 1987 p. 60)*

1984 Directive concerning the approximation of the laws relating to the permissible sound level of current generators for welding (revised 1985) *(OJ L 300 1984 p. 142) (OJ L 233 1985 p. 16)*

1984 Directive concerning the approximation of the laws of the Member States relating to the permissible sound level of electric generators (revised 1985) *(OJ L 300 1984 p. 149) (OJ L 233 1985 p. 18)*

1984 Directive concerning the approximation of the laws of the Member States relating to the permissible sound level of pneumatic jackhammers, etc. (revised 1985) *(OJ L 300 1984 p. 156) (OJ L 233 1985 p. 20)*

1984 Directive concerning the approximation of the laws of the Member States relating to the permissible sound level of lawnmowers (revised 1987 and 1988) *(OJ L 300 1984 p. 171) (OJ L 117 1987 p. 22) (OJ L 081 1988 p. 69 and p. 71)*

1986 Directive concerning the sound level of household equipment *(OJ L 344 1986 p. 24)*

1986 Directive on the limitation of noise emissions from earth-moving machines (revised 1989) *(OJ L 384 1986 p. 1) (OJ L 253 1989 p. 35)*

1989 Directive on the limitation of noise emissions from civil subsonic aircraft *(OJ L 363 1989 p. 27)*

1992 Directive on the limitation on the operation of certain aircraft *(OJ L 076 1992 p. 21)*

6. Chemicals, industrial risks and biotechnology

Year	Regulations, directives and decisions
1967	Directive concerning the approximation of laws, regulations and administration provisions relating to the classification, packaging, and labelling of dangerous substances (revised 1969, 1970, 1970, 1971, 1973, 1975, 1976, 1979, 1980, 1981, 1982, 1983, 1984 1986, 1987, 1988, 1990, and 1991) *(OJ L 196 1967 p. 1) (OJ L 068 1969 p. 1) (OJ L 074 1971 p. 15) (OJ L 167 1973 p. 1) (OJ L 183 1975 p. 22) (OJ L 360 1976 p. 1) (OJ L 088 1979 p. 1) (OJ L 259 1979 p. 10) (OJ L 366 1980 p. 1) (OJ L 351 1981 p. 5) (OJ L 106 1982 p. 18) (OJ L 257 1983 p. 1) (OJ L 251 1984 p. 1) (OJ L 247 1986 p. 1) (OJ L 133 1987 p. 1) (OJ L 239 1987 p. 1) (OJ L 259 1988 p. 1) (OJ L 287 1990 p. 37) (OJ L 180 1991 p. 1 and p. 79) (OJ L 228 1991 p. 67) (OJ L 338 1991 p. 23)*
1973	Directive concerning the approximation of the laws of the Member States relating to detergents (revised 1982 and 1986) *(OJ L 347 1973 p. 51) (OJ L 109 1982 p. 1) (OJ L 080 1986 p. 51)*
1973	Directive concerning the approximation of the laws of the Member States relating to the control of the biological breakdown of certain anionic active substances (revised 1982) *(OJ L 347 1973 p. 53) (OJ L 109 1982 p. 18)*
1976	Directive concerning the approximation of laws, regulations and administration provisions of the Member States relating to restrictions on the marketing and use of certain dangerous substances and preparations (revised 1979, 1982, 1983, 1985, 1989 and 1991) *(OJ L 262 1976 p. 201) (OJ L 197 1979 p. 37) (OJ L 339 1982 p. 55) (OJ L 350 1982 p. 34) (OJ L 147 1983 p. 9) (OJ L 263 1983 p. 33) (OJ L 269 1985 p. 56) (OJ L 375 1985 p. 1) (OJ L 398 1989 p. 19 and p. 24) (OJ L 078 1991 p. 38) (OJ L 085 1991 p. 34) (OJ L 186 1991 p. 59 and p. 64)*
1980	Decision on chlorofluorocarbons in the environment *(OJ L 090 1980 p. 45)*
1982	Decision on the consolidation of precautionary measures concerning chlorofluorocarbons in the environment *(OJ L 329 1982 p. 29)*
1982	Directive on the major accident hazards of certain industrial activities (revised 1987, 1988, 1990 and 1991) *(OJ L 230 1982 p. 1) (OJ L 085 1987 p. 36) (OJ L 336 1988 p. 14) (OJ L 353 1990 p. 59) (OJ L 377 1991 p. 48)*
1982	Directive concerning the details of supervision and control of environmental media affected by the derivatives from titanium dioxide production *(OJ L 378 1982 p. 1)*

1984 Directive concerning limits and quality objectives for mercury discharges with the exception of the chloralkali electrolysis industry (revised 1990 and 1991) *(OJ L 074 1984 p. 49) (OJ L 353 1990 p. 59) (OJ L 377 1991 p. 48)*

1986 Directive concerning the approximation of laws, regulations and administration provisions for the users of the principles of good laboratory practice and the control of their use in experiments with chemical substances *(OJ L 015 1987 p. 29)*

1988 Directive relating to the inspection of good laboratory practice (GLP) (revised 1990) *(OJ L 145 1988 p. 35) (OJ L 011 1990 p. 37)*

1988 Regulation concerning the export of certain hazardous chemicals from the Community or their import into the Community *(OJ L 155 1988 p. 2)*

1989 Directive relating to the standardisation modalities of the programme of reduction and ultimate prohibition of pollution through waste from the titanium dioxide industry (revised 1992) *(OJ L 201 1989 p. 56) (OJ L 409 1992 p. 11)*

1989 Regulation concerning the export of certain chemical substances *(OJ L 050 1989 p. 1)*

1990 Directive relating to the use of genetically altered micro-organisms in closed systems *(OJ L 117 1990 p. 1)*

1990 Directive relating to the intentional release of genetically manipulated organisms into the environment *(OJ L 117 1990 p. 15)*

1990 Directive relating to the interim measures applied in Germany for certain Community regulations concerning environmental protection or environmental protection related to the Community *(OJ L 353 1990 p. 59 or p. 79)*

7. Environment and natural resources

a) Administration and rational use of the environment and of natural resources

Year	Regulations, directives and decisions
1991	Regulation on advisory committee for the protection of nature (GA-NAT) *(OJ L 370 1991 p. 17)*

b) Protection of fauna and flora

Year	Regulations, directives and decisions
1978	Directive relating to the quality of fresh water which requires protection or improvement to support fical (revised 1990 and 1991) *(OJ L 222 1978 p. 1) (OJ L 353 1990 p. 59) (OJ L 377 1991 p. 48)*
1979	Directive relating to the conservation of wild birds (revised 1981, 1985, 1986, 1990 and 1991) *(OJ L 103 1979 p. 1) (OJ L 319 1981 p. 3) (OJ L 233 1985 p. 33) (OJ L 100 1986 p. 22) (OJ L 353 1990 p. 59) (OJ L 115 1991 p. 41)*
1981	Regulation on common rules for imports of whale or other cetacean products *(OJ L 039 1981 p. 1)*
1982	Regulation relating to the application of Agreements on international trade in endangered species of wild animals and plants into the Community (revised 1983, 1985, 1986, 1987, 1988, 1989, 1990 and 1991) *(OJ L 384 1982 p. 1) (OJ L 367 1983 p. 1) (OJ L 231 1985 p. 1) (OJ L 201 1986 p. 1) (OJ L 136 1987 p. 6) (OJ L 147 1987 p. 1) (OJ L 087 1988 p. 67) (OJ L 066 1989 p. 24) (OJ L 029 1990 p. 1) (OJ L 349 1991 p. 13)*
1983	Directive concerning the importation into the Member States of baby seal furs and goods *(OJ L 091 1983 p. 30)*
1986	Regulation relating to the conservation of forests in the Community against air pollution (revised 1989 and 1992) *(OJ L 326 1986 p. 2) (OJ L 165 1989 p. 8) (OJ L 217 1992 p. 1)*
1992	Regulation relating to the conservation of forests in the Community against fire *(OJ L 217 1992 p. 3)*

c) Waste treatment and clean technology

Year	Regulations, directives and decisions
1975	Directive on the disposal of waste oils (revised 1987, and 1991) *(OJ L 194 1975 p. 31) (OJ L 042 1987 p. 43) (OJ L 377 1991 p. 48)*
1975	Directive on waste (revised 1990 and 1991) *(OJ L 194 1975 p. 47) (OJ L 353 1990 p. 32) (OJ L 377 1991 p. 48)*
1976	Directive on to the disposal of polychlorinated biphenyls and terphenyls (revised 1991) *(OJ L 108 1976 p. 41) (OJ L 377 1991 p. 48)*

1978 Directive on waste from titanium dioxide produktion (revised 1982, 1983 and 1991)*(OJ L 054 1978 p. 19) (OJ L 378 1982 p. 1) (OJ L 032 1983 p. 28) (OJ L 377 1991 p. 48)*

1978 Directive on toxic and dangerous waste (revised 1990 and 1991) *(OJ L 084 1978 p. 43) (OJ L 353 1990 p. 59) (OJ L 377 1991 p. 20 and p. 48)*

1984 Directive on the surveillance and control - in the Communities - of transfrontier disposal of dangerous waste (revised 1985, 1986 and 1991) *(OJ L 326 1984 p. 31) (OJ L 272 1985 p. 1) (OJ L 100 1986 p. 20) (OJ L 181 1986 p. 13) (OJ L 377 1991 p. 48)*

1985 Directive on packaging for liquid foodstuffs (revised 1991) *(OJ L 176 1985 p. 18) (OJ L 377 1991 p. 48)*

1986 Directive on the conservation of the environment and in particular the soil on the use of sludge in agriculture (revised 1991) *(OJ L 181 1986 p. 6) (OJ L 377 1991 p. 48)*

1991 Directive relating to hazardous substances contained in batteries and accumulators *(OJ L 078 1991 p. 38)*

1991 Directive relating to the treatment of local sewage *(OJ L 135 1991 p. 40)*

1991 Directive on dangerous waste *(OJ L 377 1991 p. 20)*

8. International co-operation

Year	Regulations, directives and decisions
1975	Convention on the Prevention of Marine Pollution from landbased sources (Paris Convention) (revised 1987) *(OJ L 194 1975 p. 5) (OJ L 024 1987 p. 47)*
1977	Convention on the protection of the Mediterranean Sea against pollution (Barcelona Convention) *(OJ L 240 1977 p. 3)*
1977	Convention concerning the International Commision for the Rhine (Berne Convention) *(OJ L 240 1977 p. 48)*
1981	Agreement on spacious transfrontier air pollution (revised 1986) *(OJ L 171 1981 p. 13) (OJ L 181 1986 p. 1)*
1981	Agreement on the preservation of the living oceanic treasure of the Antarctic *(OJ L 252 1981 p. 27)*
1982	Agreement on the international trade with endangered species of wild animals and plants *(OJ L 383 1982 p. 7)*
1982	Agreement on the conservation of migratory wild animals *(OJ L 210 1982 p. 11)*

1982 Agreement on the conservation of European wild plants and animals and their natural environment *(OJ L 038 1982 p. 1)*
1982 Agreement on the preservation of salmon in the North Atlantic *(OJ L 378 1982 p. 25)*
1983 Convention on the fisheries and the protection of living resources in the Baltic and the belts *(OJ L 237 1983 p. 5)*
1984 Agreement on co-operation in combatting the pollution of the North Sea by hydrocarbons and other harmful chemicals (Bonn Agreement) *(OJ L 188 1984 p. 9)*
1986 International Convention on the conservation of tunafish stocks in the Atlantic Ocean *(OJ L 162 1986 p. 34)*
1988 Vienna Agreement on the protection of the ozone layer *(OJ L 297 1988 p. 21)*

References

Bongaerts, J. C.: Umweltpolitische Kompetenzen der EG nach Maastricht, in: Zeitschrift für angewandte Umweltforschung, Vol. 5, 1992, No. 1, p. 11-14.

Europäische Gemeinschaften: Fundstellennachweis des Geltenden Gemeinschaftsrechts, Luxemburg 1992.

Europäische Gemeinschaft - Europäische Union: Die Vertragstexte von Maastricht, Bonn 1992.

Grüner, M.: Umwelt- und Klimaschutz im Verkehr, in: Energiewirtschaftliche Tagesfragen, Vol. 40, 1990, No. 6, p. 410-417.

Kalleicher, D.: Der Einsatz ausgewählter Instrumente zur Reduktion von Abgasemissionen bei Kraftfahrzeugen - Eine vergleichende Analyse aus umweltpolitischer Sicht - Mainz 1991.

Kirchgässner, G.: Ansatzmöglichkeiten zur Lösung europäischer Umweltprobleme, in: Außenwirtschaft, Vol. 47, 1992, No. 1, p. 55-77.

Klemmer, P.: Harmonisierungsbedarf oder Zentralismus? - zu den umweltpolitischen Kompetenzen der EG -, in: Zeitschrift für angewandte Umweltforschung, Vol. 5, 1992, No. 1, p. 14-19.

Krämer, L.: Umweltpolitik, in: *Röttinger, M./Weyringer, C.:* Handbuch der europäischen Integration, Wien 1991, p. 639-670.

Neu, H.: Der EG-Abgaskompromiss - Eine kritische Bestandsaufnahme unter umweltökonomischen Aspekten -, Essen 1990.

Siebert, H.: Umweltpolitik in der Europäischen Gemeinschaft: Zentralisierung oder Dezentralisierung?, Kiel Working paper 1990, No. 429.

Sprenger, R.-U.: EG-Binnenmarkt und Umweltschutz, in: Beihefte der Konjunkturpolitik, Vol. 38, 1991, p. 27-72.

Task Force "Environment and the Internal Market: "1992", the environmental dimension, Bonn 1990.

Wicke, L.: Umweltökonomie, 3rd edition, München 1991.

A General System Theory Approach Towards a Better Understanding of Environmental Economics

Siegfried Hauser

1. Environmental economics

The production of goods and services leaves its effect on the environment. To begin with, natural resources and space become increasingly scarce; as fuel is consumed, for instance, transport is made possible and waste is generated. Ecological problems arising from the production of scarcities, and pollution attributed to economic activity result in economic problems. Environmental economics is an economic discipline which explicitly considers ecological parameters in its theories, analyses, and costing systems[1]. Environmental economics as well as resource economics present the two areas of research in which economic theory deals with the interaction between economics and the ecology[2]. For our purposes we can consider them together under the combined heading of environmental economics.

Environmental economics may be regarded under general macroeconomic as well as under management aspects. Macroeconomic considerations would include questions concerning externalities, natural resources as a form of economic assets, etc. Management considerations focus on costing, distorted competition, etc. Kapp and Pigou were early influential theorists within this special branch of economics. Both environmental economics as well as resource economics have gained considerably in their practical and theoretical importance since the 1960's, respectively the 1970's.

---

[1] See Deutscher Bundestag, "Umwelt der Bundesregierung 1971",Bundesdrucksache VI 2710 (1971), p. 63. Also consult the extensive discussion in *L. Wicke*, "Umweltökonomie, 2nd. Ed. Munich: 1989, p.8.

[2] See *Ch. Leipert*, "Natur in der ökonomischen Theorie und Praxis", Wirtschaft und Gesellschaft, Wirtschaftspolitische Zeitschrift der Kammer für Arbeiter und Angestellte für Wien 1/1988, pp. 255-264.

Environmental benefits or rather environmental conditions (the environment does not actually produce benefits) have become a scarce economic good. *Environmental economics* deals with the difficulties of including these environmental goods into the process of allocating scarce production factors to alternative usages. Environmental economics has suggested *several tools* for this purpose, among them

- campaigns to encourage environmental awareness;
- governmental correction of environmental damage, either via direct investments such as supplying sewage systems or via indirect support of environmental investments by subsidies;
- regulatory measures such as legal requirements and prohibitions;
- price solutions such as a Pigou tax[3] or pollution payments;
- quantity solutions such as tradable pollution allowances.

Resource economics as the second specifically environmental branch of economics seeks to ascertain the excavation time-table for a depletable natural resource which maximizes profits for the current owner. The correct measure of discounting future profits is open to debate. Economists of the neoclassical school assume that present consumption is preferred over future consumption. The *"ecologists" among the economists* demand a discount rate of zero in order to achieve equality between the present and the future. The *"hopeful" among economists* accept the premise that innovative technologies - and not the environment - are responsible for a continuous creation of inexhaustible resources. They conclude that scarcity is irrelevant.

Environmental problems are generally seen to have *three distinct origins:*

- causes rooted in development such as population growth and expansion of production;
- socio-economic causes such as the problems inherent in collective goods, external effects and human pollution practices;
- causes arising within the economic order deriving from market or government failure.

One must keep in mind that many environmental problems have their origins within the economic system and consequently cannot be conceptually separated. A certain standard of living for a populous economy seems to necessitate plant estate, energy consumption, transportation problems, and pollution. Put a bit drastically, even if your only desire is to sleep under bridges, it is a systemic necessity that you have access to such bridges.

---

[3] For an extensive discussion of Pigou-taxes consult *J. Weimann*, "Umweltökonomie", 2nd Ed. Berlin, Heidelberg: 1991, pp. 110 ff.

Environmental economics does not strive to create a philosophy of deprivation. Economically speaking, *its perspective remains the optimization of wealth* or well-being. The word perspective is used at this point in analogy to the awakening of a so-called central perspective during the Renaissance, which led architects, engineers, painters, and the general public to break with medieval conceptions[4]. The expression *perspective* is meant to describe *a new view of the economic cosmos, not simply a more frugal one. We need to examine if and how environmental problems can be solved within the reigning economic order*[5].

This is not supposed to simply imply an "economic" solution in the traditional sense. Isolated, individual solutions at the discretion of business management or government will not suffice. Edzard Reuter, president of Daimler-Benz, stated as much in a speech on global corporate responsibilities held at the Liberal Club in Münster on October 22, 1991. Coming from the point of view of chief executive officer of a major international company, he said, "Present challenges have reached dimensions that demand responses from business that include more than producing and selling automobiles, airplanes, or a bit of electronics." The current discussion on compensation payments to governments for protecting rain forests sheds light on the global economic dimensions involved. The ensuing demands on the sciences are that they, too, must search for global, socially acceptable, evolutionary solutions. The complex, almost chaotic world calls for the development of some kind of order.

2. General system theory as a theory of action for environmental economics

The epistemological statements made in the previous chapter are meant to be understood as a constructivistic theory in the Kantian spirit of an empiricism based on calculation, not as an attempted paradigm shift. We would like to follow Niklas Luhmann in considering *the world as a system embedded in an environment of systems*, without evoking any idea of an

[4] *Angela Schönberger*, "Architekturmodelle zwischen Illusion und Simulation", in "Simulation und Wirklichkeit", Ed. *A. Schönberger*. Cologne: 1988, p. 122.

[5] *Luhmann* is sceptical at this point, saying business will always maintain "in principal that what is economically not acceptable is economically not acceptable". *Niklas Luhmann*, "Ökologische Kommunikation". Opladen: 1986, p. 122.

involved hierarchy[6]. Society for instance can be described as consisting of several different systems such as the legal system, the economic system, the education system, the political system, the religious system, the scientific system, etc. A human being can be interpreted as a system within an environment of systems, namely as an anthropological system in an environment containing a biological, physical, social, chemical, etc. system. The natural sciences, especially biology, grasp each individual living cell as an atomic, molecular, cellular, organic system[7].

Systems are seen to be *functional-structural*, meaning that the world is comprehended as being in constant flow, as coming and going so to speak, and consequently systems are to be described as a collection of functions. Temporarily, these functions may give rise to structures. In contrast to Parsons[8], who sees the world as being structural-functional, i.e. as equipped with given structures, the position put forth here is that dysfunctions in the sense of a set structure cannot occur.

General system theory proposes that systems must be viewed as being self-referential. This means that systems are seen to possess the capability to relate to themselves and to distinguish this relationship from relationships formed with the environment. A system defines itself and then acts within an environment of other systems - environment being everything beyond the margins of the system itself. Seen from this point of view we would recognize the economic system, the legal system, the political system etc. to be "environment."

The image of a circuit is a good representation of the self-referential system "the economy," and the introduction of an ecological GNP account would initiate a revised self-definition of the system due to newly accepted economic and political values. "To define" should be read as "to demarcate" as well as "to determine." It is important to distinguish between self-defining systems - meant to be self-determined systems such as human systems - and biological systems. Biological systems can either act within certain bounda-

---

[6] See *Niklas Luhmann*, "Soziale Systeme - Grundriß einer allgemeinen Theorie", 2nd Ed. Frankfurt/M.: 1988; "Die Wirtschaft der Gesellschaft", 2nd Ed. Frankfurt/M.: 1989; "Ökologische Aufklärung - Kann die moderne Gesellschaft sich auf ökologische Gefährdungen einstellen?", 3rd Ed. Opladen: 1990; "Soziologische Aufklärung 1 (Aufsätze zur Theorie sozialer Systeme)", 6th Ed. Opladen: 1991; "Soziologische Aufklärung 5 (Konstruktivistische Perspektiven)", Opladen: 1990.

[7] See *F. Varela*, "Principles of Biological Anatomy". New York, NY: 1979.

[8] *Talcott Parsons*, "Beiträge zur soziologischen Theorie". Neuwied, Berlin: 1964, p. 47ff., 52ff.

ries, or else they are non-living systems, which only react. This is the reason why each and *every system-theoretical analysis needs to depart from the difference between system and environment*. Systems constitute and conserve themselves by generating and maintaining distance to the environment. Borders serve to control this distance, border maintenance becomes system maintenance. In this sense the system "economy" defines which ecological elements to include within its own system.This distance or *system/environment difference* arises because systems interpret themselves by their functions. The system/environment difference allows for the perception of *closed* systems, while permitting a *continuous reciprocal interaction with the other systems in the manner of a flow equilibrium*. Please observe that the expression "inter-dependence" on the contrary includes only linear interactions. Functional distinction pre-conditions the establishment of *binary codes*. Within the communication process among the systems these codes permit the evaluation of operations according to their system functionality. *The system "economy" is coded by have/not have and money is coded by payment/no payment*[9].

It is not possible to transform this simple binary Luhmann coding into systems of action. Firstly, one would need to inspect whether non-payment systems can exist next to payment systems in the economy. Secondly, we are dealing with a paradox: to be or not to be. The coding paradox is solved by the *distribution of have/not have as well as pay/don't pay to people and places*. In addition, we need to introduce *time* in the sense of *have now; pay now/have later; pay later* into the system. In evaluating the operations within the system the paradox is dissolved. *Material distribution as well as time become order functions of the system*, and consequently permit distinct solutions. Human systems operate using perception as do other biological systems, but in contrast to biological systems human systems use logic when transforming perception into action. Binary Aristotelian logic, according to which something can only be "true or false" at a given time and place, is highly complicated by considering time and distribution of wealth. By modeling time and distribution factors ("when for whom") "true/false" becomes relatively relational.

The final constitutive element to be considered at this point is the *autopoietic* characteristic. Autopoietic systems reproduce by generating their elementary units themselves. In the economic system prices, quantities, or

---

[9] *Niklas Luhmann*, "Ökologische Kommunikation". Opladen: 1986, p. 103. For a more extensive version consult *Niklas Luhmann*, "Die Wirtschaft der Gesellschaft". Frankfurt/M.: 1988.

institutions such as private property, competition rules, the money supply, the banking sector, the currency system, etc. are such elements. The system must use its elements to ensure solvency within the system. Autopoietic systems can thus be characterized as self-referential systems which continuously re-organize and re-formulate their elements from within themselves. Questions concerning order such as the question of self-regulation arise in this context. How things come together is defined within the system. This can, of course, lead to catastrophe, as the fate of the communist system demonstrates.

All this results in an organizational completeness of the systems within themselves, which stands in opposition to a material and energetic openness necessary for the production of the elements. This is valid for all dissipative systems, and the economy is a dissipative system. Economists are currently examining how ecological considerations can be incorporated into the economic system by re-organizating and re-formulating its elements. In other words we are asking whether ecological problems belong to another system other than the economic system, and whether the economy is so to speak the wrong agent to address for a solution. This debate has a long history, as does the issue of including social or fairness elements into the economic system[10].

3. "The environment" interpreted as a system-theoretical expression

"Environment" in the sense implied by environmental economics is a system-theoretical collective expression, as are "society" or "universe". Within the context of environmental economics the environment includes biological systems, chemical systems, mineralogical systems, climatological systems... Each system has its own rules and unique distinctions. Connections consist in form of conditional associations and interrelations, the analysis of which is complicated by the relevance of certain threshold values. Due to the non-linearity of the relations involved and to the unknown threshold values, which are dependent on the existing state of the system, an input-output-model can only offer a restricted description of the process, cluttered by numerous ceteris-paribus assumptions and simplified by linearizing the relationships involved. Such input-output-analyses result in the simulation of a "ceteris-paribus reality," not in an adequate description of reality and its complex associations.

---

[10] See *Manfred E. Streit*, "Wissen, Wettbewerb und Wirtschaftsordnung - Zum Gedenken an Friedrich August von Hayek", in ORDO 43 (1992), pp. 1-30.

Before embarking on further analysis, it is necessary to agree on a specific *world view or outlook*, i.e. on a rationalization of the world, on a demythologizing of nature, and on humanizing reality. Without such preliminary accords there is a danger that misunderstandings will arise, objective discourse becomes impossible, and that our debate will be impaired by diffuse concerns or eye-washing tactics.

Contrary to the mystical attitude of hunter and gatherer cultures and to the rational attitude with which the great agricultures approached the world, *our industrial- technological culture exhibits a deeply calculating attitude in rationalizing the world.* Nature has become a mere parameter of wealth consideration for human beings. One might say that nature is considered a quarry beyond the need of replenishment. People calculate using relative prices or opportunity costs when considering natural factors. This results in the development of heavily industrialized areas, regions specialized in providing services, areas offering natural resources, specific regions for tourism, growing coffee and bananas, and so on. Where relatively independent biotopes used to exist, we find today interdependent regions as a consequence of the rules governing the system.

Human beings also calculate the costs of using alternative types of fuel during production and choose that which is cheapest according to prevailing price and demand conditions. All these decisions are based on current cost and price calculations; using contemporary language, we would say they are due to synergy effects; or, as one used to say, they occur in the spirit of rationalization. Adam Smith and David Ricardo laid the foundations of this attitude in their discussions concerning labor division in needle-making or comparative costs in international trade. This gradual process of rationalization presupposes a *de-mythologizing of nature* and a de-ideologizing of all rationality. The hunters and gatherers were a culture of beneficiaries of nature, while the high agricultures were true cultivators of the environment. Our industrial-technological civilization, however, has subjected nature in the most complete sense possible to our will. This is what I refer to as *humanizing reality*, and it is accomplished by the desire to *command over the world* in the sense of managing our natural environment. The question going back to Heidegger concerning the administration or use of the world by humans has not been resolved, as nature refuses to demonstrate "neither being administered nor being available"[11]. That is to say the environment does not render us advice on the possibilities it can offer for human use, nor how one could actually make use of such possibilities. Should the human race annihi-

---

[11] *Martin Heidegger*, "Sein und Zeit", 12th Ed. Tübingen: 1972, p. 211.

late nature altogether it would only signal that we do not actually have command over the world.

Destruction of the natural environment by human beings is not necessarily a question of folly or evil of those involved, it might also have its reasons in what Bateson has called "*disease of epistemology*."[12] Concerning the relevant scientific paradigm he states, "We are now beginning to recognize certain epistemological fallacies of western civilization. In agreement with the general intellectual climate prevalent in England during the middle of the 19th century, Darwin developed the theory of natural selection and evolution, according to which the surviving unit was either the phylogenetic tree or the species, subspecies, or something of the kind. Today it is rather apparent that this is not the surviving unit in the real biological world. Environment and organism together form the unit of survival... Let us consider the consequences of the epistemological mistake of choosing the wrong unit of survival: you arrive at the conclusion species *versus* a surrounding species, or *versus* the environment in which it is active. Humans versus nature." We must avoid this fallacy by considering the reciprocal relationships between economics and ecology.

Technological and anthropological aspects come to mind when considering the two systems, economy and ecology, in the light of environmental economics. In agreement with our basic world view we need to reach an *accord* concerning the *technologically autonomous* technical, organizational, economic, ecological, etc. *processes* manifest in environmental problems and their relation to our *anthropologically conditioned* social, economic, political, ethical, etc. *actions. Within a highly complex system relationship* such as that among the natural, heavily cultivated environment and the economic system, a relationship dominated by unpredictable effects, non-linear causal relations, non-refutable contradictions, non-rationable rules, unaccountable references, and un-definable certainty, against the backdrop of such a relationship *an accord presents a creative, composite ordering achievement* between self-organization and chaos. Partial solutions often increase problems, because it is not possible to isolate certain aspects and circumstances; i.e. due to the non-linearity of relations involved we cannot return to individual parts or pieces.

---

[12] *G. Bateson*, "Ökologie des Geistes". Frankfurt/M.: 1985, pp 614ff.

4. Possible solutions considering system-theoretical aspects

A first step would consist in an examination of the compatibility of the technological, i.e. natural, environment, and the sociological, i.e. economic, system. Problems are generally due to lacking compatibility - a state that is almost to be expected. Use of naturally reclaimable resources as well as use of recycled, i.e. artificially reclaimable, materials is conducive to achieving some form of compatibility, while extraction of non-reclaimable substances as well as employment of non-recyclable materials is not. In this context it is necessary to ensure that the recycling process is properly executed. We can assume incompatibility to be the norm and should strive to achieve some kind of non- incompatibility. Non-incompatibility entails establishing non-contradictory standards in a number of areas and allows analysis of problematic points and minimizing the potential for conflict. It is important that the outlined non-compatibility strategy considers the technical and social interests involved properly, and that objective knowledge, social considerations, and humane understanding result in an effective communication process.

Establishing non-contradictory standards involves deciding on the type and scope of damage to the environment considered acceptable. It might be feasible to use dumps for non-toxic garbage if the only harm resulting for the environment was of purely geographic nature. Protests of a small group of people suffering from the subsequent effects in their immediate neighborhood would not be a sufficient ground for abandoning the measure. Just as the German Basic Law contains the social obligation of private property, so it is possible to accept a social obligation inherent in a private view of the surrounding landscape.

Establishing non-incompatibility also includes decreasing contradictions in the applications of environmental impact assessments, technology impact evaluations, and cost-benefit- analyses arising from the calculatory attitude people have towards the environment mentioned earlier.

The next step would consist in classifying the long-term effects of economic activity on the environment. This implies interpreting such effects not simply as the fancies of a group "granola nuts," but accepting these effects as given. It is necessary at least to come to an agreement as to whether solutions should be found and if so, how extensive these solutions should be. Possible classification schemes could include: effects on the climate, cumulative damage, irreparable harm, temporary harm, etc. An immediate problem arising would be that scientific extrapolations and simulations come to varying conclusions depending on the assumptions used. Scientific scenarios for global warming range from wet and mild winters in Europe to the flooding of large parts of the continent. In addition, it is possible to calculate a simulated future reality, but we are not able to fully comprehend the consequences, so that simulation results of the future are often misused for ideological battles in the present. Political administration needs to set the constitutional frame for future economic actions.

A further step would be an analysis of the global distribution of the effects of economic actions. The developing countries supply most natural resources and are highly affected by resource economic considerations. Should the developing countries seek to attain, under the current state of technological development, similar living standards as the industrialized countries enjoy today, consumption of natural resources and global pollution will multiply. This is a problem that the industrialized countries have refused to recognize at international environmental conferences. So far we have only treated relatively simple matters such as compensation payments for the protection of rain forests. Multinational treaties need to include provision of global authorities with the right to enforce and monitor international agreements, as is already practiced in military matters, and as seems to be currently happening in the relief coordination for Somalia.

The solutions offered above - information campaigns, government damage repair, legal instruments, price and quantity measures - need to be applied consistently. *Ideological debates on whether specific measures disagree with the market forces hamper rapid solutions.* Governments must realize the issues at stake and strive to translate their ideas into reality. Dogmatic debates on free enterprise were not supportive in the 19th century, either, when the legal requirement for stock companies was introduced to publish their results in support of capital formation. Pricing solutions involving the individual firm can be made more flexible than general legal measures such as fees and taxes. Price solutions can also be dosed more effectively than tax solutions involving indirect taxes. Business tend to pass these on to consumers.

Different forms of national accounting could result in suitable national product figures for measuring the true "wealth of nations." These figures have been thoroughly discussed in the literature, where it has been suggested to include ecological parameters into the calculation or to estimate affluence using various indicators reflecting standard of living. These indicators empirically determine quality of living by including health standards, education levels, social and natural environment factors in addition to material wealth, which are all factors not explicitly considered in lump-sum income or GNP statistics. One effect of the traditional, theoretically and politically narrow economic focus has been to exclude essential aspects of prosperity from administrative attention[13].

There exists no mechanism which could be integrated into the economic process to identify a "guilty party" in connection to pollution. We can, however, attempt to pragmatically utilize the concept of "parties responsible" when attributing costs or damages of specific offences. This must be taken as a means of allotting pollution responsibilities, not of assigning guilt.

Within the individual firm it is possible to put environmental audit systems into use to arrive at ecological accounting sheets for every involved company[14]. These can provide information useful to each firm and can also offer information for recalculating costs after price changes caused by agreed or government prescribed pollution prevention measures. Concepts of "lean production" or "total quality"[15] can be extended, in analogous fashion, to a "total ecological concept" of production. Such a "total ecological concept" would range from product planning and designing stages over distribution to "complete" disposal. Subcontractors and suppliers should be included in such a program. It would not be delegated to a specific department but involve all managers and employees. Information processing, vocational and continuous training, especially within task forces in the individual firm, should break down the problem and develop solutions. The national chambers of commerce could provide helpful information and training services.

5. Environmental protection: A new challenge for economists

Solutions can come from firms via the market. Automatization and rationalization have solved subsistence problems in the industrialized nations. Instead, we are confronted with a problem of over-capacity. It is quite possible that environmental products trigger off additional innovations. Intensified research, public as well as private, is essential. Microsystem technology could provide the foundations. Environmentally adequate products might become market leaders. I have heard of a company in Japan

---

[13] See *Siegfried Hauser*, "Indikatorenkonzepte zur Bestimmung der Lebensqualität", in "Energieversorgung und Lebensqualität", Ed. *H. Krümpelmann*. Villingen: 1978, pp. 137-154.

[14] See e.g. *H.-O. Henkel*, "Umwelt-Auditing bei IBM. Mit Informationstechnik zum Gesamtkonzept", in "Umwelt-Auditing", Ed. *U. Steger*. Wiesbaden: 1991, pp. 120-137; *W. Hopfenbeck*, "Umweltorientiertes Management und Marketing", Landsberg/Lech: 1990; *R. Müller-Wenk*, "Die Ökologische Buchhaltung", Frankfurt/M.: 1978.

[15] Representatives for the whole literature consult the study by *J.P. Womack/D.T Jones/D. Roos*, "Die zweite Revolution in der Autoindustrie". Frankfurt/M.: 1992.

that uses software products to produce machines. This is an intriguing idea, as it involves reversing the classical process of production, which tags software to the machine. These people are attempting the reverse by developing machines to match existing software. The idea is fascinating, too, because it lets technological facts appear less constrained, and because the idea itself, not the technical equipment involved, is the true innovation. I am also convinced it is possible to take advantage of snob effects by offering expensive environmental products.

On the macroeconomic level solutions similar to those used in the defense business are feasible. This would entail taxing part of the national product away and feeding it back into the economy for the production of filter systems and similar products or for environmental research purposes. The MITI in Japan pursues various ideas along these lines. They are considering the problems and possible solutions of the 21st century today. They are not only considering these issues, they are supporting solutions by long-term industrial policy. We must not forget, in this context, that our students' life expectancy we are educating today is the year 2050.

Of course there will be problems of transition requiring endurance in reforming production processes, as well as in reforming mental processes. These are constraints necessary for a free-market system to unfold its dynamics. The system theoretical approach allows a better dissimulation of conflicts than attempted solutions working with concepts of "true" and "false." The system theory approach encourages a rapid and flexible implementation of measures due to its low susceptibility to dogmatic misuse.

The economy can only deal with those parts of environmental problems which can be translated into the language of prices. The rest is up to politics, on a local, regional, and national level. Luhmann's code "govern/don't govern" gives a good description of the current German dilemma: no conceptional environmental administration available. Under global aspects it is necessary to introduce solvency into the international economic system to ensure that global environmental problems can be solved. In other words, the developing countries, which are non-payment-systems, need to be integrated into some type of payment system according to an economically sound solution. Dogmatic debates on whether certain measures fit into a market economy or not must make room for the enforcement of solutions in gradual, reversible, but emphatically executed steps.

A Dynamic Analysis of Global Warming

Ryuhei Okumura

1. Introduction

The relationship between economic activity and environmental destruction has been recognized as problems of external diseconomies. In the presence of externalities, the ordinary price system can not serve as an optimal allocation mechanism. However, a pigovian tax (subsidy) can remove the discrepancy between private costs and the social costs, and lead the economy to Pareto optimum. Even though there are several important problems (the problems of income distribution, information, Coase's theorem), the Pigovian tradition remains as a standard policy measure in the economy with transaction costs.

Global warming is a diseconomy which is global in scope and irreversible over long time horizons. The character of global warming makes a pigovian tax (subsidy) more difficult as a policy measure. This is because the lack of scientific evidence on the relationship between the magnitude of global warming and human activities raises the information problem immediately. The international character of diseconomy raises the income distribution problem between DCs and LDCs.

Cline (1992)[1] proposes a two-stage, contingent policy strategy. In the first phase, countries limit further expansion of greenhouse gases (carbon dioxide, methane, nitrous oxide, and chlorofluorocarbons) emission, through the adoption of such policy measures as modest carbon taxes, reduced deforestation and increased afforestation. By 2000 the international community would review the scientific analysis; if the diagnosis is confirmed, counties would move to adopt an intensified policy to limit warming. However he does not show the basis of tax rate; i.e., $5 per ton of carbon emitted.

---

[1] *W.R. Cline*, Global Warming: the Economic Stakes, Institute for International Economics, May 1992.

Uzawa (1991)[2] presents a theoretical foundation for the computation of the imputed price for greenhouse gas and for land forest. His approach puts stress on equity issues, and derives the conclusion that, "imputed prices of greenhouse gases and land forests in each country involved are determined in such a way that the ratios of imputed prices to the per-capita level of national income in each country take the same values for all countries" (p.278).

Firstly, Uzawa solves the optimal problem in the one-country case, and then extends the analysis to the multi-country case. He assumes that income per capita of each country is equalized, and applies the same formula of the shadow price of carbon dioxide(CO_2) to the multi-country case. But the accumulation of CO_2 causes externalities, so it is not certain that the same formula can be used. The purpose of this paper is to extend Uzawa's analysis to two-country world in order to consider this point.

Another important issue is the income redistribution problem in the process of stopping global warming. Even though this problem is not considered here, it remains as a vital question.

2. Uzawa model

If the causes of global warming are atmospheric concentrations of "greenhouse gases", particularly of carbon dioxide (CO_2), we should understand the global carbon cycle. Uzawa pictures it as the interchange among three major reservoirs of carbon: the atmosphere, the surface ocean, and the terrestrial biosphere. These are in equilibrium, but this equilibrium in the global carbon system is disturbed by anthropogenic activities: the combustion of fossil fuels and the depletion of land forests.

Denote by V_t the amount of carbon dioxide at each moment of time t, accumulated in the atmosphere. V_t increases due to anthropogenic activities, while a certain amount of CO_2 is absorbed by the oceans. Therefore, V_t changes according to the following equation.

$$(1) \quad \dot{V}_t = ax_t - \mu V_t$$

Where x_t = the level of anthropogenic activities, a and μ = positive constants. In this simple model, the level of anthropogenic activities implies the quantity of final consumption goods.

---

[2] *H. Uzawa*, "Global Warming Initiatives: The pacific Rim", in *R. Dornbusch* and *J.M. Poterba* ed., Global Warming, The MIT Press, 1991.

An important impact of global warming is a rise in the sea level. A sea-level rise as a result of melting of land-based glaciers and ice sheets would cause the world countries great expense for coastal protection. In some cases, it may not even be possible to protect. An increase in the atmospheric level of CO_2 induces not only global warming, but also other changes in natural and social conditions. We simply assume the concentration of CO_2 decreases the national welfare.

In the model of this section, the world consists of one country, and the population is constant. Without loss of generality, we can set the number of population as one. The utility indices of the representative individual is supposed to be,

$$(2) \quad y = u\ (x_t)\ \phi\ (V_t),\ u' > 0,\ u'' < 0,\ \phi' < 0,\ \phi'' > 0$$

The optimization problem is to maximize the discounted present value of future utility indices,

$$(3) \quad \int_0^\infty u\ (x_t)\ \phi\ (V_t) e^{-\delta t}\ dt$$

subject to the constraint (1) and the given initial condition V_0. Where the discount rate δ assumed to be a positive constant.

This problem can be solved by the method of the maximum principle. We define the current-value Hamiltonian as,

$$(4) \quad H = u\ (x_t)\ \phi\ (V_t)\ +\ q_t\ (ax_t\ -\ \mu V_t)$$

where q_t is the auxiliary variable (the shadow price of the stock of CO_2).

The first-order conditions for an interior maximum can be expressed as,

$$(5) \quad u'\ (x_t)\ \phi\ (V_t)\ +\ q_t\ a\ =\ 0$$

$$(6) \quad \dot{q}_t/q_t\ =\ (\delta\ +\ \mu)\ -\ u(x_t)\ \phi'\ (V_t)/q_t$$

The optimum time paths of consumption xt, the stock of CO_2 Vt, and the shadow price q_t are determined as the solutions to the system of differential equations (1), (5), (6).

Uzawa pays particular attention to the stationary state. At the stationary state (q_t/q_t= 0), the equation (6) can be written as,

$$(7) \quad q^{*} = u(x^{*})\ \phi'\ (V^{*})/(\delta + \mu)$$

Since the atmospheric carbon dioxide is an economic bad, q^{*} has a negative value. Set pt= -qt, we can rewrite the equation as,

$$(8) \quad p^{*} = u(x^{*})\ [-\phi'\ (V^{*})]/(\delta + \mu)$$

This is Uzawa's formula for the imputed price of the atmospheric concentration of carbon dioxide.

The meaning of the formula (8) is as follows; The emission of CO_2 increases the stock of CO_2 in the atmosphere. The stock of CO_2 reduces the national welfare over unlimited periods. The present value of this reduction of the national welfare can be calculated by discounting. Here, the effective discount rate becomes $\delta + \mu$, because a part of the stock of CO_2 is absorbed by the oceans at the rate of μ. Uzawa applies this formula to multi-country case as well. But, there is a crucial difference between one country case and multi-country case, because carbon dioxide emissions have externalities. In the next section, we consider the optimization problem in two-country framework.

3. Two-country model

In this section, we compare the Nash equilibrium path with the world-wide social optimal path in two-country framework. The Nash equilibrium solution can be understood as a market solution. The world economy consists of two countries, the country 1 and the country 2. The structure of each country is identical with the country in the section II. It is assumed that there is no international trade, no international investment and no international migration.

3.1. Nash equilibrium path

Consider each country as player of a differential game[3]. For country 1, the optimum problem is to choose his strategy $\{x_{1t}\}$ to maximize,

[3] On a differential game, see *Morton I. Kamien & Nancy L. Schwartz*, Dynamic optimization, North-Holland, 1991.

$$(9) \quad J_1(\{x_{1t}\}, \{x_{2t}\}) = \int_0^\infty u_1(x_{1t})\, \emptyset_1(V_t) e^{-\delta t}\, dt$$

subject to the constraint,

$$(10) \quad \dot{V}_t = \Sigma_{i=1}^{i=2} a_{it} x_{it} - \mu V_t$$

the given initial condition V_0 and given strategy of country 2 $\{x_{2t}\}$. Where a strategy {xit} for country (i=1,2) is a time path of a control variable (i.e. consumption). The optimum problem of country 2 is similar to country 1's, which is not repeated here.

Nash equilibrium is a pair of strategies of two countries $(\{x_{1t}^*\}, \{x_{2t}^*\})$, such as,

(11) $J_1(\{x_{1t}^*\}, \{x_{2t}^*\}) \geq J_1(\{x_{1t}\}, \{x_{2t}^*\})$, for any $\{x_{1t}\}$,
and
(12) $J_2(\{x_{1t}^*\}, \{x_{2t}^*\}) \geq J_2(\{x_{1t}^*\}, \{x_{2t}\})$, for any $\{x_{2t}\}$.

Open-loop strategies are ones for which each country chooses all the values of his control variable for each moment in time at the outset of the game. The Nash equilibrium open-loop strategies can be determined by the application of the standard optimal control methods.

Form a Hamiltonian for each country,

$$(13) \quad H_1 = u_1(x_{1t}) + q_{1t}\left[\Sigma_{i=1}^{i=2} a_1 x_{1t} - \mu V_t\right]$$

Applying the standard first-order conditions of optimal control theory to (13) gives rise to the equations,

$$(14) \quad u_1'(x_{1t})\, \emptyset_1(V_t) + q_{1t} a_1 = 0$$

$$(15) \quad \dot{q}_{1t}/q_{1t} = (\delta + \mu) - u_1(x_{1t})\, \emptyset_1(V_t)/q_{1t}$$

which together with (10) yield five equations for determining the five time paths $\{x_{1t}^*\}$, $\{x_{2t}^*\}$, $\{q_{1t}^*\}$, $\{q_{2t}^*\}$, $\{V_t^*\}$. Again, we pay special attention to the stationary state. From (15), we can derive the equation (16).

$$(16) \quad q_1^{\infty} = [u_1(x_1^{**})\, \emptyset_1'(V^{**})]/(\delta + mu)$$

This is the same formula as in the Uzawa model case. Therefore, Uzawa's formula is suitable to an equilibrium of a decentralized private decision system rather than a worldwide social optimum in multi-country case.

3.2. Worldwide social optimal paths

We define a worldwide social optimal problem as, maximize

$$(17) \quad \int_0^\infty \left[\Sigma_{i=1}^{i=2}\, u_i\,(x_{it})\ \phi_i\,(V_t) \right] e^{-\delta t}\, dt$$

subject to

$$(18) \quad \dot{V}_t = \Sigma_{i=1}^{i=2}\, a_i\, x_{it} - \mu V_t$$

and a given V_0. The current-value Hamiltonian for this problem is,

$$(19) \quad H = \Sigma_{i=1}^{i=2}\, u_i\,(x_{it})\ \phi_i\,(V_t) + q_t \left[\Sigma_{i=1}^{i=2}\, a_i\, x_{it} - \mu V_t \right]$$

The first-order conditions for an interior maximum are

$$(20) \quad u_i'\,(x_{it})\ \phi_i\,(V_t) + q_t\, a_i = 0$$

and

$$(21) \quad \dot{q}_t / q_t = (\delta + \mu) - \Sigma_{i=1}^{i=2}\, u_i\,(x_{it})\ \phi_i'\,(V_t)/q_t$$

Now the shadow price of CO_2 in the stationary state is,

$$(22) \quad q_\infty = \Sigma_{i=1}^{i=2}\, u_i\,(x_{i\infty})\ \phi_i'\,(V_\infty)/(\delta + \mu)$$

This formula is clearly different from the Uzawa's formula. The shadow price in this worldwide social optimum case is higher than the one in Uzawa's case. This comes from the externality of CO_2 accumulation.

4. Conclusion

In this paper, we examined the important contribution by Uzawa to estimate the shadow price of CO_2. The explicit extension of the one-country Uzawa model to the two-country world showed that the estimated value by Uzawa was underestimated.

General Equilibrium Analysis of CO_2 Levies and Emission Rights[1]

Yuko Arayama

1. Introduction

The theoretical base from which to approach environmental issues is an analysis of economic externalities. The seminal works by Prof. Pigou showed that firms with negative externalities must be taxed in order to equalize private and social marginal costs and that firms with positive externalities should be subsidized again in order to equalize private and social marginal costs. Needless to say by equalizing private and social marginal costs the social optimum is attained.

The results derived by Prof. Pigou are so conclusive that almost all his successors have used his theoretical reasoning when examining troublesome environmental issues.

His successors were by no means wrong as long as the environmental issues remain local and static. However major topics in environmental concerns can not be local at the current time. For example, arguments relating to the necessity of regulating CO_2 emissions caused by the fear of global warming are obviously global. If recent environmental problems are related to global externalities rather than "classical" local externalities, it is necessary to reexamine the validity of applying Pigouvian intuition, with its local perspective, to global environmental issues.

Many authors have tried to examine the theoretical aspects of externalities in a general equilibrium framework. Bhagwati and Srinivasan (1983) demonstrated simple general equilibrium analysis for production externalities

[1] The first draft of this paper was firstly presented at 14th Seminar of the Faculties of Economics of Nagoya and Freiburg University on March 31, 1993. The author is grateful to Mr. *K. Taketoshi*, Mr. *T. Miyanaga*, Mr. *T. Hattori* and Mr. *H. Kumoi* for many useful comments and technical assistance.

for a small open economy, which distinguished between "output-related externality" and "factor-use-related externality." Shibata and Shibata (1988) also handled production externalities in terms of a so-called "fixed capital model." Baumol and Bradford (1972) have shown that detrimental externalities could affect the convexity of the production possibility frontier and that those could results in a non-convex production possibility frontier. Baumol (1972) has also investigated the effects of taxation and the control of externalities in a general equilibrium set up. Smith (1974) provided an exposition of stationary general equilibrium of a replenishable natural resource in a two-commodity world. Hazilla and Kopp (1990) performed a general equilibrium analysis of the social cost of environmental quality and provided an empirical analysis of the U.S. Clean Air and Clean Water acts.

Instrument choices in environmental policy have been argued by Baumol and Oates (1971), Dewees (1983), McGartland and Oates (1985), McGartland (1988) and O'Neil, David, Moore and Jones (1983). Effects of policy measures on income distribution were examined by Dorfman and Snow (1975), and Gianessi, Peskin and Wolff (1979).

One of the principal problems related to environmental issues is in the domain of negative externality and effective range of policy measure. Peltzman and Tideman (1972) concluded that spatially uniform prices for environmental resources will be particularly inefficient because population tends to cluster in the same areas as economic activity. Hoel (1991) tried to approach global environmental problems by evaluating the effects of unilateral actions taken by one country in terms of game theory.

The rest of this paper will be organized as follows. In the first section Pigouvian tax will be brief surveyed and a possible explanation offered as to why arguments on CO_2 levies and emission rights have lost any theoretical links to the discrepancies between social and private marginal costs, which is the central concern in Pigouvian tax.

In section two, we will develop an economic model which allows us to reinterpret Pigouvian analysis in terms of a general equilibrium. This attempt to extend Pigouvian analysis from a partial equilibrium to a general equilibrium is indispensable since environmental issues are global rather than local. In the third section the economic implications provided by Pigouvian tax in a partial equilibrium are interpreted in a general equilibrium framework. The last section reexamines policy measures such as CO_2 levies and emission rights in terms of a general equilibrium framework.

2. Why CO_2 levies or emission rights?

Various serious environmental issues exist. However we will limit our argument only to the CO_2 issue here, mainly because CO_2 is the most typical and general example of a global externality.

As far as CO_2 is concerned, it is very rare to impose Pigouvian tax on the commodities whose production process is characterized by heavy CO_2 emissions. Why is it so?

There could be three major explanations for this. First, many people (including many economists) believe that CO_2 is the major cause of global warming, but that this has not yet been proved scientifically. As a result of this causal ambiguity it is extremely difficult to estimate the social cost of CO_2 emission. Second, CO_2 might not be a big problem at flow base. CO_2 might contribute to global warming simply because CO_2 could accumulate. If CO_2 is not a big concern at flow base, any additional amount of CO_2 newly created in order to increase the production of a CO_2 emitting commodity may not result in a large discrepancy between private marginal cost and social marginal cost in the production X. Finally, almost no production process is free from CO_2 emission. Therefore, all commodities must be taxed in order to eliminate the difference between social and private marginal costs.

Diagram 1 depicts a basic idea of Pigouvian tax. Marginal evaluation of consuming X is equal to private marginal cost (PMC, later on) at point "a", however, social marginal cost (SMC, later on) is far beyond this marginal evaluation. Therefore, Pigouvian tax (P-tax), which is equal to the length between point "b" and "c", should improve social welfare by the amount of shaded triangle "a-c-e". The fundamental characteristics of Pigouvian analysis become immediately clear: 1) It is assumed that the social cost of the externality can be estimated; 2) the analysis remains static, and 3) the analysis remains in a partial equilibrium framework.

In contrast to these fundamental characteristics: 1) There is no established measure to estimate the social cost caused by CO_2, 2) CO_2 can accumulate over time, and 3) global warming "caused" by CO_2 is global and not local at all in its nature. Because of these limitations, Pigouvian theory can hardly provide a basis for the analysis of global environmental issues.

This specific situation concerning CO_2 and state of the art in economic theory in general has driven a wedge between the idea of socially optimum level of CO_2 emission and policy measures to ensure the optimum level of CO_2 emission is attained. Consequently, regulating the *total amount* of CO_2 emissions has been recognized as the only relevant target of environmental policies. Considerations relating to *social optimum* have been entirely neglected in the discussion at any level. Needless to say, many economic analyses concerning CO_2 levies and emission rights have nothing to do with externalities. They are merely a simple application of microeconomic theory without externalities.

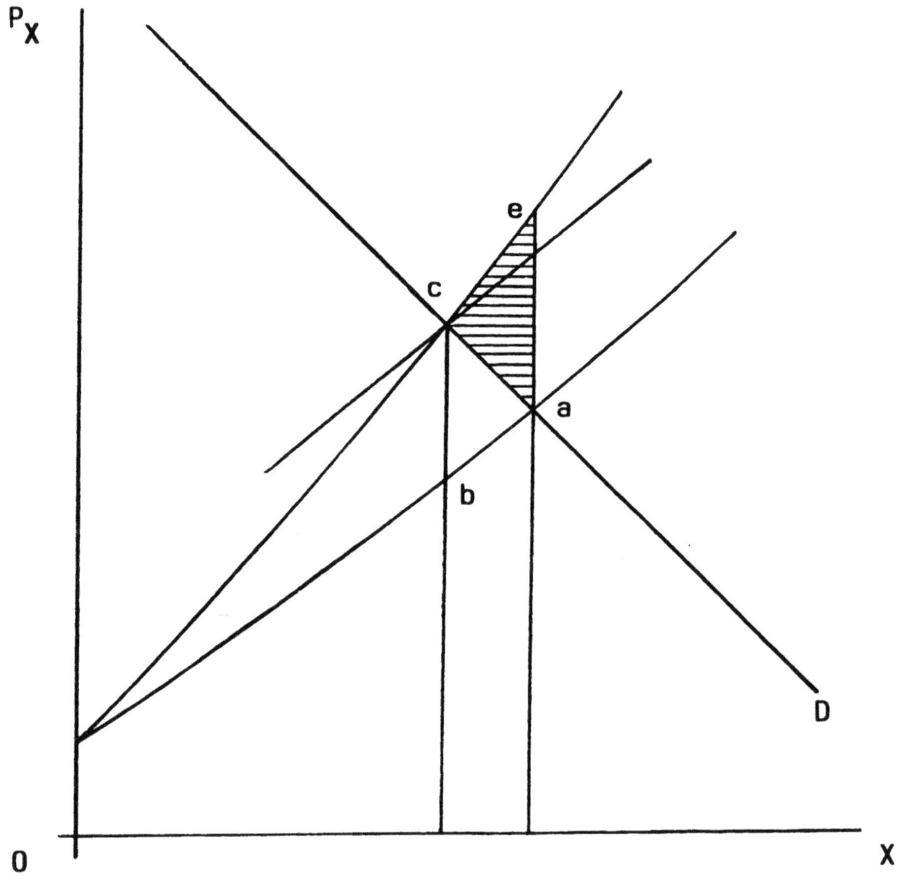

Diagramm 1: Pigouvian Tax in a Partial Equilibrium

3. Social marginal cost in general equilibrium

The static nature of Pigouvian analysis can be easily modified into a dynamic application. On the other hand, Pigouvian analysis can hardly provide a theoretical basis for global analysis of environmental issues mostly because it remains in a partial equilibrium framework. In order to recover the latter deficiency, a general equilibrium model with externalities will be developed in this section.

Economic model

The economic model adopted here heavily depends on the idea developed by Bhagwati and Srinivasan (1983) and Shibata and Shibata (1988). Namely, the nature of externalities is assumed to be "factor-use-related" and short-run.

Our economy consists of two sectors, X-sector and Z-sector. X-sector is a polluter in the production of commodity X, which results in an increase in CO_2 in the air in proportion to the amount of energy (possibly oil or natural gas) consumed. Z-sector also uses energy as its factor of production, but it is not a polluter. All the carbon contents in oil and natural gas are transformed into materials in a commodity Z. Therefore, production of Z never increase the amount of CO_2 in the air.

CO_2 *in the air* does degrade the environment of a country. X-sector is not affected by CO_2 in the air, so that productivity in X-sector does not decrease regardless of the quantity of CO_2 emitted. On the other hand, Z sector is vulnerable to the amount of CO_2 in the air, therefore its productivity decreases as the amount of CO_2 increases. Production functions and factor endowment of an economy are given as follows:

$X = Fx\,(Ex, Kx)$ -------- (1) prod. function in X

$Z = e(Ex)*Fz\,(Ez, Kz)$ -------- (2) prod. function in Z

$Ex + Ez = E$ -------- (3) energy constraint

$Kx + Kz = K$ -------- (4) capital constraint

Fx(.) and Fz(.) are homogenous in degree one in capital and energy. Equations (1)-(4) can represent the actual production possibilities.

Environmental factor, e(Ex), in production function for Z is a shifting factor which represents the level of environmental degradation in the air.[2]

[2] The environmental Factor takes a positive value of less than one, since efficiency of production in Z-sector is degraded due to the negative externality.

E and K are the energy and capital endowment respectively. Assumptions on factor intensities will be provided when it becomes necessary.

Short-run social production possibility frontier

The above economic model follows the standard Heckscher-Ohlin-Samuelson model and has the characteristics of the long-run equilibrium. Before starting a long-run analysis of the model, we will firstly analyze the short-run nature of this model by assuming capital is a sector specific factor in each sector. Due to the existence of factor specificities, we call this situation short-run in the rest of this paper.

When amounts of sector specific factors of production, Kx and Kz, are given at a certain level, we can derive a short-run production possibility frontier. By neglecting the negative externalities in polluting sector X, a short-run production possibility frontier (SR-PPF, later on) can be derived through the usual procedure as is shown in Diagram 2. Since we neglect negative externalities, Fx and Fz^0 are the production functions in each sector. As a change in energy allocation between two sectors, combination of the maximum amount of X and Z is given by the PPF locus.

On the other hand, we have to take the effect of negative externalities in Z sector into consideration in order to derive a short-run social production frontier (SR-S-PPF). The larger is X sector's production, the larger is the amount of CO_2 exhausted by X sector and the smaller is the production efficiency in Z sector. Therefore, the production locus will shrink when Ex increases as is shown in Fz^1, Fz^2, and so on. By connecting the corresponding points, we will get a SR-S-PPF locus.

SR-S-PPF can take various shapes as is shown in the lower diagram in Diagram 3. Speed of shrinking in production efficiency due to a CO_2 increase in the air is the major factor to determine the shape of SR-S-PPF. Diagram 3 also shows a correspondence between the production possibility frontier and the marginal cost. Each social marginal cost (SMC) numbered from 1 to 4 corresponds to SR-S-PPF numbered from 1 to 4, respectively.

Long-run social production possibility frontier

The derivation of the long-run social production possibility frontier is shown in Diagram 4. Three bench mark points, "h", "i" and "j", are utilized in the diagram. Point "h" indicates the allocation where all capital endowment is used as a sector specific factor of production in Z sector. On the contrary,

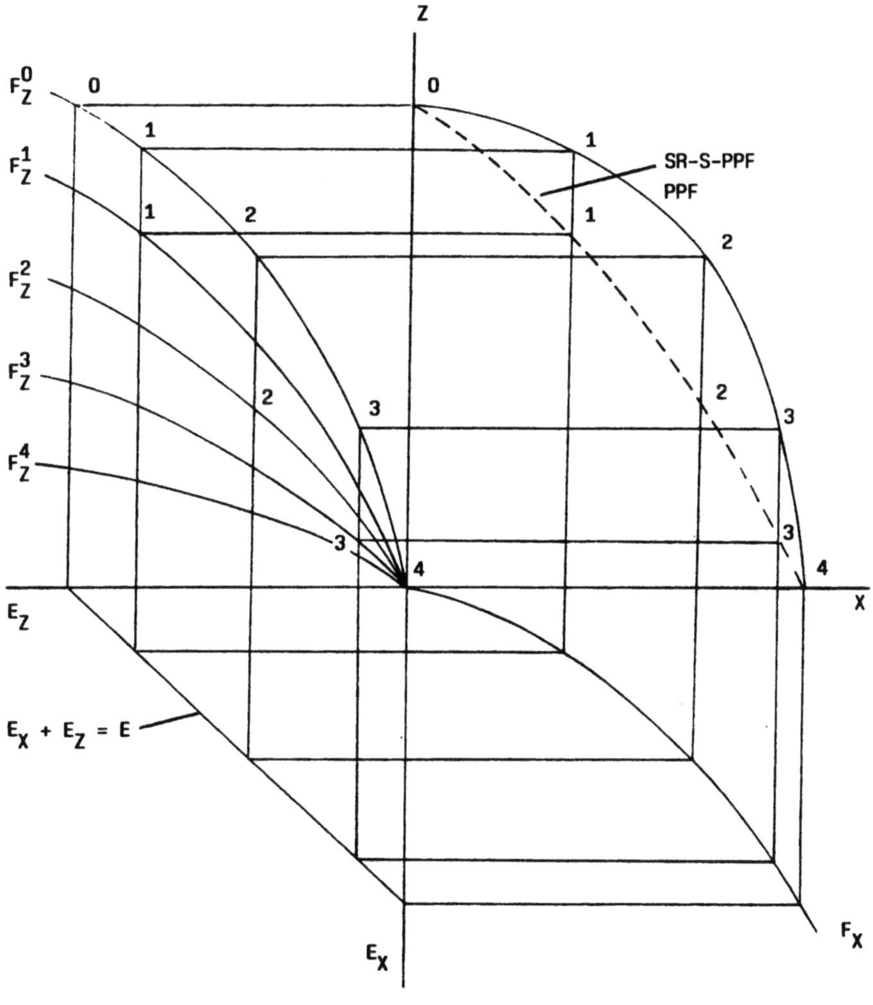

Diagramm 2: Derivation of Short-Run P-PPF and Short-Run S-PPF

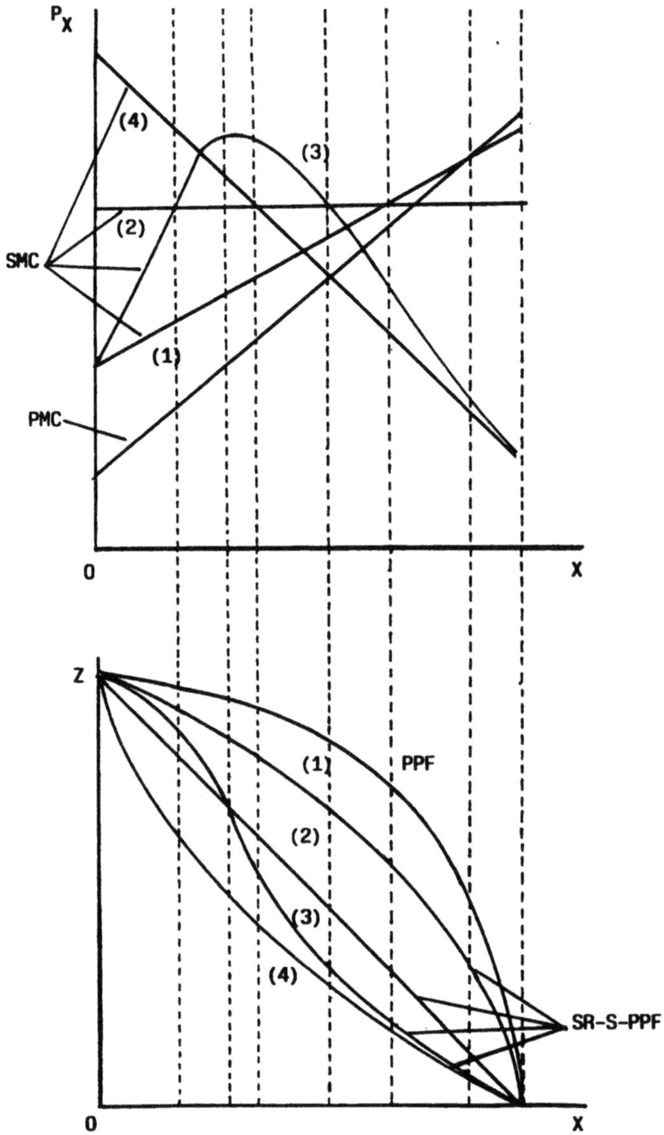

Diagramm 3: Correspondence between Social-PPF and Social Marginal Cost

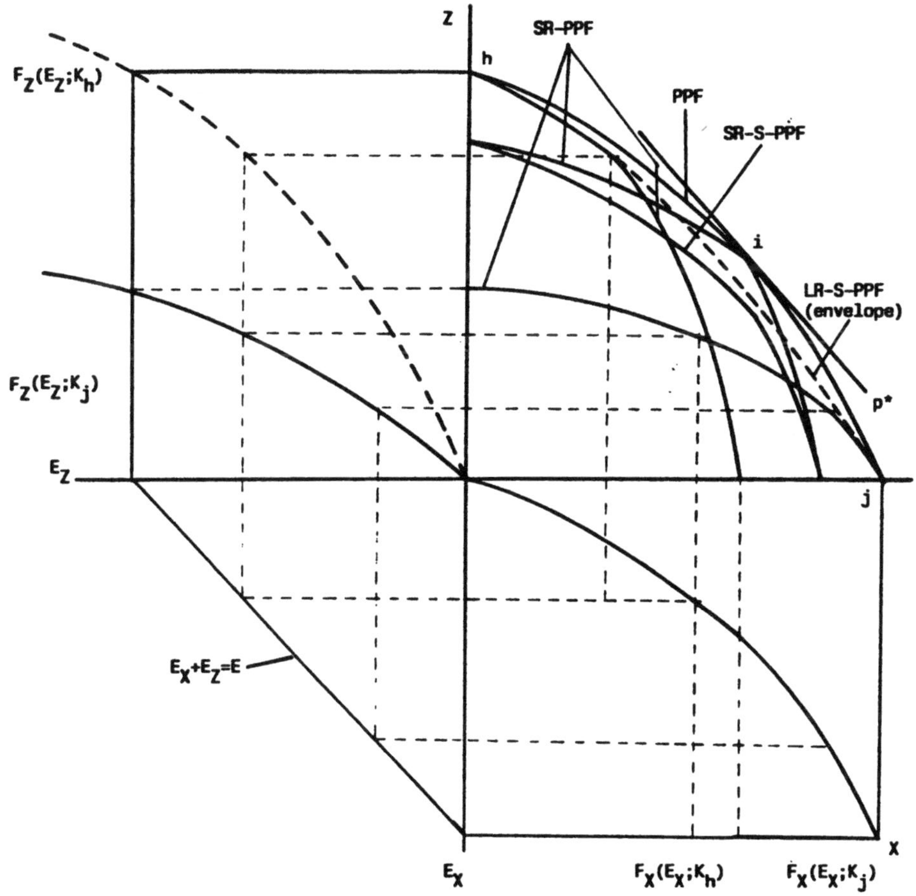

Diagramm 4: Derivation of Long-Run S-PPF

all capital endowment is utilized in X sector at point "j". At point "i", each sector is allocated a certain amount of capital as a sector specific factor. Now, we suppose that the relative price Px^* is given initially, and the price starts increasing afterwards. If each sector has its specific factors, production changes along the SR-P-PPF locus. If not only energy but also capital can move between two sectors freely (and this situation could arise in the long-run), production moves along the LR-PPF locus. Due to this correspondence between SR-PPF and LR-PPF, it turns out that the LR-PPF locus is an envelope of SR-PPF.

In the previous subsection, we have already derived SR-S-PPF from SR-PPF. By applying this procedure to all the SR-PPF loci, we can ultimately derive the long-run social production possibility frontier (LR-S-PPF) as an envelope of SR-S-PPF. Once LR-S-PPF is derived, the long-run social marginal cost (LR-SMC) could be obtained as a slope of the line which is tangent to LR-S-PPF.

4. Pigouvian tax and its interpretation in a general equilibrium

This section intends to interpret the economic implications brought by Pigouvian tax in a general equilibrium framework. This apparently difficult task becomes possible by utilizing notions of SR-PPF and social production possibility frontiers.

Pigouvian tax in a general equilibrium

The upper diagram in Diagram 5 looks intentionally very similar to the diagram which explains the economic implications of Pigouvian tax for social welfare. It thus becomes easier for us to compare the economic messages from Pigouvian tax in partial and general equilibrium. However, this diagram contains more information than the ordinary diagram of Pigouvian tax, since PMC and SMC in the upper diagram are derived from SR-PPF and LR-S-PPF in the lower diagram which is obviously standing for a general equilibrium framework. A partial analysis deliberately ignores the existence of other commodities in order to keep the analysis clear and simple. In contrast to this, a general equilibrium approach incorporates all commodities into the analysis in order to examine the economic interactions between the quantities consumed, the quantities produced, prices and so on.

The lower diagram reveals the economic effect of negative externalities in the production of X. If the existence of the negative externalities is not

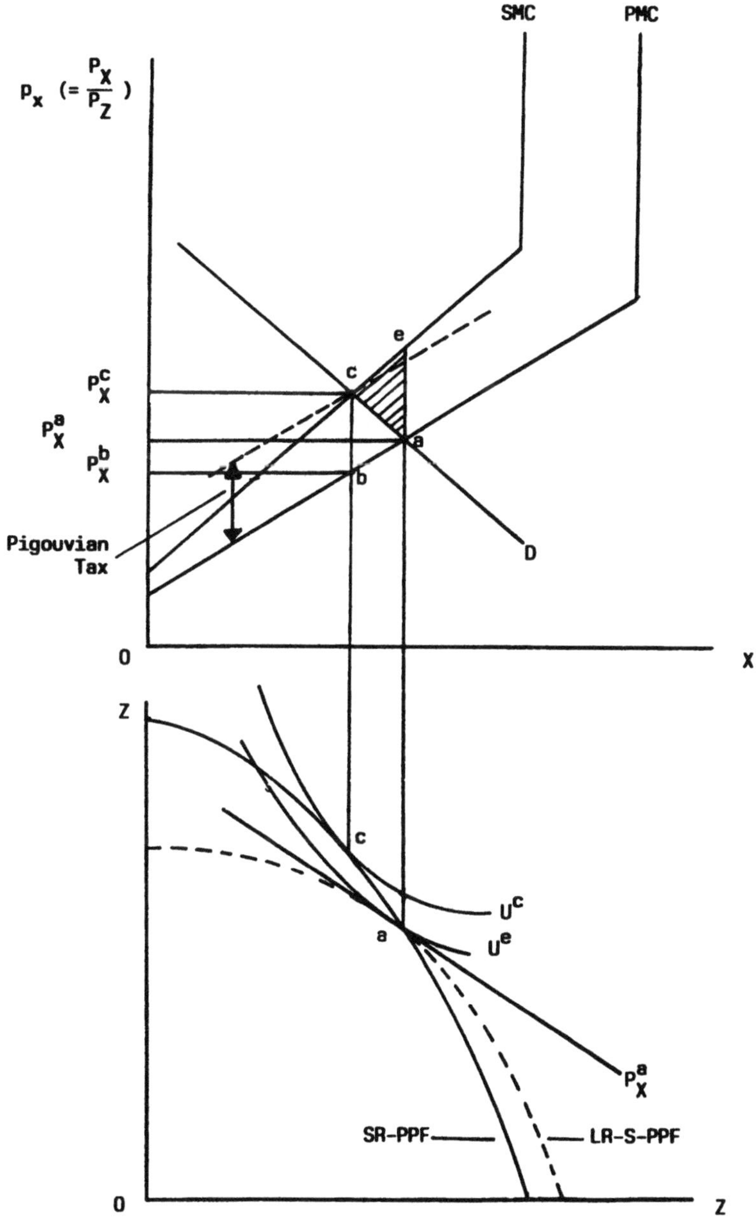

Diagramm 5: Pigouvian Tax and its Interpretation in a General Equilibrium

taken into considerations, social welfare is maximized at point "c" where the social indifference curve is tangent to LR-S-PPF. Therefore the point of production which neglects the existence of negative externality, "a," is not an optimum. If the negative externalities are taken into considerations, the actual marginal cost for the economy is given by the slope of LR-S-PPF instead of the slope of the line tangent to SR-PPF at "a". Therefore, it becomes apparent that social optimum is attained at point "c" where the social indifference curve is tangent to S-PPF, the true production possibility frontier which takes the cost of externality into account. Thus it is also obvious that producing and consuming X at the level indicated by "a" is sub-optimal, since the social indifference curve which passes through "a" locates in a lower position compared with that which passes through "c".

As is explained in the earlier section, a decrease in the efficiency of production in the Z sector due to the negative externalities caused by the X sector can be attributed to the discrepancy between SR-PPF and S-PPF. This reasoning seen in a general equilibrium framework makes the economic identity of negative externality much more clear than that in a partial equilibrium. Namely, Pigouvian tax is a policy measure which *intervenes in the commodity market* to induce incentives for larger equilibrium quantity of Z and a smaller equilibrium quantity of X in order to adjust the discrepancy between private and social marginal costs caused by negative externalities.

5. Emission rights and CO_2 levies

This section proposes a general equilibrium analysis of emission rights and CO_2 levies. The ultimate purpose of this section is to make a social welfare comparison between a Pigouvian tax, emission rights and CO_2 levies possible and to analyze the income distribution under each scheme of controlling CO_2 emission.

Emission rights

Emission rights is a policy measure which could exactly fix the amount of energy input in polluting sectors as far as the emission rights are effectively binding. If the emission rights constraint is not binding (in other words, the emission rights are not purchased at any positive price), the economy could perform as if it had no emission rights regulation. Therefore, effectively binding emission rights will make energy sector specific. If this factor specificity created by emission rights is regarded as permanently effective, long-run equilibrium of the economy can be characterized by a "fixed capital model" rather than the standard Heckscher-Ohlin-Samuelson model.

Diagram 6 is drawn to correspond to this long-run characteristic of emission rights. The amount of emission rights is set at a long-run equilibrium level indicated by "#" on PPF. Since emission rights are not binding between "0" and "1" along LR-PPF, this part of production possibility corresponds to PPF developed in the previous section.[3] On the other hand, at any level of production beyond $X^{\#}$ emission rights are effectively binding, so that effective production will be switched from Fx to Fx/E.R. at $X^{\#}$. LR-PPF is derived by utilizing this production function. A LR-S-PPF with emission rights is derived by simply applying the method use before.

Diagram 6 allows a simple comparison of social welfare between a Pigouvian tax and emission rights. It reveals that emission rights are the more efficient policy measure if LR-S-PPF/E.R. locates above LR-S-PPF. The intuition of this result is obvious. Since CO_2 is created by utilizing one of the factors of production, energy, direct intervention on the factor market could be more efficient than a Pigouvian tax which intervenes in the commodity market rather than the factor market.

CO_2 levies

Diagram 7 depicts a derivation of LR-PPF and LR-S-PPF provided that CO_2 levies are imposed on energy use in the polluting sector. Since the Z sector does not exhaust CO_2 in its process of production, the Z sector is exempted from CO_2 levies.

These CO_2 levies can be analyzed as distortions in the factor market. Namely, production possibility tends to shrink in the direction of origin in the presence of factor market distortions as is shown in Diagram 7. The locus of PPF/Levies locates inside of PPF. LR-S-PPF/levies can be derived through the ordinary procedure. The locus of PPF/Levies shrinks due to the inefficiencies in factor allocations caused by CO_2 levies. On the other hand, efficiency in production in the Z sector can be restored to some extent thanks to saving in energy consumption in X sector. Therefore the total effect of CO_2 levies can not be determined without knowledge of the relative strength of each effect.

---

[3] In Diagram 6 capital is assumed to be a mobile production factor. This interchangeable choice of the mobile factor will not affect the fundamental conclusions of the model, since both PPF and LR-S-PPF are the envelope of the corresponding SR-PPF and SR-S-PPF respectively.

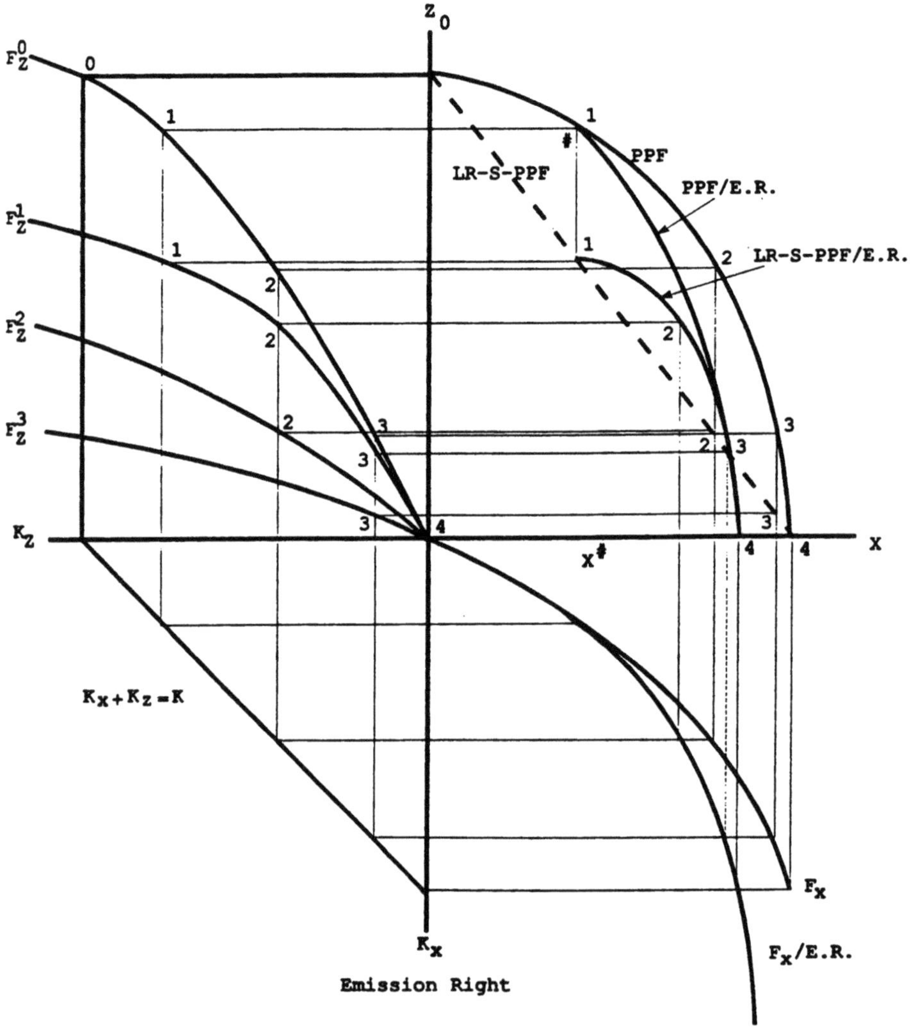

Diagramm 6: Derivation of Social PPF with Emission Right

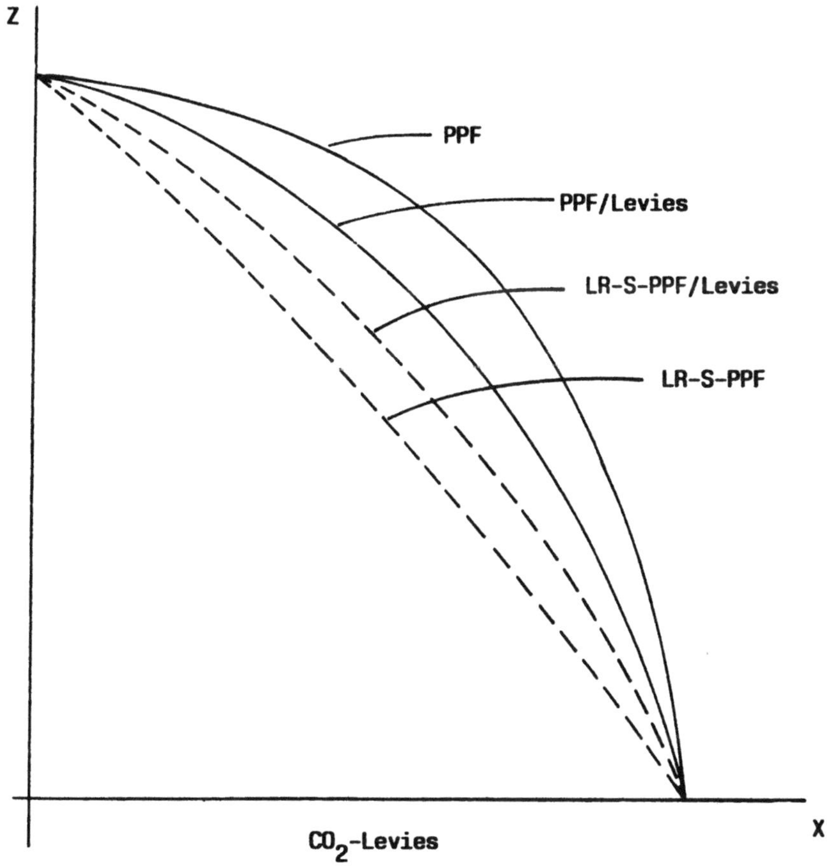

Diagramm 7: Derivation of Social PPF with CO_2-Levies

6. Concluding remarks

This paper intends to make a general equilibrium analysis of CO_2 emissions. Special attention was paid to the analysis of emission rights and CO_2 levies so that we could return the argument of externalities to the discussion of environmental issues. The model proposed in this paper is incomplete in many aspects, however, I believe that the idea of social cost or social optimum is able to regain its role again in a general equilibrium framework.

References

Cropper, L.M./W.E. Oates, "Environmental Economics: A Survey," Journal of Economic Literature (June, 1992): 675-740.

Coase, R.H., "The Problem of Social Cost," Journal of Law and Economics (October, 1960): 371-84.

Barnett, A.H., "The Pigouvian Tax Rule under Monopoly," The American Economic Review (December, 1980): 1037-41.

Baumol, W.J., "On Taxation and The Control of Externalities," The American Economic Review (June, 1972): 307-22.

Baumol, W.J./D.F. Bradford, "Detrimental Externalities and Non-Convexity of the Production Set," Economica (May, 1972): 160-76.

Baumol, W.J./W.E. Oates, "The Use of Standards and Prices for Protection of The Environment," Swedish Journal of Economics (March, 1971): 42-54.

Bhagwati, J.,/V.K. Ramaswani, "Domestic Distortions, Tariff and the Theory of Optimum Subsidy," Journal of Political Economy (February, 1963): 44-50.

Bhagwati, J.,/T.N. Srinivasan, "Production Externalities," Lectures on International Trade, (The MIT Press 1983) ch.18.

Buchanan, J.M., "External Diseconomies, Corrective Taxes, and Market Structure," The American Economic Review (March, 1969): 174-77.

Chacholiades, M., International Trade Theory and Policy, (McGrow-Hill, 1978), ch.20

Dewees, D.N., "Instrument Choice in Environmental Policy," Economic Inquiry (January, 1983): 53-71.

Dorfman, N.S./A. Snow, "Who Will Pay for Pollution Control? - The Distribution by Income of The Burden of The National Environmental Protection Program, 1972-1980," National Tax Journal (March, 1975): 101-15.

Gianessi, L.P./H.M. Peskin/E. Wolff, "The Distributional Effects ofUniform Air Pollution Policy in The United States," The Quarterly Journal of Economics (May, 1979): 281-301.

Hamilton, J.H./E. Sheshinski/S.M. Slutsky, "Production Externalities and Long-Run Equilibria: Bargaining and Pigouvian Taxation," Economic Inquiry (July, 1989): 453-71.

Hazilla, M./R.J. Kopp, "Social Cost of Environmental Quality Regulations: A General Equilibrium Analysis," Journal of Political Economy 98 (August, 1990): 853-73

Hoel, M., "Global Environmental Problems: The Effects of Unilateral Actions Taken by One Country," Journal of Environmental Economics and Management (January, 1991): 55-70.

Johnson, H.G., "Optimal Trade Intervention in the Presence of Domestic Distortions," *Baldwin* et al, Trade, Growth and the Balance of Payments: Essays in Honour of Gottfried Haberler (Chicago: Rand-Mcnally, 1965).

Lee, D.R., "Efficiency of Pollution Taxation and Market Structure," Journal of Environmental Economics and Management (September, 1975): 69-72.

Lee, D.R., "Substituting Pollution Taxation for General Taxation: Some Implications for Efficiency in Pollutions Taxation," Journal of Environmental Economics and Management (December, 1986): 338-47.

McGartland, A.M./W.E. Oates, "Marketable Permits for The Prevention of Environmental Deterioration," Journal of Environmental Economics and Management (September, 1985): 207-28.

McGartland, A.M., "A Comparison of Two Marketable Discharge Permits Systems," Journal of Environmental Economics and Management (January, 1988): 35-44.

Mumy, G.E., "Long-run Efficiency and Property Right Sharing for Pollution Control," Public Choice 35 (1980): 59-74.

Mussa, M., "Factor Market Distortions and the Shape of Transformation Curve," Econometrica (July 1966): 686-98.

Mussa, M., "Tariffs and Distribution of Income: The Importance of Factor Specificity," Journal of Political Economy (November/December 1974): 1191-203.

O'Neil, W./M. David/C. Moore/E. Joeres, "Transferable Discharge Permits and Economic Efficiency: The Fox River," Journal of Environmental Economics and Management (December, 1983): 346-55.

Peltzman, S./T.N. Tideman, "Local Versus National Pollution Control: Note," The American Economic Review (December, 1972): 959-63.

Shibata, H., "Pareto-Optimality, Trade and Pigouvian Tax," Economica (May, 1972): 190-202.

Shibata, H., "Pareto-optimality and Gains-from-Trade:A Further Elucidation," Economica (February, 1974): 71-8.

Shibata, H./A.Shibata, Koukyou Keizaigaku (Public Economics), Toyokeizai 1988.

Smith, V.L., "General Equilibrium with a Replenishable Natural Resource," Review of Economic Studies (1974): 105-15.

Ueda, K./H. Ochiai ed. Kankyo Keizaigaku (Environmental Economics), Yuuhikaku 1991 (in Japanese).

Uzawa, H./M. Kuninori ed., Economic Analysis of Global Warming, Economic Affairs, Vol.3 University of Tokyo Press, 1993 (in Japanese).

Weitzman, M.L., "Optimal Rewards for Economic Regulation," The American Economic Review (September, 1978): 683-91.

Internalization of Environmental Costs for Sustainable Development - Learning from the History of Fighting Sulfur Dioxide in Japan -

Yoichi Nishijima

1. Internalization of environmental costs for sustainability

It is said that Japan is environmentally advanced. It is also said that Japan has been successful in internalization of environmental costs, consequently improving the environment. Undoubtedly, Japan has controlled a good portion of pollution areas and is leading the world in developing and implementing environmental technologies.

Outside, Japan is challenged by *technologies for the protection* of the global environment, while inside it faces the need for the transition to a recycle-type society. In an age when the requirements for environmental protection are getting more severe every year, how should industry tackle the problems of getting the environment into business? The Second World Industry Congress on Environmental Management (WEICEM II) held in Rotterdam, April 1991, declared that corporate environmental management should be exercised based on free competition. Does this imply that, like Japan, foreign countries are beginning to internalize environmental costs? Environmental development is indispensable for humankind. However, this development cannot be justified if it spoils the Earth, the basis of the environment, whether it is local or global, neglecting our responsibility to pass the environment as sound as possible to the future generations. Also, environmental destruction cannot be justified in the sense that the resource-supplying "South" is exploited by the benefiting "North". To solve these problems, the concept of the sustainable development has come to be widely accepted. This development is sustainable if it is conducted while maintaining the resources and taking actions to protect the environment from the waste produced from the use of the resources. To make development sustainable, economic activities also need to be made sustainable. For a sustainable economy, it is required to know, create, and use an autonomously working economic system. One example is the inclusion of the environment in the internal system of economics as if acquiring the capabilities to live or sustain oneself in one's body. An animal is more advantageous than a plant or vegetable in that the animal has internalized its nutrition acquiring capability as its feet.

To be specific, internalization of environmental costs is defined as putting the environmental costs in the market economies to internalize them to the price-constituting factors. It is a fact that Japan has been successful in somehow internalizing the environmental costs, which have been generally considered incompatible with the market economies. What are the causes of Japan's having been able to handle environment as one of the internal economies? Although many admit it is imminent to protect the global environment and realize recycle-type societies, they mention the impossibility of such undertakings. The key to overcoming such a pessimistic view is handling of the environment as one of the internal economies. It is expected that the environmental protection policy of Japan will go in this direction.

2. Japan's awakening to environment - Experiences of tragedies caused by pollution -

After World War II, Japan adopted an industrial promotion policy with emphasis placed on industrial restoration and economic growth. However, in the process of attaining these goals, little attention was paid to environmental protection. This negligence led to disasters to the environment from around 1955 onwards: air pollution by sulfur oxides (Yokkaichi city), water pollution by mercury compounds (Minamata), and soil pollution by cadmium (Jintsugawa), amongst others. Pollution-triggered diseases spread from 1965, followed by frequent pollution law suits. This promoted the provision of antipollution measures by means of the establishment of environmental criteria and compensation for the victims of pollution diseases. These ex post facto measures could not prevent the pollution-caused damages from spreading and produced unfavorable frictions with society. As a result, there are more than 100,000 officially certified patients of pollution diseases, and their compensation amounts to 100 billion Yen annually. What an unjustifiable cost for industrial development this was!

These lessons taught us that, when comparing the cost of compensation paid for the damage caused by improper antipollution measures with the cost of preventive measures, the former is far larger than the latter. Although it may be improper to express the sufferings of victims simply in terms of money, the research "Japanese Experiences on Pollution" done by the global environmental economy study group estimated, with respect to the three major pollution cases mentioned above, the cost of damages caused by pollution for which no counter measure has been taken and the cost of the preventive measures sufficient to control pollution. The results were represented in annual cost comparisons.

According to this calculation, the air pollution from sulfur dioxide (SO_X) in Yokkaichi city produced more than 1,200 patients officially certified by the Pollution-related Health Damage Compensation Law and imposed an annual compensation of 1,330 million Yen. Furthermore, the countermeasures amounted to an annual total of 14.8 billion Yen including the investment in plants and equipment, their operating cost, and the public direct and indirect costs. It is assumed that, if the pollution were allowed to spread with no effective countermeasures taken, the cost to overcome the problems would amount to an annual total of 21.1 billion Yen. With the Minamata case (water pollution), the research estimated that the damage would amount to an annual total of 12.6 billion Yen, while the countermeasures, if taken, would cost only 130 million Yen annually, less than 1/10 of the damages. The comparison would be 2,500 million Yen to 600 million Yen for the Jintsugawa soil pollution.

According to the estimates made by Professor Yoichi Kaya, Tokyo University, the compensations for the damage which would have been caused by not taking the effective action against the emission of sulfur dioxide (SO_X) in Japan would be about 10 times higher than the cost of taking the countermeasures.

Thus, in any case, the antipollution measures can be or should be economically justified. Analysis shows that economic development while controlling pollution is better than development ignoring environmental protection in terms of cost and its effectiveness.

In reality, in the Yokkaichi case, the heavy oil desulphurization facilities were built, low sulfur content fuels were acquired, and flue gas desulphurization plants were introduced, eventually achieving the final target set by the total SO_X controlling act as late as in 1976, or 17 years after the start of the operation of the petroleum refinery and petrochemical complex. This will be discussed in more detail in Section 5.

3. Japan's limited environmental capacity

Environmental capacity is defined as the capacity of a country or area to contain the total emitted harmful substances regulated by the emission control laws and environment protection criteria, plus a reserve. If the absolute amount of emissions in a particular country or area at a point of time is greater than its environmental capacity, its environment will deteriorate. This premise is the condition in which some of the emitted harmful substances are neutralized by nature. The environmental capacity of a particular country or area, classified by air, water, and soil, depends on its area, population density, types of industries, and natural conditions.

Japan is an island nation and, therefore, different from those continental countries in handling environmental issues. Although the use of seas around it as waste dumping sites should not be allowed, they may provide a natural cleaner of the properly processed emissions. Japan's environmental capacities are characterized as follows:

(1) Air: Japan is an island nation and therefore more advantageous in diffusing pollutants than continental countries whose emitting pollutants into the air directly affects surrounding countries. The continental countries must internationally establish mutual environmental cooperations in addition to developing environment-protecting technologies.

(2) Water: Japan is one of the most rainy countries in the world and has many rivers, which pour into seas in a shorter time than those long rivers found in continents. This, along with long coastlines, contributes to the natural clean-up of pollutants.

(3) Land: because of its relatively small territory, limited populated area, high population density, and geographically concentrated industries, Japan's environmental capacity for land is very limited. To overcome this problem, Japan has been reclaiming the land from the sea and converting it into industrial and housing areas. The sea is also used for the land reclamation for burying incinerated wastes, known as the Phoenix Project.

In spite of these advantages, the small territory, high population density, and geographically concentrated industries increase the environmental load per unit area. This means that pollutants exist in proximity, posing a higher risk of deteriorating the environment. Also, these conditions greatly differ from one location of the country to another. For example, the Kanto and Kansai seaside industrial zones, Japan's industrial center since its modernization about 100 years ago, are now finding it very difficult to welcome those industries which may endanger the environment. Environmentally unfavorable industries are trying to get out of these areas because of the ever stricter environmental protecting regulations, at both national and local level. The industrial output from these areas combined was 50% of all Japan's output in 1965. Twenty five years later, the figure dropped to 40%.

Because the relocations of industries and work forces cannot be made quickly, Japan has been obliged to develop environmental protection technologies and systems that can withstand the strict environmental criteria and the reserved environmental capacity of each region. The technological problems remaining in each region must be solved and, at the same time, a new social system must be built to expand environmental capacity. Legal arrangements have just started for one of the requirements for a change in the social system for environmental protection, including the Law for Promotion of Utilization of Recyclable Resources or simply the Recycling Law, the revision of the Waste Disposal and Public Cleaning Law, and the coordination of the associated national laws to the Basle Convention.

In spite of its favorable natural conditions, the high population density and the geographically concentrated industries are forcing Japan to bear a large environmental cost. To pay the cost, the environment must be handled as one of the internal economies.

As compared with continental countries where the import and export of pollutants take place daily in the form of the polluted air and water, Japan has been advantageous in making the environment into an internal economy without going through the steps for bearing the international division of the environmental cost.

4. Dependence on overseas resources and its impact on environmental protection

The total amount of the resources dealt in the world is estimated to be 7 billion tons a year. About 1/4 (1/6 in terms of GNP) of them, 1.7 billion tons are used in this narrow country mainly for industrial production. The domestic resources account for 2/3, or 1.2 billion tons, mostly consisting of building materials and glass. The imported resources of about 500 million tones are crude oils, coals, iron ores, grains, and foods. Ninety eight percent of these resources are used for industrial production and the remaining two percent for agricultural production.

As a result, about one billion tons of resources stay in Japan for a relatively long period as durable goods, 300 million tons are used as energy, and 100 million tons leave this country as exports. The wastes amount to a total of 400 million tons, of which 160 million tons are recycled, making this island country heavier by about 200 million tons a year. The waste which is left unrecycled contributes to worsen the environment, a fact not yet generally recognized.

One of the features of Japan's resource and environmental problems is a high net productivity. For example, an imported raw material of about 60,000 Yen is manufactured and exported at about 400,000 Yen a ton. The high value is added by the roundabout production consisting of many processes. Because of the high final added value, the cost of environmental protection, for example, the handling of the waste generated from each manufacturing process, may be considered as an added value, thus giving the ground for getting environment into the internal economies.

As shown in the resource distribution mentioned above, about one billion tons are being accumulated as capital goods, permanent building structures, and the like, both privately and socially. This amount is the positive stock in the annual flow of the resources, while 200 million tons of waste provides the negative stock. This negative stock offsets Japan's future environmental capacity. This point must be considered in substantiating the social capital, which in turn presents the important point in solving environmental problems.

In other words, the handling of the huge amount of solid wastes currently produced and to be produced in the future is a critical problem to be solved. There is a long-term projected need to be carried out aiming at the reuse and recycling of the wastes.

Japan has made relatively free and advantageous selection in procuring raw materials overseas. Because of its rather poor natural resources, Japan has gradually replaced expensive domestic resources with cheaper and better overseas resources. The stable procurement and the selection of materials which are low in pollutant content or can be neutralized environmentally with ease have contributed to the reduction of the environmental protection cost. Also, locating the major industrial zones on seasides has been reducing the cost of transporting raw materials from overseas to the production facilities in this country.

It can be said that these conditions are advantageous in terms of environmental protection. Being poor in natural resources has turned out to be advantageous in environmental protection. It should not be attributed to sheer luck. It is the result of the nation's wisdom of survival through the total destruction of industries by the war and the subsequent hardships. Turning bad conditions into good results is the real thrill of engineering.

Recently, the Yen evaluation has made more Japanese corporations shift part of their production bases overseas where it is easier to procure the necessary resources and labour. The problem is that low added value industries are moving overseas along with environmental pollution. Some point out that this pollution export is saving Japan's environment. As an environmentally advanced country, Japan should show that it can protect the overseas environment and is actually doing so.

Global environmental issues are closely related to resource issues. Japan is procuring the necessary natural resources, or international commodities, based on the market mechanism. The answer to the question as to whether the addition of environmental cost to the product prices is also applied to international commodities is probably negative. It would be difficult for the producing countries to get these commodities, the environmental costs of which are internalized. If the environment is being polluted or destroyed globally, then all of the cost for environmental protection should be shared internationally. In other words, environmental costs should be internalized on a global basis and with international consensus.

5. A case of environmental protection - Actions against SO_X -

In 1959 Japan's first petrochemical complex started operation. In line with the operation, the pollution caused by the SO_X emitted from the plants became a serious social problem. The countermeasures were not fully taken and made effective until 10 years later.

In 1975 - 1980, the application of the total amount regulation helped mostly achieve the target environmental criteria. However, it took another 10 years for the class I area specification to be lifted. It took a total of 30 years for the countermeasures against the SO_X-triggered air pollution to be included in the internal economies (Figure 1).

First, the installation of flue gas desulphurization units throughout Japan largely solved the air pollution caused by SO_X. The number of installations at the end of March, 1990 was 1,843, 33 units (about 2%) more than the previous year, with the total processing capacity of 178.8 x 10 6 NM3/H, 2.5 NM3/H (about 1%) higher than the previous year. Figures 2, 3, and 4 show the situation by industry, by facility concerned, and the transition in installations from 1970 to 1988, respectively. Figure 5 shows the installations by processing capacity. As for the processing capacity, the units of 10 to 40 x 10 3 NM3/H account for 41% of all installations, while the units of 5 to 100 x 10 3 NM3/H account for 71%.

As shown in these diagrams, the installation of flue gas desulphurization units has fully spread in the 20 years from 1970 in terms of industries, facilities, and scale. Currently, the existing units, except for the large units attached to coal burning large thermal plants, are entering the phase of discard or replacement.

The next point is the legislation that attempted to solve the problems caused by the polluted air and eventually worked as a main factor in the internalization of environmental costs. The Basic Law for Environmental Pollution Control, enacted in 1967, states the prevention of health damages which may be caused by pollution and defines environmental pollution as damages to the health or living environment caused by pollution of the air, water, or soil as a result of industrial and other activities. In 1969, the Law for Pollution-related Health Damage Relief was enacted. In 1972, the Law for Pollution-related No-fault Liability was enacted to hold the polluter responsible for the pollution whether it was made intentionally or not. In the same year, judgement was passed on the Yokkaichi city pollution suit that the polluting facilities are jointly responsible for the damages caused by the air pollution.

The Pollution-Related Health Damage Compensation Law enacted in 1973, specified the class I area as an area in which the air is seriously polluted over a wide range and the disease caused by the air pollution occurs frequently. In 1978, 41 locations were specified as class I areas throughout the country. However, the practice of antipollution measures reduced the emission of SO_X in these locations (Figure 6), consequently lifting the specification in 1988. In legislation, this law was revised to the Law for Pollution-related Health Damage Compensation and Others. Based on the new law, the pollution-related health damage compensation system shifted emphasis from the compensation on an ex post facto basis to the prevention of health damage.

6. Acquiring the economic means for environmental protection

The fact that airpollution problems caused by SO_X have been settled indicates that the internalization of environmental costs has taken place with some restrictions. For the Japanese economy, a big problem of handling solid wastes remains to be solved in order to realize a recycle-type society. This also requires such internalization. Based on the results of the successful antipollution activities over the past 30 years, the following paragraphs discuss the factors of the internalization of environmental costs to solve this problem.

Starting with the pollution problems, Japan's environmental problems have involved energy and resource saving problems, which have been solved mainly by technological innovations. However, the generally accepted view or opinion is that the environment is an external economy, and the investments into antipollution and environmental protection activities are negative ones, neither bringing any profits nor improving the nation's economy. Is this view true?

6.1. The internal processing by enhanced productivity

The above-mentioned environmental protection measures executed throughout the nation's economy have not blocked Japan's high economic growth. Although the investments in the environment, which were considered not to directly contribute to production, were expected to raise prices, the wholesale price index has been kept stable over a long period.

In other words, environmental protection has advanced, but economic growth has continued at the same time. As shown in Figure 7, the Japan's economic growth continued at an annual average of 8% or more from the 50's to 60's. Over the 20 years from the first half of the 70's, the Japanese economy continued to grow at an annual average of 4% or more.

Achieving the environmental protection without pushing up prices was assured by Japan's economic vitality. As shown in Figure 8, if the overall average of the Bank of Japan's overall wholesale price index is 100 in 1985, then in 1970, when antipollution measures began to be executed it was about 50 and in 1990 it settled to about 90 after the oil crises.

Figure 9 shows the international comparison of wholesale prices. The comparison is made with the index in 1970 being 100, when Japan's environment investment began mainly in heavy oil desulphurization units. In the 20 years to date, Japan's index is 185, which is the lowest figure in the comparison. Germany is 204. America, Canada, and France are on the order of 300. Great Britain and Italy are on the order of 800. This means that, with Japan, the environmental costs expended in various forms worked to expand the economy in the form of effective demand creation as the income effect, not as the price effect in the rise of wholesale prices. This proves that environmental protection has been progressing without involving any macro economic drawbacks.

Japan's successful environmental protection within the tolerance of the price hike indicates that the environmental investments have been absorbed by its economic vitality. Environmental protection indeed requires money.

However, production consists of various factors. An increase in productivity due to a certain factor can offset the cost increase by other factors. The value of maintaining the environment can be established by applying technological innovation, for example. It can be said that, in Japan, environmental costs acquired or spent in various forms have been internally processed in enhanced productivity rather than regarded as the price effect of wholesale price increases. That is, it can be concluded that the inclusion of the environment in the internal economies at the macro economic level has been realized. The discussion of the economic value of the enhanced productivity in this process is beyond the purpose of this paper.

6.2. Including environmental investment into economic growth factors

The White Paper of Environment published in 1977, when investment in the facilities consisting mainly of the heavy oil desulphurizing equipment came to the end of the first stage, reported that the effects of the antipollution cost to the macro-economy had been absorbed in the process of economic growth, and had only a limited impact on the economy. Furthermore, the regulations have promoted the development of antipollution technologies, for which Japan has been capable enough technologically and financially.

The investment in technological innovations related to the environment was a factor in activating the nation's economy. In the 1970's, a total of 5,200 billion Yen was invested in the antipollution facilities, with a peak investment of 1,000 billion Yen in 1975 as shown in Figure 10. This brought about a demand creating effect (for example, the creation of the antipollution industry) contributing to gross national product as well as propagation effects to the related industries. With more than 30 heavy oil desulphurizing plants built since 1970, the technology for processing a large amount of hydrocarbon fluids at high temperatures and pressures was developed, enhancing the level of antipollution technologies.

It is true that these investments raised the heavy oil prices, reducing the demand. However, this introduced liquefied natural gas as an alternative energy source, whose consumption steadily increased to 35 million tons in 1990, with investments in the processing facilities amounting to a total of 2,000 billion Yen at present value. At the same time, the export of the facilities for liquefying, storing, and shipping the gas in the producing countries and the building of ships for transporting the liquefied natural gas also amounted to 2,000 million Yen. The negative effects of the antipollution investments were offset or more than offset by the positive investments in the alternative energy industry.

The first energy crisis or oil embargo by OPEC in 1973 encouraged energy saving investments. Energy saving means to save the input of energy including water, electricity, and steam in the production of the same product. Although it involves added facilities, energy saving decreases the variable expenses (including the operating cost) which more than offsets the rise in fixed costs, resulting in a large cost reduction per unit of the product. In terms of the nation's economy, the energy consumption in crude oil equivalent per 100 million Yen of GNP dropped from 224 kiloliters in 1973 by 35% to 141 kiloliters in 1988, lowering the energy cost to 3% of the GNP as shown in Figure 11.

In addition to the energy saving, resource and labor savings were carried out throughout the industries. The secondary effect of the technological innovation, or the cost reduction, had changed the nature of the antipollution investments from negative to positive. The net positive effect was the advance in pollution control technologies.

From then on, environment-related investments have been continuing in the context of "from pollution to environment"; that is, from the prevention of pollution to the development of alternative resources and energies, to the energy, resource, and labour savings, and to environmental protection on a global basis. These investments have helped enhance economic growth. In other words, the environmental costs has been internalized through the antipollution and environmental protection investments.

7. Role of the government in promoting environmental protection and private corporations' policy making

The administration-advocated co-operation between industries and academic circles has become a pattern after World War II. This pattern has also been working well in solving the pollution and environmental issues. The Japanese government has always taken a long-term view for difficult problems such as environmental problems, and steadily formed the systems for the co-operation with those concerned in order to solve these problems. As for global environmental issues, Japan proposed the Earth Restoration Project in 1989, which then developed into the Greenhouse Effect Prevention Project determined by a Cabinet meeting. To back up this project, the government started a long-term development of the necessary technologies, including fixing CO_2. As to the technological transfer, an organization, supported by both the government and private concerns, has began to work on executing the transfer. With the air pollution and water contamination problems settled for the time being, waste dumping has emerged as a central issue of environmental protection. The legal arrangements necessary for solving this problem are being prepared quickly, including the establishment of the recycling law, the revision of the waste disposal law, and the domestic legislation of the Basle Convention.

In the private sector, private enterprises led by economic organizations (for example, Keidanren's Global Environment Protection Charter) are seriously tackling environmental problems. Each industry has already settled the details of the actions for environmental protection. At the individual corporation level, the environment has been included in top management priorities and is in the execution stage. Most Japanese corporations believe that tackling environmental issues will not be effective unless it is based on a medium-term managerial attitude not affected by period profit and loss account statements. This belief seems to be proved right. To execute the government's long-term concepts is the role of private enterprises. To prove them to be true is the role of academic circles.

The government's guidance of private enterprises, including the tackling of environmental issues, results in the internalization of environmental costs. The knowledge and means obtained by scholars' looking at the global environment made possible through such technologies as artificial satellite communications and satellite probing provide the "visible hands," rather than the classical "invisible hands," to connect individual corporations, which enables them to internalize the environmental costs. For example, the industries concerned confirm with each other that they will observe, as long as economically justifiable, the environmental criteria set by the government, and let individual enterprises execute the criteria proved to be proper by scholars. The co-operation between the government and the private sector is effective in environmental issues.

The result of installing flue gas desulphurization units shows that many associated industries have faithfully observed the environmental criteria, making effective the domestic SO_X emission control. This has led to the preservation and enhancement of the environment and the vitalization of the economy. In other words, the facts proved that the environment has affirmative effects on the economy. The warm south wind bringing the economic vitalization, rather than the cold north wind forcing the investment in the environment, has worked well in tackling the environmental issues. The existence of the south wind was made known by academic circles, and the engineers carried out the concept.

8. Work habit of the Japanese and their willingness to accept technologies

It can be said that the internalization of environmental costs is realized only when the necessary conditions are prepared, and they act on each other positively. In the history of environmental protection, this achievement made in a relatively short period is worth noting. It may not too much to say that this achievement has been a miracle. It is not sufficient to attribute this achievement to political and economic factors only. A more important key may be found in the philosophy of diligence peculiar to the Japanese. As Shichihei Yamamoto pointed out in his book "On Diligence - the Motivation of the Japanese," the Japanese are traditionally characterized by the philosophy of diligence, which is said to have been formed about 250 years ago, in the Edo era, by such mentors as Shosan Suzuki and Baigan Ishida. It is not the job of this paper to delve too far into this philosophy, but suffice to say that since the Edo era the Japanese have not been working for money alone, but for the joy of working itself, which is sometimes sublimated to art.

The Japanese people's willingness to accept technology, or the rational method to reconstruct natural laws into means useful for human beings, may be another reason for the successful internalization. One well-known example is the introduction of a matchlock to a southern island of Japan by a Portuguese missionary about four hundred years ago. Two years later, there were several hundred thousand Japan-made Tanegashima's, called after the island, all over the country. It can be called Japanese tradition to domestically produce a large amount of goods at a low cost based on imported technologies, or acquire technologies as problem-solving tools, improving them, and developing unique ones.

The combination of the Japanese people's diligence and the willingness to accept new technologies has been realized in various things. The internalization of the environmental costs is one of these realizations, which is being positively evaluated in Japan's environmental protection.

9. Japan's future international contributions

As an economic superpower and an environmentally advanced country, Japan is responsible for leading the world in solving environmental problems. Japan has survived by manufacturing quality- and price-competitive products. It is true that Japan is now requested to make international contributions in the one field of environments which is no more out of bounds in manufacturing any products. It is not comfortable to be asked just for money simply because of Japan's economic position. In addition to financial contributions, there are other international contributions such as material, technological and human ones. Selection of contribution types must be made by considering all those requests and abilities.

The fact that "art of diligence" has also been displayed in environmental reservation in Japan may suggest a line of direction to which Japan should proceed from today when a real contribution is requested for sustaining the global environment. It is very important that technologies combined with diligence spread through contributions by those people having traditional Japanese culture in the background. Technologies are not transferred as if they were just a simple material, but have been produced and conveyed by human brains and hands. Any technology is indeed very much humanistic. Environmental technologies should be transferred abroad by experienced Japanese.

Most important is that the transfer of Japan's environmental technologies must accompany know-how obtained from its production technology experiences especially when they are transferred to developing countries. As pointed out above, production and the environment are not independent of each other. The transfer of environmental protection technologies alone will not satisfy the need of developing countries. Environmental technologies alone cannot find their proper position without enhanced productivity. It is necessary to transfer the environmental protection technologies while observing and enjoying the fruit of the transferred production technologies. Not only technical documents but also personal actions is necessary.

It is desired that the people who carry out the tasks of international contributions be those veterans who experienced the industrial restoration after World War II and have survived the pollution war. Proposed here is the execution of international contributions through an organization of those veterans who find their missions in understanding the situations of developing countries, transferring the necessary technologies and know-how, and training the staff of these countries. The transfer of environmental protection technologies coupled with know-how based on Japan's hard-earned production experiences is believed to be the true international contribution for the above reasons. This contribution should be led by those senior people who have overcome difficulties of every kind in their prime time and have survived the post-World War II with the philosophy of diligence.

10. Remaining issues

In summary, the internalization of the environmental costs started and was established from the fact that compensation for patients of pollution diseases was up to ten times more expensive than pollution countermeasures. Furthermore the pollution abatement costs, or environmental costs in a more appropriate sense, have been absorbed by the propagation effects on production technology due to extensive efforts such as research and development in environmental technologies as well as general enhanced productivity. Thus, the analysis concludes that the environmental efforts have not substantially raised total costs and have been internalized in the market economy.

It has been made clear that a lot of factors that enable the internalization of environmental costs exist. However technologies or regulations do not suffice alone. In addition to recognizing values of the environment, it is necessary to have a higher level of production technologies which can cover the costs of environmental preservation. Social systems also play an important role in assembling people to the goal of environmental preservation. Japanese fundamental characteristics such as the cooperating attitude of influential people in industries, schools and governments as well as the nation's traditional characteristics of diligence in work and acceptance of technologies have been pointed out.

Thus, we should proceed from now on to take advantage of the results of analysis on those success factors. However, there still remain other aspects which are beyond the previous analysis.

Consider the airpollution preventing technologies, for example, the SO_X problem seems to have been overcome as shown in Figure 1, while NO_X has not yet met the environmental criteria. This indicates that laws and regulations alone are not enough for overcoming environmental problems. With large-scale facilities, a technology to inject ammonia into the exhaust gas in the presence of catalysts is practiced. However, no appropriate technology has been found to control the NO_X emitted from small-scale units, especially from Diesel engines. Technological development is urgently required in this area.

As for the handling of large amounts of solid wastes currently produced and to be produced in the future, a long-term planning must be developed in the hope of eventually realizing a RECYCLE society which will reduce the amount of wastes, re-use wastes, recycle them as resources, and return them harmless to the environment. Solid wastes pose a new type of environmental problems, which may be classified as municipal or consumer types. In order to solve these problems including river quality deterioration by home wastes, individuals should be more conscious of the environment and the reconstruction of social systems should be done in the direction of a new environment friendly community. Enterprises with production as their means can resort to technological countermeasures to the environment even after it gets worsen, while individual citizens should think in preventive terms of not worsening the environment to begin with.

We are now in the midst of the borderless age, where every country relies on each other economically and environmentally. The inclusion of every aspect on a global scale is now desired. Even so, issues of production and environment vary between countries. In making international contributions, it is paramount to pursue measures for success by analyzing these inherent factors.

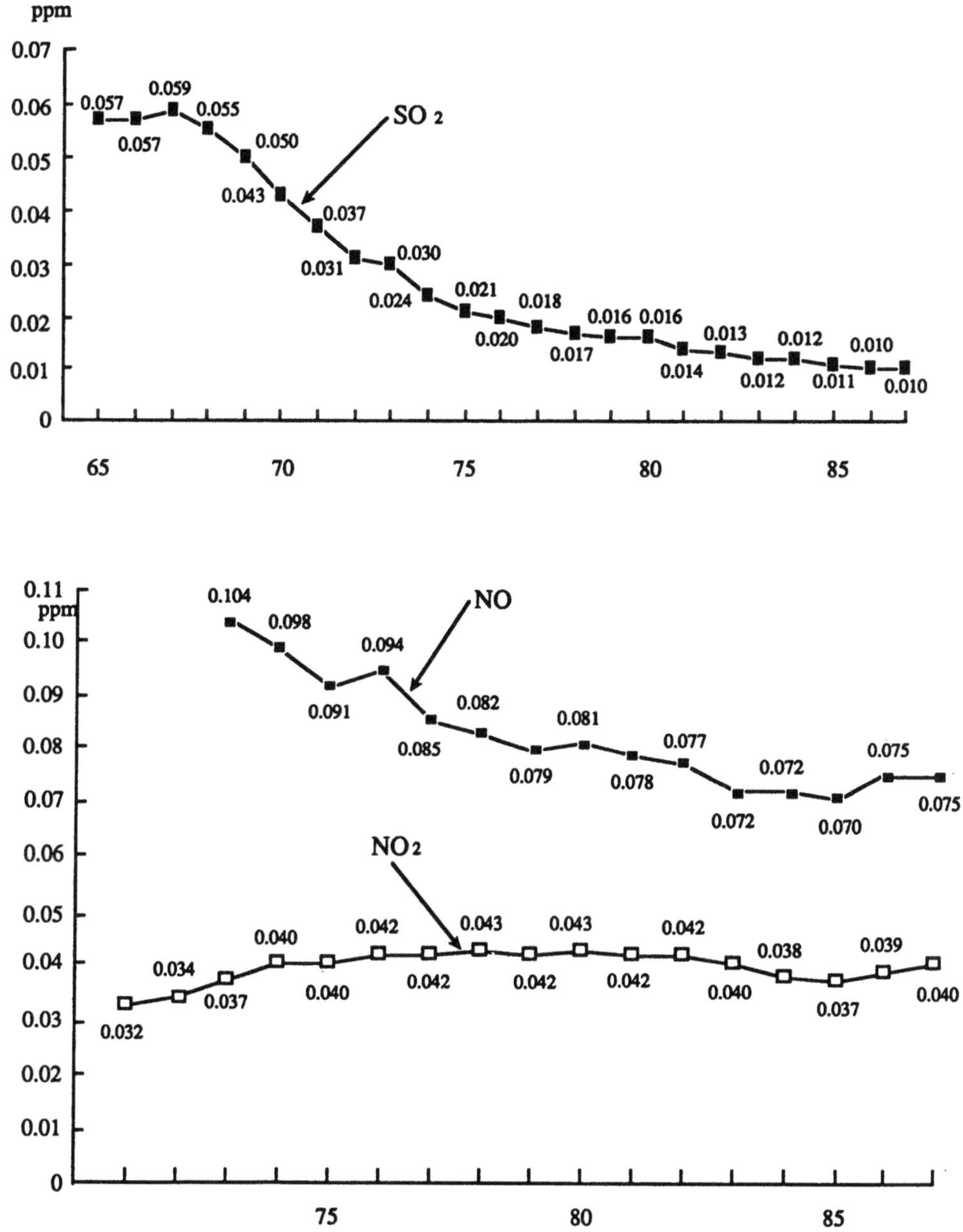

(Environmental Protection Agency)

Figure 1: SOx, NOx Emission

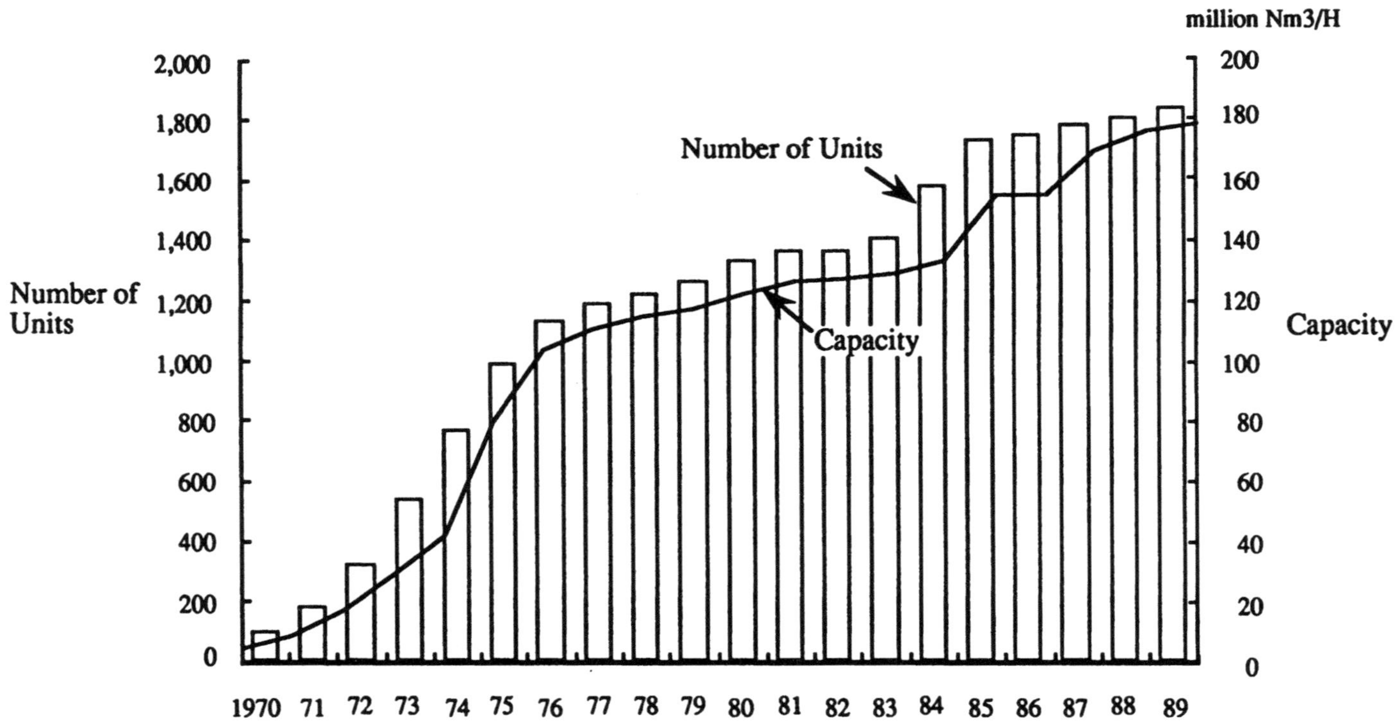

(Environmental Protection Agency, Nov. 1991)

Figure 2: Progress of Flue Gas Desulfurization Unit Installation

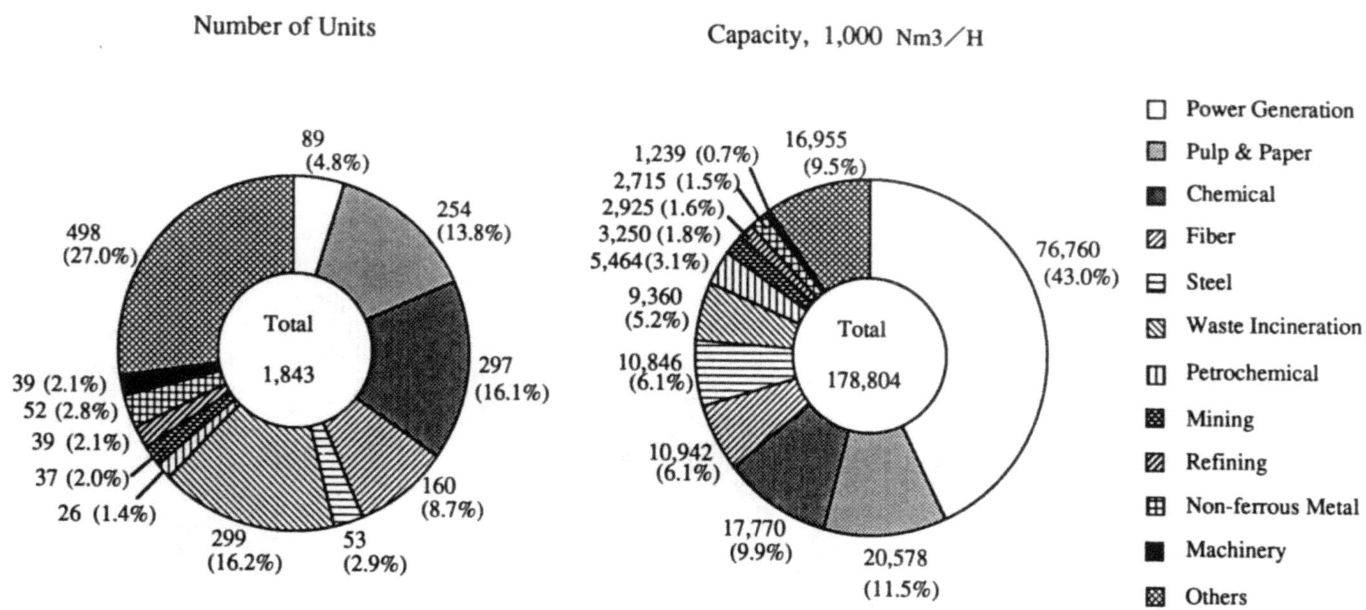

(Environmental Protection Agency, Nov. 1991)

Figure 3: Flue Gas Desulfurization Unit Installation by Industry

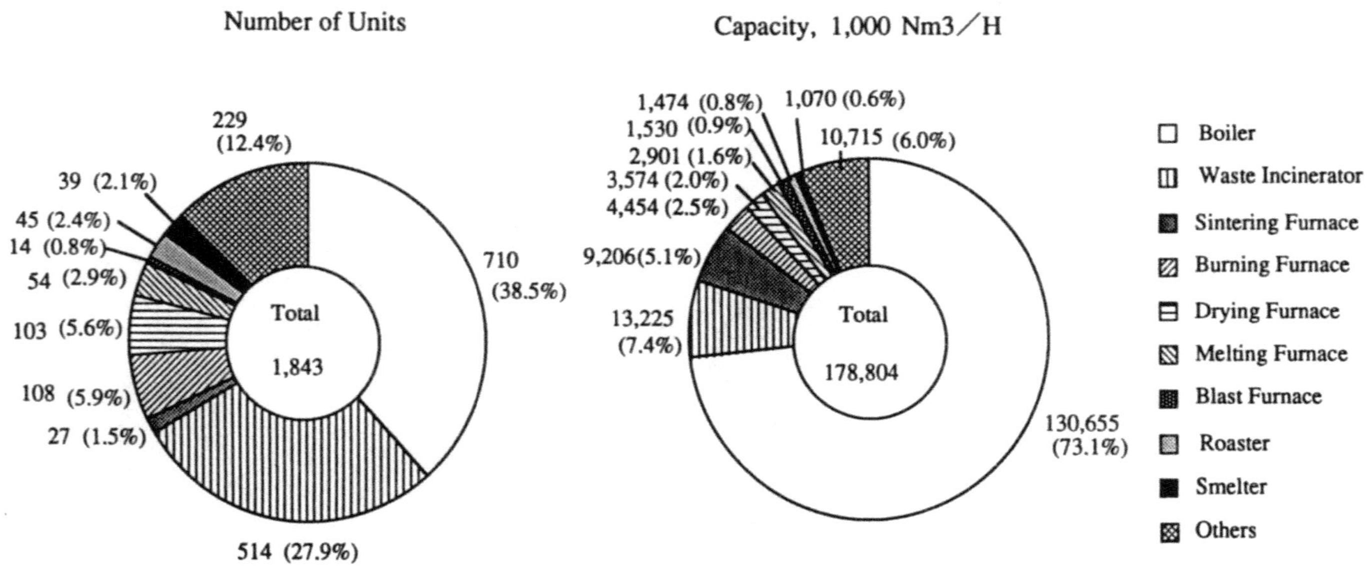

(Environmental Protection Agency, Aug. 1990)

Figure 4: Flue Gas Desulfurization Unit Installation by Flue Gas Sources

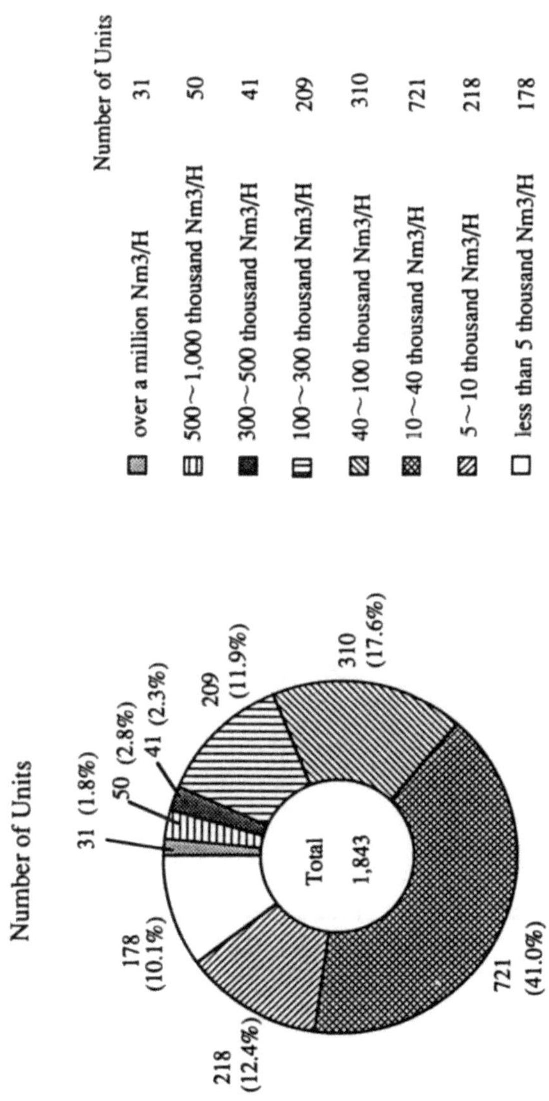

(Environmental Protection Agency, Nov. 1991)

Figure 5: Flue Gas Desulfurization Unit Installation by Unit Capacity

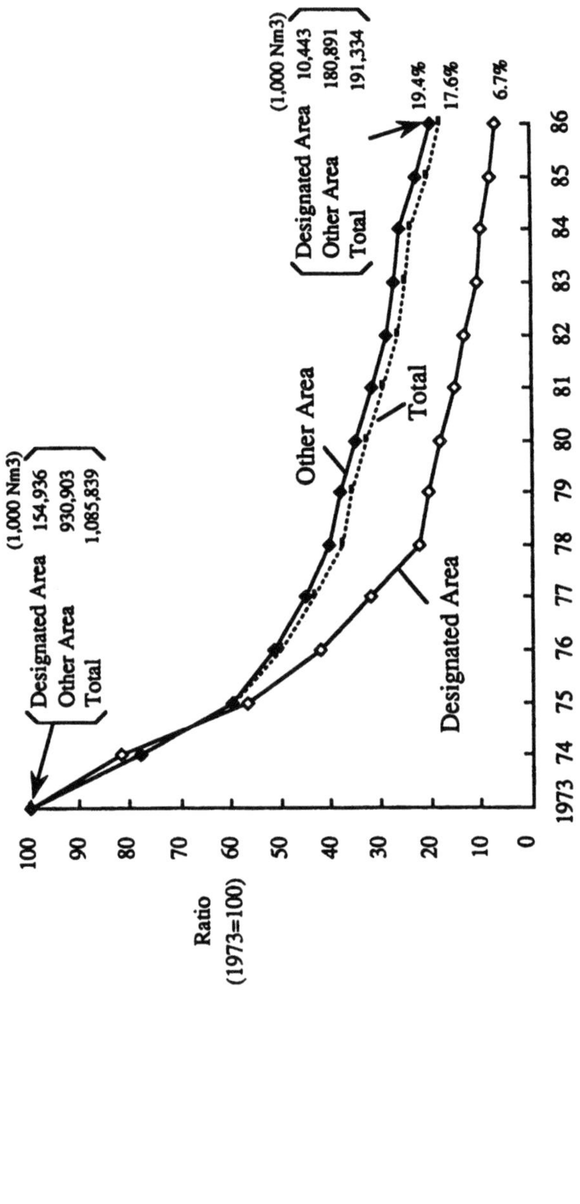

(Environmental Protection Agency)

Figure 6: SOx Emission in Japan

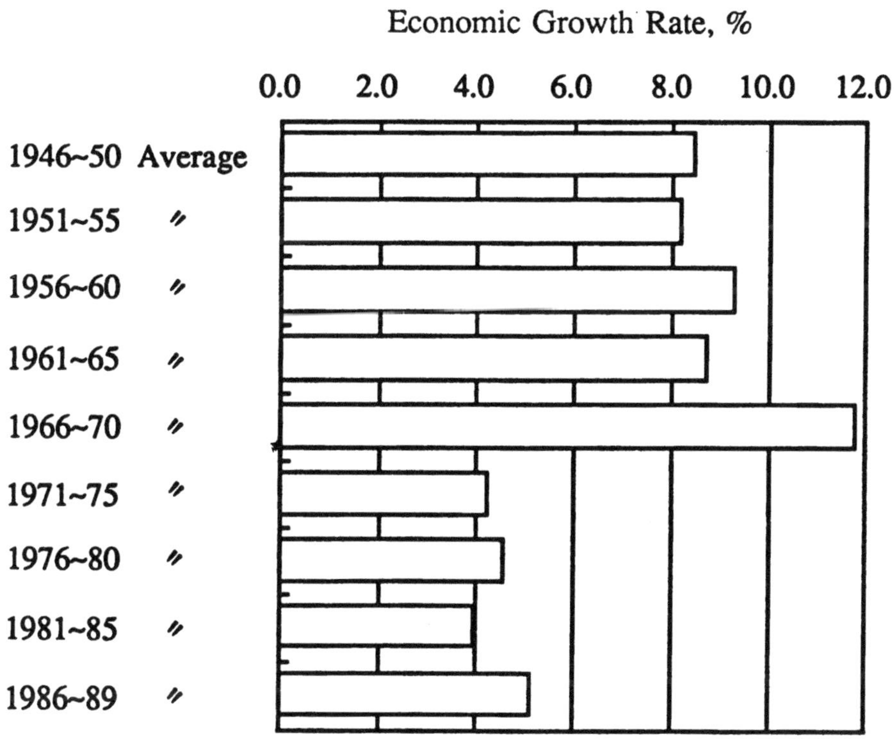

Figure 7: Average Economic Growth Rate for Five Years

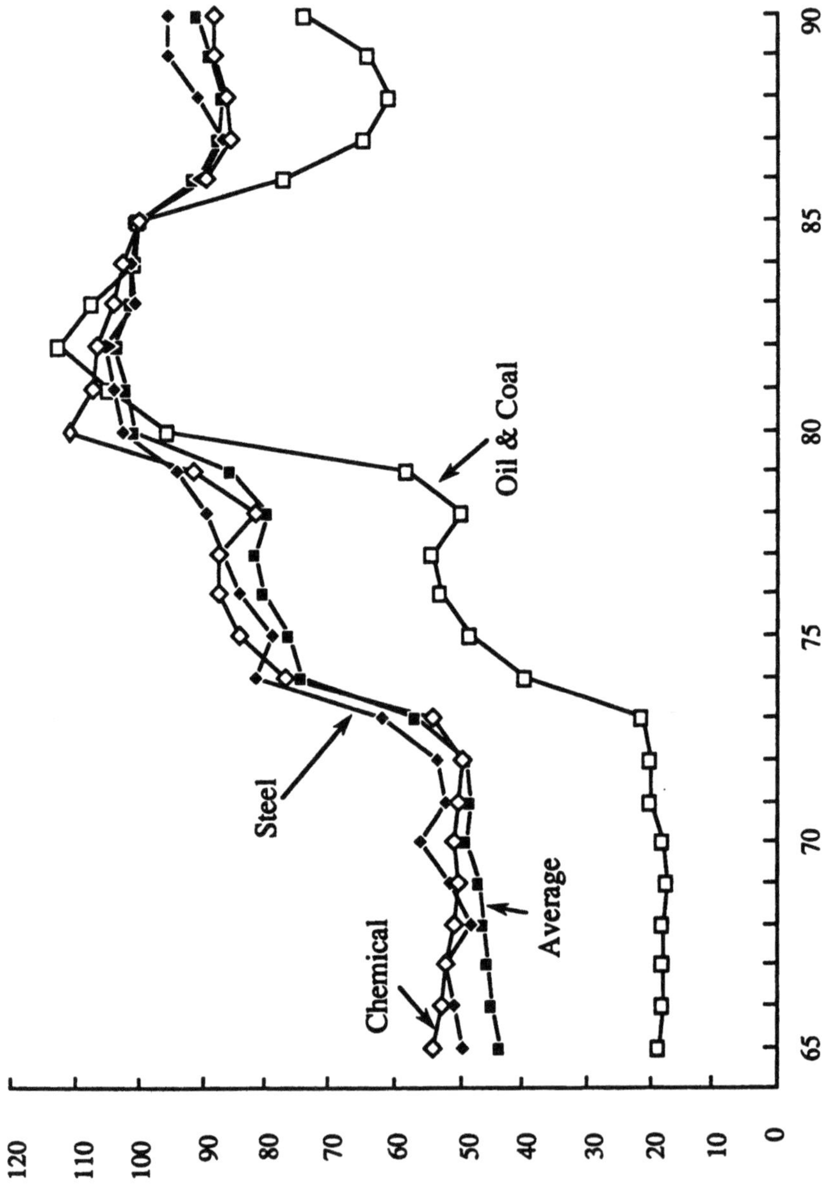

Bank of Japan

Figure 8: Wholesale Price Index (1985 = 100)

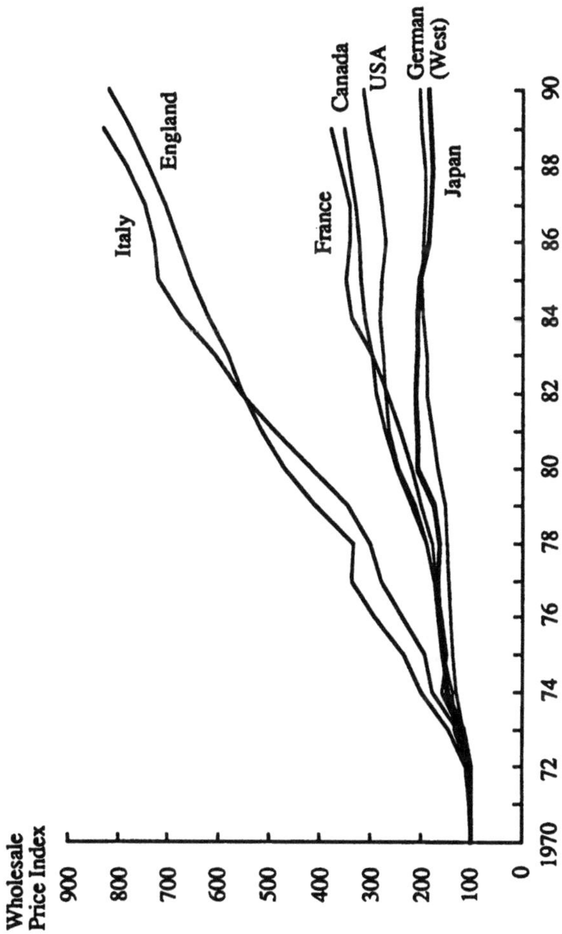

Figure 9: Trend of Wholesale Price Index in OECD Countries
(1970 = 100)

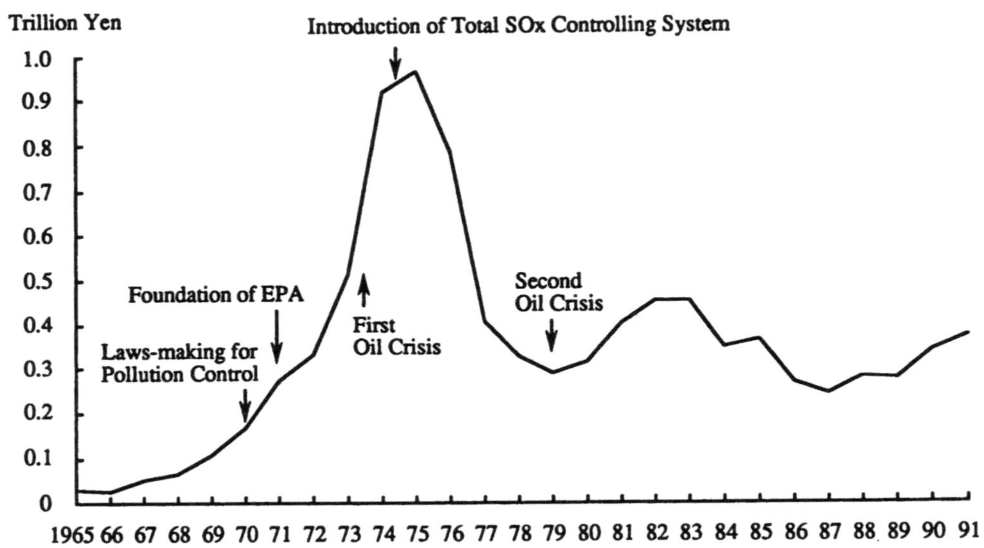

Remarks 1. "Trend of Pollution Abatement Investment in Private Sector" surveyed by MITI.

2. Object : Companies whose capital are more than 100 million yen in mining and manufacturing industry.

3. 1965--1989 : Actual, 1990 : Forecast, 1991 : Planning

Figure 10: Trend of Pollution Abatement Plant Investment

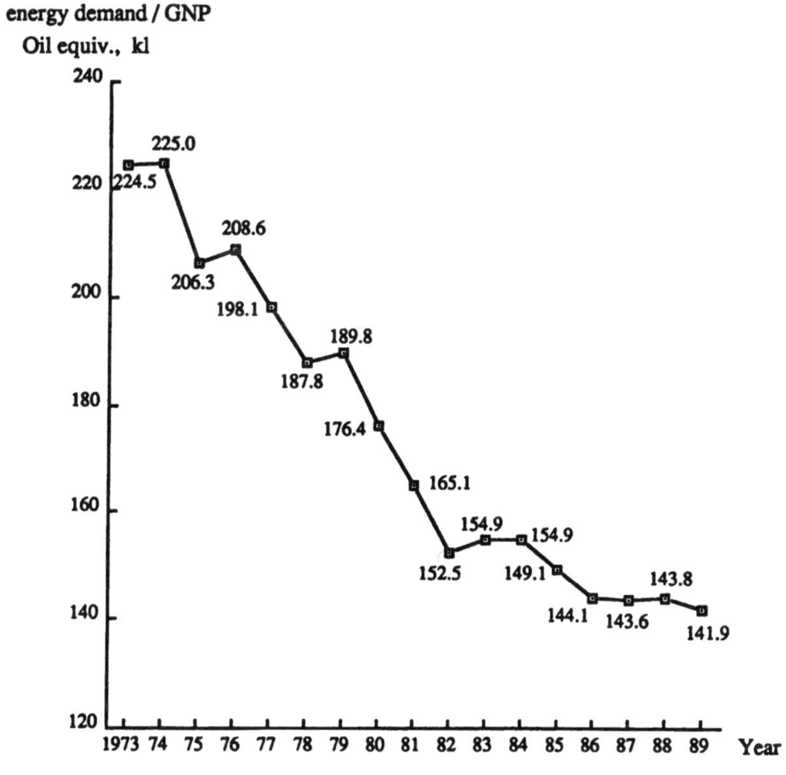

Energy per GNP = energy demand / GNP (100 million YEN)

(Source) Ministry of International Trade and Industry

Figure 11: Energy Consumption per GNP in Japan

References

The Second World Industry conference for Environmental Management. (WEICEM II)

Japan's Experiences on Pollution, the Global Environment and Economics Study Group, Godo Shuppan Publishing.

A paper submitted by Prof. *Yoichi Kaya* to the Rome Club's Tokyo convention.

Establishment of Total Amount Regulation Method for SO_x Reduction in Yokkaichi Area and its Effect on the Health of Residents, Kankyo Kenkyu (Environmental Research), 45 (1983).

The Guide to Pollution-Trigerred Health Damage Compensation and Prevention, Pollution-Trigerred Health Damage Compensation System Study Committee, the Environment Agency, Shin Nihon Hoki Publishing.

White Paper on Earth, World Watch, 1990 and 1991 Editions.

The Water Resources of Japan, the Agency of National Land, Printing Bureau of the Ministry of Finance.

The River Environment of Japan, the Environment Agency, Printing Bureau of the Ministry of Finance.

The Industrial Statistics Table, MITI, Printing Bureau of the Ministry of Finance.

Political Economics on Global Environment, the Global Environment Study Committee, the Environment Agency, Diamond Publishing.

Recycling of Industrial Wastes, Atsuhiro Honda, Energy Saving Center.

The White Paper on Environment, Printing Bureau of the Ministry of Finance (1977).

On Diligence - Motivation of the Japanese, *Shichihei Yamamoto*, PHP Institute.

Transfer of Environmental Technology
- Transfer Technology and Roles of Non-profit Institutions -

Yoshida Takeshi

1. Introduction

Technology transfer has been recognized as critical to long-term and sustainable development of firms by not only researchers, but also by practitioners and managers. However most research shows that it is not an easy task and a number of hurdles exist, which must be tackled and solved. Therefore in considering the transfer of environmental technologies, we will encounter and have to solve the same difficulties. Worse, there are additional inherent problems of environmental technologies.

Thus, we will first make a clear distinction between problems of technology transfer and those of environmental technologies. Secondly, we examine such problems in detail. Thirdly, we propose that a mediating non-profit institution, that facilitates transfer by providing their various functions, is one of the best solutions and the most important and effective mechanisms. Finally, we will describe as an example one such institution for environmental technology in Japan.

2. The problems and solutions of technology transfer

2.1. Problems of technology transfer

Technologies are formed by explication or theorization of experiences through experiments, or application of scientific findings on a trial-error basis. Consequently they consist in a variety of explicit and/or tacit knowledge (know-how) so that technology transfer may mean transferring of this knowledge.

Though knowledge has various forms and can be categorized in numerous ways, it is effective to think of it consisting of three main constituents:

firstly, the embodiment of knowledge-resources, tools, machinery, goods and services, behavior and know-how of their actual use; secondly, what we usually think of knowledge, including theories, facts or information about cause-and-effect relationships and meta-knowledge to generate, transform and use knowledge; finally, schema, or cognitive framework through which one can interpret and understand one's own reality, and create facts or data.

Usually, the first part of knowledge can be transferred more easily than the others because of its observability. Reversely, the interpretation frameworks are most difficult to acquire and transfer. It is true that resources or products are readily procured. But as know-how or technique is tacit or uncodable (Attewell, 1992), even products, if they require much know-how for their use or manufacture, are not considered to be mobile and transferable parts (Hamel, 1991; Badaracco, 1991). In order to accomplish the transfer of tacit knowledge completely, the relations between the parties involved (providers and receivers of knowledge) become longer-term and their technological and social interactions become denser and more iterative (Tornatzky and Fleischer, 1990) than exchange relations within markets. Reversely, unless they embrace such stable settings for transfer, tacit know-how cannot cross boundaries.

Transfer of what we call knowledge - the second part of knowledge - needs the settings mentioned above further, because there are very few, if any markets of knowledge transaction. Exchange of knowledge as information is quite different from transactions in other commodities. Information is not observable in itself and we cannot understand its content and real value without acquiring it. If the sellers behave in an opportunistic way (Williamson, 1975) markets do not emerge.

In this sense information exchange cannot exist without mutual trust between parties. Consequently, an alternative to markets, i.e., organization - results (Williamson, 1975). However organizations are neither a perfect nor often a viable solution in order to acquire all needed knowledge because organization is often a costly and time-consuming task and organizations, once structured or institutionalized, are apt to become inflexible compared to elastic market transactions. As a result, in order to solve this dilemma, or to maintain both mutual trust and flexibility, interorganizational relationships among a few parties - licensing, strategic alliances, long-term buyer-supplier relations - increasingly become the prevailing phenomena.

Finally, there are much greater difficulties in transferring frameworks upon which one's interpretation of real worlds, or reality is based. These are deeply embedded in an individual's behavior and the basic assumptions of an individual's framework are taken for granted and have been a source of self-identification for a long time. Another framework cannot be valued and understood objectively and open-mindedly. Consequently, transfer of frameworks is more arduous.

2.2. Solutions to barriers of technology transfer

Attewell (1992) proposes a knowledge-barrier institutional-network approach consisting of nine propositions. Five of them are concerned with our arguments. Firstly, organizational learning is partly a consequence of immobility of technical knowledge. Secondly, the burden of developing technical know-how (organizational learning) becomes a hurdle to adoption. Thirdly, given such hurdles, the relationships between supply-side and user organizations in a network go beyond selling and buying equipment. Fourthly, mediating institutions come into existence if technical knowledge is scarce and/or organizational learning around a technology is burdensome. Finally, mediating institutions capture economies of scale in rare event learning.

Tornatzky and Fleischer (1990) argue that technology deployment takes place within contexts and the determination of the type of most effective deployment mechanisms must be based on such contexts. According to them, there are five elements of contexts. 1. the nature of the technology; 2. characteristics of users; 3. characteristics of deployers; 4. boundaries within and between deployers and users; 5. characteristics of communication and transaction mechanisms.

Furthermore, they argue that technologies are inseparable from the cultural and social settings in the following aspects. (1) Their use is conditioned by the cultural norms and values, and social roles and practices; (2) The core, invariant elements of the technologies themselves may be as much social as they are physical. In this sense technology is characteristic of immobility because understanding of cultural and social factors and content of technology transfer are inescapable, but very hard work for those who are not familiar with them.

Hamel (1991) points out that there are three determinants of learning outcomes: a collaborative intent that refers to a firm's initial propensity to view collaboration as an opportunity to learn or not, and thus the desire to learn; transparency, that is the openness of each partner and thus the potential for learning; and receptivity to a partner's capacity for learning. He also suggests that the greater the need to learn, the higher the barriers to receptivity and argues that in order to replicate the skills of a partner, a firm must be able to identify the intermediate learning steps' between its present competence level and that of its partner.

From these arguments we point out that there exists three main factors that encourage or discourage technology transfer: firstly, the ability and motivation of transferrers (supply-side) to clarify tacit knowledge, transform it into explicit one and then move it; secondly, the capacity and aspiration of recipients (demand-side) to absorb and re-invent knowledge; and finally, mediating mechanisms or institutions. These play an important role in facilitating the transfer of complicated technologies between actual or potential, providers and recipients through capability-building, framework-sharing and/or trans-cultural interaction of both parties, providing intermediate learning steps through training or lectures, and making experiments on rare events or trials that most small organizations cannot afford. Not infrequently they may act as role models that other organizations are willing to follow and standard setters that determine the direction or path of technology evolution.

There are structural, cultural, geographic, and procedural barriers to the success of the information exchange (Tornatzky and Fleischer, 1990). As a result, boundary-spanning functions are required to flow information between boundaries. The greater gaps between the parties in culture, geography, procedures, structures and power, the higher walls and the more required are the boundary-spanning organizations that are able to break down these walls. Thus for technology transfer the capability and motivation of the providers and recipients are important, but more important are mediating institutions that promote the transfer or learning of technology, which are communication and transaction mechanisms (Tornatzky and Fleischer, 1990) that most often are apt to be ignored. If they did not exist, the speed and efficiency of transfer would decrease, and it would take longer to grasp the transferred technology completely and utilize it to the full extent of its power.

3. The inherent problems and solutions of environmental technology transfer

There are two ways of solving those difficult problems such as environmental protection that have far-reaching effects on many people and community as a whole but which no one as an individual has an ability and willingness to solve.

One is that through national or local government policy the introduction of environmental technology or anti-pollution facilities into plants or operating processes becomes compulsory. Another is to change frame of reference of firms and societies, that is, to shift away from beliefs that its introduction imposes high costs on firms or societies to thoughts that it may provide an opportunity of generating new products and/or process, or innovation.

In order to generate substantial changes environmental technology transfer and diffusion may be necessary, but not sufficient. At the same time the beliefs, goals, assumptions, mentalities and attitudes that drive individuals and firms activities', as well as daily practices and tools used to accomplish them need to be altered (Schmidheiny, 1991) and then diffused, learned and shared among all people in all societies.

As creating and implementing a complex advanced technology requires both individual and organizational learning (Attewell, 1992), so does transferring a technology. In addition, environmental technology transfer needs community or society learning. It is said that the organization and society have learned only when individual knowledge and know-how have become personified in organizational and social routines, practices and beliefs, and individuals have communicated and exchanged them with one another within organizations or societies. This will take for a very long time through face-to-face communications or one-to-one technology transfers. In order to breed such change, more education, publicity and examples of success of its introduction are needed.

We suggest that non-profit institutions play an important role in realizing technology transfer. It is difficult for profit organizations to take these solutions into consideration, because they cannot and did not treat and propose public policy, and do not have a device of promoting society-wide change of framework.

There are two main types of environmental technologies: end-of-pipe technology and cleaner production technology (Schmidheiny, 1991). The aim of the former is not to handle the source of pollution and production processes directly, but to eliminate harmful by-products such as smoke, NOx, SOx and so on. Examples of the technology are filters, scrubbers, treatment plants and incineration.

The latter is concerned with eliminating the source directly and improving the processes of pollution occurrence themselves. This can be divided into four categories: operation of machinery and production systems in the most efficient manner; material substitution; manufacturing modifications; and resource recovery or re-use.

Because the environmental technology, especially end-of-pipe technology prevent deterioration of atmosphere and various pollution, most people think it is indispensable in constructing power plants or producing products. But even if its necessity is recognized, frequently it is impossible to make further investments because of frequent capital scarcity. In spite of sufficient money to acquire technologies, additional introduction costs of technologies can barely be permitted in terms of cost management. But "when viewed within the context of sustainable development, environmental concerns become not just a cost of doing business, but a potent source of competitive advantage."(Schmidheiny, 1992, p.86).

As a result, not in terms of day-to-day practices and tactics, but corporate strategy and objectives, managers have to estimate the effects of environmental technology on effectiveness and performance of their companies. Even if calculation of costs or ROI (Return on Investment) is needed, it is necessary to do so not on a short-term, but on a long-term basis.

There are also three broad types of obstacles to the spread of pollution prevention realized by a cleaner technology within industry (Schimdheiny, 1992): economic problems, that is, scarcity of capital; lack of information or data about performance of pollution prevention technology; and management attitude - a prevailing belief that environmental protection is a peripheral issue and a diversion from basic corporate goals.

In order to overcome these obstacles, the mechanisms or institutions that specialize in each problem must be established because concentrated efforts, specialized knowledge and know-how, strong leadership and high reputation, and ample money help solve such tough, complicated and intransigent problems.

4. Functions of non-profit institutions

So far we have investigated the meaning of non-profit institutions when transferring environmental technologies. Next, let us consider technologies for technology transfer (Tornatzky and Fleischer, 1990). However in this section we do not develop a theory of technologies for technology transfer (we will call it transfer technology) completely and generate the methodology for analyzing it. We only consider relations between its function and the roles which non-profit organizations play.

Its chief functions are the followings: (1) promoting transfer and (2) breaking down obstacles to transfer.

The first function is embodied by information technology and organizational design: firstly, development and installation of information systems and tools for knowledge transfer and accumulation (construction and utilization of network, and development of various advanced information technologies, such as knowledge base, multimedia and data base).

Secondly, design of new organizational arrangements, such as the establishment of research and development centres (R & D) for environmental improvement and R & D related to transfer technologies, and places for training and education of environmental technologies and even environmental policies and law.

Finally, there exists what is called organizational and interorganizational development (Yoshida, 1993). This includes the development of techniques to facilitate human interactions among parties involved in technology transfer, smooth barriers of communication, share common problems, change attitudes and thought toward pro-environmentalism and produce proper decision-making procedures and tools for developing cleaner production technologies and cleaner products.

Depending on the type of technology, the transfer technology varies. For example, transfer of "end-of-pipe" technology or methods can be accomplished through the construction of equipments or plants with a high probability of success and reasonable cost, but cleaner production technology cannot do so because of the necessity of a deep understanding of the scientific bases of technology and all the processes of production.

As a result, the latter needs many more devices and systems for transfer, more complicated, sophisticated and expensive transfer technology, and longer time to transfer than the former does. More opportunities for training and education and longer time horizon are needed. This is effective for long-term, but not efficient for short-term.

The end-of-pipe methods may be a more realistic solution. It is hard to acknowledge the necessity and value of the cleaner production methods. But it is the balance between the present and the future, or ecology and economy that is required. In developing countries, pollution already occurred has to be rectified and at the same time cleaner technology must be developed to produce outputs of low cost and high quality.

We propose that transfer of end-of-pipe technology is likely to be the most successful between firms on a commercial basis, but that the transfer of cleaner technology should not for the three reasons. Firstly, much and varying tacit know-how is required to utilize the technology because the understanding and knowledge of all functions of the machinery and manufacturing processes are indispensable. Secondly, as even firms themselves with such newly emerging technologies do not comprehend all their functions, they still have to learn by doing (Arrow, 1962) and by using them (Rosenberg, 1982), and be gathering data or information. It is natural that they can not teach others anything not fully known to themselves. Finally, when a cleaner technology is under development, it is not transferable because of secrecy and unrealizable profit. Firms will not give others technology that does not yet bear any fruit. From this viewpoint the emergence of non-profit organizations is worth while.

The most powerful engines for promoting technological innovations are likely to be profits and so firms will occupy crucial positions, but they can not always play an important role in transferring innovations for above reasons. Thus, non-profit institutions, which can destroy the obstacles (tacitness of knowledge, incompleteness of information about how to use technology and secrecy) of transferring cleaner technologies should exist. These institutions can provide education and training repeatedly and over a long period, so that some tacit knowledge will be flow across boundaries.

It is easier for the non-profit organizations to collect considerable data and information about a technology from firms having such data than from other profit organizations, because they are not likely to appear as competitors even if they have acquired information.

Due to their non-profit character, they are not likely to hesitate in teaching and moving technology under development and reversely they may teach it to other organizations positively in order to give publicity to outcomes and acquire reputation. Thus the exchange of advanced knowledge among research institutions may take place more easily.

Moreover, firms often have few incentives to invest a lot of money to generate transfer technologies and disseminate them even if they already possess them. Therefore, non-profit institutions are engaged either in making R & D for transfer technologies by themselves, or inducing firms to do so by subsidizing them, and at the same time they are deeply committed to dissemination activities.

Tornatzky and Fleischer (1990) emphasize the social content and context of innovation and technology deployment. Thus, we stress the need of doing research and development on social science, specifically organizational science and its applications (i.e., theories of organizational design, intra and inter-organizational development and organizational behavior, and practices based on them).

The institutions for technology transfer or transfer technology should have purposes or departments for R & D on organizational science and devote much more money and human resource to non-technological aspects of technology transfer.

5. Institutions for transfer of environmental technology in Japan

The International Center for Environmental Technology Transfer (ICETT) is located in Yokkaichi City, Mie Prefecture, near Nagoya city. It was first established as a foundation under the jurisdiction of Governor of Mie Prefecture in March, 1990 with a fund donated by Mie Prefecture, Yokkaichi City and many firms. In February 1991, this center changed to the foundation under the jurisdiction of the Minister of International Trade and Industry (MITI).

The main purpose of ICETT is to provide the following activities on the basis of Japan's industrial technology in order to contribute to the conservation and development of the world economy.

1. Training in global environment conservation technology, and R & D related to technology transfer.

2. Smooth transfer of technology appropriate to the conditions in foreign countries.

3. Comprehensive proposal for preventing destruction of and improving environment. And its expected operations are the following.
   (1) Training and instruction in technology
      (a) Receiving trainees, and dispatching instructors
      (b) Research and development for training programs

   The aims of this operation are to transfer the technology that has already been developed and are proved to be effective, and to create the most effective training programs for teaching the environmental technologies.

   (2) Research and development;
      (a) R & D related to transfer of technology overseas
      (b) Joint R & D with industries, universities, institutes in Japan and overseas
      (c) Transfer of environmental conservation technology utilizing ODA expenditure
      (d) Joint R & D with overseas researchers on specific nations and regions
      (e) R & D for environmental improvement based on overseas needs.

   Some operations pertain to transfer activities themselves directly and to R&D for environmental technology and for transfer technology. Some relate to join actions or co-operation which contributes to technological break-through and the nurture of specialized scientists and technicians that matters to both transfer and creation of technology. The others concern the formation of stable interactions, that is, networking, among scientists and engineers with various backgrounds (new organizational configurations).

(3) Investigation and information furnishing
 (a) Investigation into needs and seeds related to transfer of technology
 (b) Gathering and furnishing technical information

In order to transfer technology, the mediating institutions have to detect those who wish for technology, investigate whatever their needs are, and inform those people of their needs, if they can not perceive them themselves. Thus, a lot of information is collected externally, processed, stored within the institutions and supplied to outside. The information stored needs to be accessible to outsiders.

(4) Human exchange and dissemination.
 (a) International exchange for research and training
 (b) dissemination and awareness enhancement

Because interpersonally direct face-to-face communication can convey richer information than formal written communication, human exchange as a way of transferring complicated technologies, such as environmental technologies is also effective, with the limitation that it takes long time and high cost and its impact is narrow.

6. Discussion

ICETT have already had most of all the functions and purposes required to transfer environmental technologies, but in fact only a few actually work. In addition, what they have done are related to technological aspects of transfer, and instructions on history or general explanations or air/water pollution in Yokkaichi or other places in Japan.

For one reason, ICETT itself has not had so much experience in transferring technology, because a few years have passed since its establishment. But it is more important that it does not recognize technology transfer as an organizational, social or cultural phenomena. If it did recognize its importance, it would list R & D for social context and content of transfer as one of the main purposes.

Nonetheless, that does not seem to deteriorate the importance of the institution, because we do not think it insignificant to move out experience and anti-pollution technology to other counties. In order to change out thoughts and attitudes, information gathering and dissemination, human interactions and joint R & D, even if centred on technological facets, are not said to be dispensable.

For the transfer of environmental technologies and other technologies, we need to keep the balance between a physical and an organizational aspect. If not, machine and equipment introduced may sit forever in the warehouse or may be pulled out of a production line and tossed into the scrap yard (Tornatzky and Fleischer, 1990). Only environmental technologies can not be the exception to this rule.

References

Attewell, P., "Technology Diffusion and Organizational Learning: The Case of Business Computing", Organization Science, Vol. 3, NO. 1, 1992

Arrow, K., "The Economic Implications of Learning by Doing", Review of Economic Studies, 29, 166-170, 1962

Badaracco, J.L. Jr., The Knowledge Link: How Firms Compete through Strategic Alliances, Harvard Business School Press, 1991

Hamel, G., "Competition for Competence and Inter-partner Learning Within International Strategic Alliances", Strategic Management Review, Vol. 12, 1991

Rosenberg, N., Inside the Black Box: Technology and Economics, Cambridge, Cambridge University Press, 1982

Schmidheiny, S., Changing Course: A Global Business Perspective on Development and the Environment, Cambridge, The MIT Press, 1992

Tornatzky,L./M. Fleischer, The Processes of Technological Innovation, Lexington, MA: Lexington Books, 1990

Yoshida Takeshi, "Sosikikan Kaihatsuron (On Interorganizational Development)" , in Japanese, Keizai Kagaku (Nagoya University), 41-1, 1993

Williamson, O.E., Markets and Hierarchy, Free Press, 1975

Environmental Activities among Lay People
- The Analysis of the Attributes of People Who are Aware of Environmental Activities -

Midori Aoyagi

Abstract

In this paper we analyze environmental activities among lay people, especially housewives. We use the questionnaire survey on the housewives in Japan. We compare six groups of household according to their husband's occupation in order to determine what determines becoming involved. Multinominal logit probability models are estimated on data from the questionnaire survey in 1991. The findings are that having children, occupation and income class are the significant factors that determine participation in the activities.

I. Introduction

Environmental activities among lay people is becoming more important issue than before in Japan. In the past, people who were involved in environmental movements were considered to be "left-wing", or were affected by and suffered from health problems that might be caused by pollution of air and water. Now it becomes more general and one of the important issues of the world, to which everyone refers to.

Past environmental problems might be expressed as the problems of pollution and destruction of nature, so that the PPP (Polluter Pays Principle) is the fundamental principle to solve each problems. However this is not the case, for we are both polluter and victim. Our day-to-day activities affect the environment, but at the same time we suffer from the damage. What should we do?

Some people have reached the conclusion that they must act for the environment and begin to be involved in these actions. They have formed groups to act effectively. Most of them are what we call CBO (Community Based Organizations), sometimes NGO (Non Governmental Organization). Our question is then, what kind of people are most likely to participate in these actions? Our purpose is to clarify the attributes of people who are involved in these activities, because we would like to analyze what determinants predicts who participates in such activities to encourage citizen's activities.

2. Participation in environmental activities among lay people

According to the Agenda 21 by the Brazil Summit, the Japanese government will establish GEF (Global Environmental Fund) to support not only Japanese but also international NGOs. At the Summit NGO played an important role and have great influence large parts of society. Thus the Japanese government began to realize the importance of citizen's movement to improve our environment.

Sherkat (Sherkat 1991, 1992) used the Youth-Parent Socialization Panel Study in U.S. to analyze people's participation in the environmental movement, protest movement in mid 60's. By Multinominal Logit Regression, he found that white, higher GPA score, in the college track, northern and less religious students were more likely to participate environmental movement than others. Also, Diekmann (Diekmann 1992) made a survey covering Berne and Munich about environmental actions and participation in those movement. He concluded that people who were more likely to be female, from Berne rather than Munich, have closer contacts with neighbours, be higher educated, and tended to more REB (Responsible environmental Behavior).

Kabashima (Kabashima, 1988) investigated the politics participation in Japan. He used the Social Movement Survey and showed that highly educated persons are more likely to have a deep and broad knowledge of politics, but that the voting rate is not as high as expected. Farmers or those who manage small factories tend to go to vote. He concluded that, compared to farmers, highly educated people are often executives of larger firms and their costs of voting are high comparing to his/her benefit. As for Japanese environmental actions, few studies have been made of the attributes of participants in larger sample. Today, responsible environmental activities are to be taken by everyone who uses the earth's limited resources and information about the environmental effects caused by our activities should be provided to citizens. We have to discover what kind of people are most likely to be interest, and who will not be. This is the purpose of our study.

3. The modelling of choice

We use a discrete choice model to explain the behavior of people (Manski and McFadden, 1983). Generally the model will be written P(i | z,q), where i is an alternative in infinite choice set C, z denotes a real vector characterizing the choice set and decision maker, P gives conditional probability that in the choice context characterized by z alternative i will be select. q denotes the parameter vector from observations of the choices made by samples of decision makers. We consider the population model f(i,p). If the marginal distribution p(z) is defined, we can write

$$f(i,z) = P(i/z,q)\ p(z)$$

According to Cosslett (Cosslett, 1981), "the only probability models used in practice are the well known logit and probit models". Suppose we adopt the multinominal logit form of the probabilities, we can write,

$$P(i/z,\theta) = \frac{\exp V_i(z,\theta)}{\sum_{j=1}^{M} \exp V_j(z,\theta)}$$

where M is the number of alternatives. V represents the attractiveness or desirability of alternative i. In the random utility maximization model it is the average utility (for all subjects with the same characteristics z) of alternative i. In practice it generally has the linear form,

$$V_i(z_i,\theta) = \sum_{\alpha} z_{i\alpha}\theta_{\alpha} = z_i\theta$$

for i=1,..........M.

4. Data

The data were obtained from the questionnaire survey on 5,000 housewives in Japan in August 1991. Environmental activities include waste, recycling, nature and water conservation, and other environmental concerns are asked with face sheet (income, age educations, so on). The effective responding rate was 80,5%, so that sample size is 4,026 (see figure 1). All samples are divided into 6 clusters according to the husband's occupation and occupational situation. One reason is that in Japan, occupational situation is highly correlated with age and education. The other reason is the calculation efficiency. Each cluster has a significant difference in each character (figure 2).

Area	All japan (47 Prefectures)
Respondents'	Upper 2 persons ordinary family (single family are excluded)
Sample size	5,000
Sampling Method	Stratified 2 stage sampling
Survey Method	Interview by interviewee at each respondent's home
Period	August 10-12, 1991
Respondence rate	Effective 4,025 (80,5 %)

Fig. 1 The Questionnaire Survey

The cluster 1 is the "Pension or interest income/professional (no kids) family". This cluster consists of two groups. The main income resource of the first group is pension or interest, and their mode of age is upper 60s. This group might be the retired group. The other group's main occupation is professional, such as lawyer or medical doctor. The difference from cluster 6a (also professionals) is that most of them live without or have no children.

The second cluster is "farmer's family". The mode of age is also upper 60s. The significant difference from other clusters is that their educational background is lower, the average family size is the largest among the clusters, and their participant rate of environmental activity is also lower than other clusters.

The third cluster is "white-collar worker's family (general)". These form the majority of our sample, also of Japanese society. 36,4% of their wives work part-time, which is the highest rate among the clusters. Also 22,72% of wives work full time, this is also the highest rate.

The fourth cluster is "white-collar worker's family (manager class)". Their mode of income class is upper 10 million Yen, most of them have graduated from university or completed graduate school. The rate of participation of environmental activities is highest among the clusters.

The fifth cluster is "merchant/domestic factory family". Most wives are working in their family business, and their participation rate is not so high.

NO.	family type	No. of samples	Income Class (10000 yen) (mode; %)	living in a house (%)	husband's age (mode; %)	education of husband (mode;%)	education of wife (mode;%)	persons in a family (%)	participation (%)	Occupational situation of wife (%)
1	**Pension & interest/ professions (no kids)**	474	~400 (46.4)	86.50	60~ (78.7)	High school (38.0)	High school (47.7)	3.17	19.62	non **61.0%** part-time **17.72%** family business **10.97%** full time job **9.70%**
2	Farmer's family	270	400~ 700 (44.8)	97.41	60~ (47.0)	Junior High school (61.1)	Junior High school (56.7)	4.50	15.56	Non **16.6%** Part-time **1.48%** Family business **62.22%** Full time **9.63%**
3	white-color worker's family (general)	1549	400~ 700 (45.7)	73.27	40~50 (36.2)	High school (48.9)	High school (52.3)	3.98	22.01	Non **35.5%** Part-time **36.34%** Family business **5.42%** Full time **22.72%**
4	white-color worker's (manager class)	301	1000~ (48.5)	81.06	50~60 (46.2)	University, Graduate School (52.8)	High school (62.1)	3.95	27.57	Non **47.1%** Part-time **31.56%** Family business **7.97%** Full time **13.29%**
5	merchant/ domestic factory family	569	400~ 700 (31.6)	86.99	50~60 (32.2)	High school (51.5)	High school (55.0)	4.08	20.21	Non **19.3%** Part-time **12.65%** Family business **57.47%** Full time **10.54%**
6	Professions family (with kids)	179	400~ 700 (45.3)	64.25	30~40 (45.3)	University, Graduate School (59.8)	College, professional School (39.1)	4.18	25.70	Non **53.0%** Part-time **26.25%** Family business **5.59%** Full time **15.08%**

Fig. 2: The Summary of Clusters

The last cluster is "professional family (with kids)". Their "living in a house rate" is the lowest, and mode of age is the youngest. Both husbands and wives are most educated in each cluster. Most of them have (a) child(ren) and the non-working rate of the wife is the highest.

This gave a brief background of each clusters. Using this information, we then tried to investigate what attributes can explain the wives' participation in environmental activities.

5. Result

Here, we include in "environmental activities": waste problems (including recycling movement), nature conservation group (this includes forest, water, air etc.), bird watching, and so on. According to the our questionnaire survey, the waste problems amount to about 92%. We estimated the parameters of each logit, response variable is "participation in environmental activity", and explanatory variables are "live with child(ren)", "wife's occupation", "family income", "education (both husband and wife)" and "age (both husband and wife)". We used "CATMOD" command in SAS to estimate these parameters (SAS Inc., 1988).

1) Cluster 1

The significant explanatory variables are husband's age, occupational situation of wife. The wives who are occupied in their family business are more likely to participate in activities (see figure 3).

2) Cluster 2

The significant explanatory variables are housewife's education, child. Those who have (a) child(ren) that go to kinder garden or school are more likely to join the activities (see figure 4).

3) Cluster 3

The significant explanatory variables are child and income. Those who have (a) pre-school child(ren), or their income class are upper 4 million Yen are more likely to be involved in the activities. Especially, in the under 10 million Yen income class family, the wives whose children are before school are more likely to be involved. And in the upper 10 million Yen income class family, they tend to be involved if they have no such a child (see figure 5).

CLUSTER1 (Pension & interest income families/professions and no kids families) MODEL=[ACTIVE][CHKJOB][SEAGEC][ACTIVE*CHKJOB][CHKJOB*SEAGEC] LIKELIHOOD RATIO $\chi 2$=2.89 (p=0.97162) sample size=429					
U^{ACTIVE}_{i} (p=0.0001)	Active	i=1 (non-active)		i=2 (active)	
		0.678652		-0.678652	
U^{CHKJOB}_{j} (p=0.0001)	occupation of housewife	j=1 (non)	j=2 (part-time)	j=3 (family business)	j=4 (full time job)
		0.770404	0.0535802	-0.084422	-0.7395622
U^{SEAGEC}_{k} (p=0.0001)	husband's age	k=1 (~50 yr's old)	k=2 (~60 yr's old)	k=3 (60 yr's old ~)	
		-0.888437	-0.204081	1.092518	
$U^{ACTIVE}_{i}{}^{CHKJOB}_{j}$ (p=0.1777)		j=1 (non)	j=2 (part-time)	j=3 (family business)	j=4 (full time job)
	i=1 (non-active)	0.0405883	0.0070879	-0.429156	0.3814798
	i=2 (active)	-0.0405883	-0.0070879	0.429156	-0.3814798
$U^{CHKJOB}_{j}{}_{SEAGEC_{k}}$ (p=0.0575)		j=1 (non)	j=2 (part-time)	j=3 (family business)	j=4 (full time job)
	k=1 (~50 yr's old)	-0.343352	-0.29682	0.131406	0.508766
	k=2 (~60 yr's old)	-0.022322	0.351958	-0.109254	-0.220382
	k=3 (60 yr's old ~)	0.365674	-0.055138	-0.022152	-0.288384

Fig. 3: The Estimation of the Parameters from Log-Linear Model (Cluster 1)

Cluster 2 (Farmer's family) MODEL=[ACTIVE][HKSCHL][CHILD][ACTIVE*CHILD][CHILD*HKSCHL] LIKELIHOOD RATIO χ 2=3.16 (p=0.6760) sample size=269						
U^{ACTIVE}_{i} (p=0.0001)	Active	i=1 (non-active)			i=2 (active)	
		0.611158			-0.611158	
U^{HKSCHL}_{j} (p=0.0002)	housewife's education	j=1(junior high)		j=2(high school)	j=3(upper college)	
		0.500346		0.386143	-0.886489	
U^{CHILD}_{k} (p=0.0031)	Children	k=1 (No kids)	k=2 (baby)	k=3 (kinder garden)	k=4 (Elementary school)	k=5 (junior high & high school)
		0.654762	-0.517495	-0.205671	0.509078	-0.440674
$U^{ACTIVE,CHILD}_{i\ k}$ (p=0.0174)		k=1 (No kids)	k=2 (baby)	k=3 (kinder garden)	k=4 (Elementary school)	k=5 (junior high & high school)
	i=1 (non-active)	0.464723	0.311755	-0.499587	-0.012307	-0.264584
	i=2 (active)	-0.464723	-0.311755	0.499587	0.012307	0.264584
$U^{CHILD,HKSCHL}_{k\ j}$ (p=0.0001)		k=1 (No kids)	k=2 (baby)	k=3 (kinder garden)	k=4 (Elementary school)	k=5 (junior high & high school)
	j=1(junior high)	0.872958	-0.026341	-0.478833	-0.112095	-0.255689
	j=2(high school)	-0.251681	-0.094461	-0.141487	0.446793	-0.462526
	j=3(upper college)	-0.621277	0.120802	0.62032	-0.334698	0.718215

Fig. 4: The Estimation of the Parameters from Log-Linear Model (Cluster 2)

Cluster 3 (white-color worker's family-general)
MODEL=[ACTIVE][CHILD][INCMCC][ACTIVE*CHILD][CHILD*INCMCC
LIKELIHOOD RATIO χ2=0.00 (p=1.00) sample size=1549

Parameter	Variable	i=1(non-active)	i=2(active)
U^{ACTIVE}_{i} (p=0.0001)	Active	0.680476	-0.680476

Parameter	Variable	j=1(Have no child under high school)	j=2(have a child before high school)
U^{CHILD}_{j} (p=0.0001)	Children	-0.303915	0.303915

Parameter	Variable	k=1 (~4Million Yen)	k=2 (~7Million Yen)	k=3 (~10Million Yen)	k=4 (10MillionYen~)
U^{INCMCC}_{k} (p=0.0001)	Income Class	-0.036198	0.72619	0.10236	-0.792352

Parameter		i=1 (non-active)	i=2 (active)
$U^{ACTIVE,CHILD}_{i\ j}$ (p=0.0615)	j=1(no child b. H.S.)	0.728101	-0.728101
	j=2(have a child b. H.S.)	-0.728101	0.728101

Parameter		k=1 (~4Million Yen)	k=2 (~7Million Yen)	k=3 (~10Million Yen)	k=4 (10MillionYen~)
$U^{ACTIVE,INCMCC}_{i\ k}$ (p=0.0589)	i=1 (non-active)	0.150333	-0.001789	-0.133268	-0.015285
	i=2 (active)	-0.150333	0.001789	0.133268	0.015285

Parameter		k=1 (~4Million Yen)	k=2 (~7Million Yen)	k=3 (~10Million Yen)	k=4 (10MillionYen~)
$U^{INCMCC,CHILD}_{k\ j}$ (p=0.0006)	j=1(no child b. H.S.)	-0.121429	-0.152646	-0.048079	0.322154
	j=2(have a child b. H.S.)	0.121429	0.152646	0.048079	-0.322154

Parameter			k=1 (~4Million Yen)	k=2 (~7Million Yen)	k=3 (~10Million Yen)	k=4 (10MillionYen~)
$U^{ACTIVE,INCMCC,CHILD}_{i\ k\ j}$ (p=0.1542)	i=1 (non-active)	j=1(no child)	0.0834215	0.0371777	0.0681041	-0.1887033
		j=2(have a child)	-0.0834215	-0.0371777	-0.0681041	0.1887033
	i=2 (active)	j=1(no child)	-0.0834215	-0.0371777	-0.0681041	0.1887033
		j=2(have a child)	0.0834215	0.0371777	0.0681041	-0.1887033

Fig. 5: The Estimation of the Parameters from Log-Linear Model (Cluster 3)

4) Cluster 4

Income and child are the significant explanatory variables. The families whose income are upper 7 million Yen are more likely to be involved (see figure 6).

5) Cluster 5

Wife's occupation and child are the significant explanatory variables. The families whose children are before junior high school are more likely to be involved (see figure 7).

6) Cluster 6

Age of wife and child are the significant explanatory variables. The families whose children are pre-school age are more likely to be involved (see figure 8).

Cluster 4(white-color worker's family(manager class)) MODEL=[ACTIVE][INCMCC][CHILD][ACTIVE*CHILD][INCMCC*CHILD LIKELIHOOD RATIO(χ 2=5.95 (p=0.7452) sample size=301						
U^{ACTIVE}_i (*p=0.0001*)	Active	i=1(non-active)		i=2(active)		
		0.406126		-0.406126		
U^{INCMCC}_j (*p=0.0931*)	Income Class	j=1 (~7Million Yen)	j=2 (~10Million Yen)	j=3 (10Million Yen~)		
		-0.233539	-0.022408	0.255947		
U^{CHILD}_k (*p=0.0001*)	children	k=1 (No kids)	k=2 (baby)	k=3 (kinder garden)	k=4 (Elementary school)	k=5 (junior high & high school)
		1.32465	-1.30444	-0.814808	0.55993	0.234718
$U^{ACTIVE}_i{}^{INCMCC}_j$ (*p=0.0375*)		j=1 (~7Million Yen)	j=2 (~10Million Yen)	j=3 (10Million Yen~)		
	i=1(non-active)	0.177091	0.14318	-0.320271		
	i=2(active)	-0.203394	0.202072	0.320271		
$U^{CHILD}_k{}^{INCMCC}_j$ (*p=0.1705*)		k=1 (No kids)	k=2 (baby)	k=3 (kinder garden)	k=4 (Elementary school)	k=5 (junior high & high school)
	j=1 (~7Million Yen)	-0.241366	0.61335	0.0240025	0.0532582	-0.4492447
	j=2 (~10Million Yen)	-0.092494	-0.226389	0.0360154	-0.106579	0.1856965
	j=3 (10Million Yen ~)	0.33386	-0.386961	-0.0600179	0.0533208	0.2635482

Fig. 6: The Estimation of the Parameters from Log-Linear Model (Cluster 4)

Cluster 5 (merchant/domestic factory family) MODEL=[ACTIVE][CHJOB][CHILD][ACTIVE*CHJOB][ACTIVE*CHILD][CHILD*CHJOB] LIKELIHOOD RATIO $\chi 2$=8.22 (p=0.8292) sample size=531						
U^{ACTIVE}_{i} (*p=0.0001*)	Active	i=1 (non-active)		i=2 (active)		
		0.622634		-0.622634		
U^{CHJOB}_{k} (*p=0.0001*)	occupation of wife	j=1 (non)	j=2 (part-time)	j=3 (family business)	j=4 (full time job)	
		0.0724346	-0.353649	1.08562	-0.8044056	
U^{CHILD}_{k} (*p=0.0001*)	Children	k=1 (No kids)	k=2 (baby)	k=3 (kinder garden)	k=4 (Elementary school)	k=5 (junior high & high school)
		0.973026	-0.373465	-0.776801	0.698572	-0.52133
$U^{CHJOB}_{k}{}^{CHILD}_{k}$ (*p=0.0683*)		k=1 (No kids)	k=2 (baby)	k=3 (kinder garden)	k=4 (Elementary school)	k=5 (junior high & high school)
	j=1 (non)	-0.210477	0.768896	0.104789	-0.26989	-0.393318
	j=2 (part-time)	-0.049086	-0.120698	0.24319	-0.106171	0.032765
	j=3 (family business)	0.0585613	-0.061969	0.0566833	-0.063837	0.0105614
	j=4 (full time job)	0.2010017	-0.586229	-0.4046623	0.439898	0.3499916
$U^{ACTIVE}_{i}{}^{CHILD}_{k}$ (*p=0.0437*)		k=1 (No kids)	k=2 (baby)	k=3 (kinder garden)	k=4 (Elementary school)	k=5 (junior high & high school)
	i=1 (non-active)	0.210528	-0.085377	-0.25565	-0.073328	0.203827
	i=2 (active)	-0.210528	0.085377	0.25565	0.073328	-0.203827

Fig. 7: The Estimation of the Parameters from Log-Linear Model (Cluster 5)

Cluster 6 (Professions family(with kids)) MODEL=[ACTIVE][CHILD][HKAGE][ACTIVE*CHILD][CHILD*HKAGE] LIKELIHOOD RATIO $\chi 2$=2.87 (p=0.4121) sample size=178				
U^{ACTIVE}_{i} (p=0.0001)	Active	i=1 (non-active)	i=2 (active)	
		0.620979	-0.620979	
U^{CHILD}_{j} (p=0.0001)	Children	j=1 (Have no child under school)	j=2 (have a child before school)	
		-0.78101	0.78101	
U^{HKAGE}_{k} (p=0.0314)	housewife's age	k=1 (20～30)	k=2 (30～40)	k=3 (40～)
		-0.397939	0.298594	0.099345
$U^{ACTIVE,CHILD}_{i,j}$ (p=0.2752)		j=1 (Have no child under school)	j=2 (have a child before school)	
	i=1 (non-active)	0.158094	-0.158094	
	i=2 (active)	-0.158094	0.158094	
$U^{CHILD,HKAGE}_{j,k}$ (p=0.0943)		k=1 (20～30)	k=2 (30～40)	k=3 (40～)
	j=1 (Have no child under school)	0.284003	-0.285131	0.001128
	j=2 (have a child before school)	-0.284003	0.285131	-0.001128

Fig. 8: The Estimation of the Parameters from Log-Linear Model (Cluster 6)

6. Discussion

For most of clusters, the child is the one of the significant explanatory factors. There are several reasons considered why children play an important role in the decision to participate in environmental activities. The one is our definition of "environmental activities". Over 90% of respondents answered that they join "waste problems". This includes not only general waste problems, but also includes recycling.

Now in Japan, one of the main recycling bodies is the PTA (Parents and Teachers Association). To co-operate with recycling, the most easy way for those who have children is to take part in their school activities. This reason is for cluster 2, cluster 3, cluster 5.

The information that the wives seek is considered to be a weak but important reason, especially for young mothers. In cluster 6, wives who have (a) pre-school child(ren) are more likely to be involved in activities. They are relatively younger compared to other clusters. They are a relatively sensitive to environmental pollution and the related health problems. They seek information of what is safe for their children. They tend to join groups that give them this information.

As for other significant explanatory variables, the income class, age, occupation of wife are adopted. In cluster 3, this is the most major cluster, the person who belongs to the higher income class is more likely to participate in activities. But people who have no pre-school children are less likely to have no children, the person who belongs to high income class but has no pre-school children is less likely to do so.

In cluster 1, wives who are occupied in the "family business" are more likely to participate the activities. Other explanatory variables are not directly significant to participation.

In conclusion, the significant variables that affect wives' participation in environmental activities are children (whether they have children and the children go to school or not), income class (wives in the higher income class family are more likely to be involved), age, education, occupational situation. The latter three variables do not directly affected participation.

The cluster of white-worker's general class family (cluster 3) is also a major cluster of our survey, and we could not analyze whole sample at a time. But as they are central to our society, if we continue studying their behavior, we will be able to see analyze a major part of our society.

References

Cosslett, Stephen R.: Efficient Estimation of Discrete-Choice Models, in: *Manski, Charles F./ Daniel McFadden* (ed.): Structural Analysis of Discrete Data with Econometric Applications, The MIT Press, Cambridge, Massachusetts, 1981 (Fourth Printing 1990).

Diekmann, Andreas: Solving Social Dilemmas by Moral or Economic Incentives? Results of a Survey and Field Experiment of Responsible Environmental Behavior, presented at the 1992 annual meeting of the American Sociological Association, 1992.

Kabashima, Ikuo: Participation in Politics, Modern Politics Series, University of Tokyo Press, 1988, in Japanese.

Maddala, G.S.: Limited-dependent and qualitative variables in econometrics (Econometric Society Monographs 3), Cambridge University Press, 1983.

Manski, Charles F./Daniel McFadden (ed.): Structural Analysis of Discrete Data with Econometric Applications, The MIT Press, Cambridge, Massachusetts, 1981 (Fourth Printing 1990).

Matsuda, Noriyuki: The Multivariate Analysis for Qualitative Variables, ASAKURA publications, 1988, in Japanese.

Parsons, G.R./Mary Jo Kealy: Randomly Drawn Opportunity Sets in a Random Utility Model of Lake Recreation, Land Economics, Vol. 68, No. 1, February 1992.

SAS Institute Inc.: SAS/STAT User's Guide, Release 6.03 Edition, SAS Institute Inc., 1988, in Japanese by SAS Institute Japan.

Sherkat, Darken E./T. Jean Blocker: Environmental Activism in the Protest Generation: Differentiating Sixties Activists, presented at the 1991 annual meeting of the American Sociological Association, 1991.

Sherkat, Darken E./T. Jean Blocker: Protest and Alternation: Sixties Activities in Adulthood, presented at the 1992 annual meeting of the American Sociological Association, 1992.

Organizing for Environmental Management

Tamiki Kishida

I. Introduction

Since World War II many countries have made a great effort to increase their national production, and some countries have enjoyed economic growth in the 1950s and 1960s. As a necessary result environmental problems arose, primarily in the form of pollution or public nuisance. However environmental problems at those time were mitigated mainly because of the oil crises in the 1970s. In the 1980s, with the age of globalization accelerating the borderless and interdependent world economy, world-wide environmental problems were brought about which we need to deal with in order to sustain our only earth. Thus the trend of environmental problems can be divided into two stages. The first stage was the nation-wide pollution control. The second was the global level of environmental protection. In accordance with this macro trend in environmental problems, the shift of firms' responses was brought from population control to environmental management, and firms diversified their methods to cope with environmental problems.

My focus is on organizational and strategic features of environmental management. We can, for example, identify three strategies of environmental management. First is the internal measures within the respective firm, which in most cases is associated with cost reduction. Second is the so-called philanthropy which includes altruistic activities promoting the public interest in the community. The examples are birds protection, greening activities, formalization of holidays for voluntary activities. Third are the measures concerning the business proper. This means a trend toward the environmental protectionist firms and ecological business. In this paper, these trends are analyzed firstly in the macro perspective with reference to some research conducted in the 1970s and 1990s. Secondly, recent responses of six Japanese firms to environmental management of organizations are examined. Finally, some conclusions and implications of organizational adaptation to its environment are argued.

II. Macro characteristics of environmental management

The environmental characteristics of Japanese firms at the end of 1960s and early 1970s were as follows:
1. Japan's national territory was limited and population density was high.
2. Heavy and chemical industries were located intensively in the urban areas.
3. The financial basis of local governments was weak and social capital inadequate.

The investment of Japanese firms in pollution control was immature mainly because the cause-effect relationships of pollution were so vague, and the price mechanisms were so difficult to work that firms' incentives to invest in pollution control were weak. We conducted three research projects in 1971 concerning investment in pollution control.

The first research was done by the Ministry of International Trade and Industry (MITI) in 1971. Questionnaires were sent to all firms with more than 300 employees. The results were:
1. The investment of polluting industries (thermal power generation, steel, petroleum, petrochemical, mining, nonferrous metals, and paper manufacturing) was 107.5 billion yen (85%).
2. Of total investment the percentage for pollution control was 5,0% in 1969, and 5,8% in 1970.
3. The investment in air dominated (66,9%), second was in water pollution control (24,6%).

The second research was conducted also in 1971 by the Japan Development Bank. 384 main firms were involved, with whom the Bank carried out transactions.
1. The total amount of the investment for pollution control was 171.3 billion yen in 1970, and 274.1 billion yen in 1971.
2. The percentage of investment for pollution control was 4.7% in 1970, and 6.3% in 1971.
3. The investment for air pollution control was 27-28% in 1971.

Thirdly, the Long-term Credit Bank of Japan carried out research on 200 main transaction firms in 1971.
1. The investment for pollution control increased to 20.0% in 1971 as compared with that in 1970.
2. The percentage of investment to pollution control increased by 4,9% in 1970, and 5,8% in 1971.
3. The percentage of pollution control investment in polluting firms were 14,0% (oil refining), 8,6% (paper manufacturing), 8,3% (nonferrous

metals), 6,8% (steel), 6,5% (chemical), 4,1% (electricity) and 4,0 (petrochemical).

The above research showed that firms tried to manage the increase in cost due to investment in pollution control by rationalization and mark-ups. However there were few firms that planned to go abroad and begin local production as a means to avoid pollution.

With the ascent of the age of globalization, especially after G5 in which yen appreciation was admitted in 1985, Japanese firms developed their plant abroad.

The Keidanren (Federation of Economic Organizations) established a "Charter of Global Environment" in April 1991. In its introduction it is stated that we must resolve the world problems of poverty and population and maintain a global environment which allows sustainable development. It also recommends (1) formalization of the proper conditions of the environment and the annual internal audit, (2) mitigation of environmental pollution in every process of R & D, production, and marketing, (3) technological development for saving energies and resources, (4) transfer of pollution control technology, (5) minimizing the diffusion of pollution from accidents, (6) community activities, enlightenment, and PR on environmental protection, (7) the consideration of environmental conditions accompanied by the international development of business, (8) the contribution of firms to the national environmental policy.

Secondly, in 1991 the Japanese government also established the act of promoting the use of recycled resources and revised the act of disposal of industrial wastes. For example automobiles and electric appliances were registered as first level products that should be designed easy recycling and steel and aluminum cans were directed as second level products that must have labels showing the promotion of recycling.

Thirdly, the Environment Agency conducted research of the environmental protection of firms in 1991.

1. Questionnaires were sent to 2,080 firms and the number of respondents was 319.
2. Samples were on most part manufacturers (57,4%), retailers (9,7%), finance and insurance (8,5%), and construction (8,2%).
3. Concerning the state of the art of the environmental unit or department:
   (1) 64,6% of firms had already established environmental units. The larger the sales, the larger the rate of establishment of environmental units, and 74% of manufacturing firms and of retailers have already those environmental units, though only 30% of finance and insurance forms have them.

(2) The time of installation of those units was in the early 1970s (18,0%) and after 1990 (56,8%).
(3) Circumstances of installation: 47,1% built new organizational units for general environmental problems, 17,8% revised the former pollution control units in 1970.
(4) In 60% of the firms, top management was responsible to the units; president and board chairman (60,4%), chief manager (27,4%), and section chief (6,7%).
(5) The number of full time staff: less than three (39,4%), less than 10 (58,6%). The number of part-time staff: less than 10 (56,2%), 11-12 (14,4%).
(6) Goals and activities of those units were a) information collection (87,5%), b) employees enlightenment (75,5%), report to the executives (56,7%), referral of the employees' opinions (40%), PR(40%) and environmental audit (40%).
(7) Social contribution activities was conducted (69,0%). The contents of those activities were community activities (67,3%), support of the existing fund or association (40,9%) and campaign activities (24,1%). The larger the sales of the firm, the larger the social contribution activities. The rate of social contribution activities was 92% in the construction firm, followed by retailers, finance and insurance, and manufacturing.
(8) Concerning consideration of local environments when Japanese firms extended their businesses abroad: the rate of firms going abroad was 45,8%. Among them the rate of firms that were active in protecting the local environment was 65.8%. 91,1% observed local environmental regulations. 39,0% implemented environmental assessment, while 48,6% did not.
(9) The technology transfer abroad was implemented by 43,3% of firms and 87,6% dispatched some personnel.
(10) Internal system of environmental management: 32,6% put regulations in some statutory forms, 29,5% had more severe goals than the governmental regulations, 29,2% conducted an internal audit of environmental problems. 66,1% educated and enlightened on environmental protection within the firm. 52.0% exchanged some information with other firms in the same industry.
(11) The impact of environmental protection on the performance was evaluated positively (31,7%) and negatively (11,6%).

III. Environmental management of Japanese management

This chapter analyzes micro-level firm's responses to the environmental problems with special emphasis on the organizational units for environmental management.

1. Nissan Automobile Corporation

Nissan established the environmental energy office within the first department of technology in 1972. In 1990, the energy/safety technology department was built in order to examine the satisfaction of the standards and regulations. The traffic institute in 1991 and the environmental energy institute in 1992 were another two units that tackled environmental problems. These four units directly belong to the executive in charge.

In addition to these self-contained units, a variety of committee activities are laterally performed. Here, working groups are formed by topic, e.g. CFC, milage, and CO_2. These two types of activities are integrated through respective environmental action plans.

2. NEC Corporation

The most important target of environmental management in NEC is to integrate environmental protection activities into development in the sense that designers are responsible for waste from the stages of design, development, production, through to product disposal.

In 1970 the pollution control department was established and in 1974 the institute of pollution control technology was installed. These units have now been extended to the institute of resource/environment technology in 1980. Technology development and environmental businesses are tied as networks through the company-wide committee of environmental technology.

The departments of environmental management promote self-management and the preventive management of environmental problems without any responsibility for raising profit. Under these units two unique systems are implemented. One is a system of environmental audit, which consists of the general audit performed by the department of environmental management, the audit connected by each plant and the business audit implemented by each division. These activities are promoted as the company-wide Kaizen (improvement) activities. Another is the management of industrial wastes called ABCD disposal management. The person in charge of industrial wastes is selected with 3 for each plant. This person is to manage all the processes of collection, transportation, intermediate disposal and final disposal.

3. Fuji Photo Films Corporation

Fuji developed a disposable camera in 1986 and now has the 80% market share in this area. In 1987 Fuji revised the design for recycling, and introduced a recycling system in 1990. The rate of re-use is 70% in the case of the new product, which was named Ecoshot in 1992. Films are sent back to the recycle centers after developing, decomposed and classified as re-use products or recycling ones, metals and electric batteries are also re-used. The dismantling lines were designed by the very design unit that made this production line. The central unit for environmental management is the promotion department of environmental safety.

4. Kirin Brewery Corporation

In 1974 an environmental office was installed in order to save energy, and the department of social environment was established in 1991 to perform the role of the corporate citizen. This department, as a staff unit, supervises the environmental activities of all the Kirin corporate group members.

Whenever used empty bottles are collected, 5 yen per bottle is to be paid back, so that the rate of recovery amounts to 98%, and those bottles collected are all re-usable. The rate of recovery of aluminum cans is 42.5%. Kirin is searching for a more effective means of recovery. All the factories promote the activities of collecting empty used cans. Kirin also sends educational videos to high schools and local governments.

5. Fujita General Construction Corporation

General construction industry has destroyed the environment in that it has utilized 70% of total timber consumed. Fujita tackled with environmental businesses, environmental management, and social activities.

Fujita developed Athletics, Refuse & Parking System for ecological urban development. The garbage disposal plants were built under the park, a parking lot was made beside the park, and athletic facilities have been established on the park. The most important characteristic of this system is the non incineration of garbage. The global environmental office was installed in 1989 primarily to improve the corporate image and for reasons of risk aversion. This office belongs to the headquarter of technology and cooperates with the institute of technology. Furthermore interdepartmental activities are promoted by the project and the workshop.

6. Tokyo Electric Power Company

Tokyo Electric Company has 156 hydroelectric, 29 thermal and 3 nuclear power generation facilities. It sold 220 billion Kw/h in 1991. The pollution problem in the 1960s initiated the effort to cope with the environmental protection. The fuel committee was installed in 1962, followed by a variety of committees for pollution control, and the integrating section was established in 1968. In the last twenty years, the shift from pollution control to the environmental management has been conspicuous. For example, the headquarters of pollution control changed its name to the headquarter of environmental management.

The main organizations for environmental management are:

(1) Headquarter of Environmental Locations; this unit, as corporate staff, collects various information and discusses those measures. It also prepares memoranda between the company and the local government. The head is appointed by the managing director.

(2) Workshop for Global Environmental Problems; the main members are managers and assistant managers of the concerned departments. In this workshop, members exchange information and discuss company-wide measures. The sub-chief of the headquarter of Environmental Locations is concurrently the responsible person.

(3) Laboratory of Global Environment of Technological Development; all members have masters or doctoral degrees and the global warming mechanism and CO_2 removal technology are studied.

(4) Committee for Waste Disposal; members consist of section leaders, managers of the environmental departments, and managers and sub-managers of the concerned functional departments.

(5) CFC problem Working Group; This group belongs to Workshop for Global Environmental Problems. The chief is the section leader of environmental technology. Here the members study the real state of CFC usage and discuss the direction of measures.

IV. Summary and implications

In this article, we analyzed the macro trends of environmental management and introduced the micro organizational level treatments. Firstly, the shift from pollution control to environmental management was clearly observed with the rise of the age of globalization. Secondly, Japanese firms established independent units of environmental management to cope with the global environmental problems. Firms have diversified their strategies to cope with environmental problems.

Two implication are to be deserved. One is concerning the concept of environment. Generally, environment is considered as the limitation for the specified firm to cope with. Ecological approach often intends to preserve status quo of the environment, so that it may fix the environmental conditions. However firms must and can formulate strategies to define and deal with their respective environments. Therefore the specified environment must be enacted by the firm. It is important for us to consider the strategic role of the environment especially when we tackle sustainable development where the symbiosis between economy and ecology is inevitable.

Another is the organizational arrangement of environmental management. On the one hand it is important to establish independent units in order to deal with environmental problems outside the existing power relations. On the other hand, environmental units must be able to relate closely with the existing departments and divisions. Recently environmental management has been extended to the networks of corporate group and beyond. Personnel of environmental units of 22 Large American firms also formed GEMI (Global Environmental Management Initiative) to promote efficient global environmental problems in the world. Among the members are Digital Equipment, AT&T, and Apple.

References

R.A. Hopkinson, Corporate Organization for Pollution Control, The Conference Board, 1970.

The Environmental Agency, White Paper on Environment, 1990.

Morishita Ken, Environmental Management of Firms, NOMA, 1992.

Miyamoto Ken-ichi, Environment and Development, Iwanami, 1992

M. Redclift, Sustainable Development, Routledge, Chapman & Hall, 1987.

Designing Environmental Protection within Organizations in the Federal Republic of Germany - Concepts and Perspectives -

Hans-Josef Brink

1. The ecological dimension of organizational action

Organizations as social institutions help formal and informal constituents to pursue their interests. According to this perspective, organizational action has a direct or indirect means-ends relationship with those constituents' interests. Constituents' interests become concrete as a result of organizational goal setting within the formal statement of organizational objectives, but are also reflected in the individual preferences of internal and external constituents, if those constituents do not find their interests reflected in the organization's objectives. As the empirical research on goal setting has shown, constituents' interests are generally not uni-dimensional, which means that they are not limited exclusively to economical interests in terms of securing income permanently.

Organizational action fields and their possibilities of using organizational instruments are constrained by contextual conditions of different kinds. Those conditions are either given by external constituents and therefore externally determined or result from earlier organizational decision. Since the parameters are usually goals, conditions, or instruments, they can only be defined within a concrete decision making process or within a class of decision making processes. Thus, only conditional, but not unconditional statements ents or forecasts about the efficiency of organizational action are possible.

Since the decision parameters are not constant, the processes will become increasingly complex. The parameters develop in various ways, which means the decision paths cannot - or almost not - be forecasted. Academic research on the complexity of organizational action requires pluralistic, preference-oriented models, which lead to situational relativism of the supported results and the derived recommendations.

The critical discussion about leadership in organizations, especially in firms, has to be oriented towards the demands of the relevant constituents. This way, values and attitudes as well as the needs of those constituents can be expressed directly. Besides the economic dimension in terms of earning income and the disposition of scarce resources, today's organizations face more and more social and ecological demands. Hence, it is increasingly important that academics include social and ecological dimensions of organizational action in their research.

The discussion about the environment in various countries differs with respect to intensity. In the Federal Republic of Germany, this discussion started in 1970 and has gained impetus and scope ever since. Michael (1990) suggests five different periods of environmental dispute in Germany during this time span.

Contrary to environmental economics, business schools have only begun to develop models concerning the organizational protection of the environment and of environment management towards the end of the 70's. Scientific publications within the German literature emphasize several different aspects. Until the middle of the 80's, models of more or less technocratic character were developed. In these models, however, environmental protection is mainly seen as an expensive and legal restriction. Hence, organizational adaptation to the legal system and its actions is the main focus of these models. Since then, integrative and overlapping models of environmental protection have increased the scope of the old models or even replaced them.

In socio-cultural models, environmental protection is associated with the social responsibility of organizations. Strategic models stress environmental protection as competitive strength and, therefore, argue for strategic action of organizations. Evolutionary models, on the other hand, view environmental protection as an implicit part of the environment. In this context, the concept of sustainable development is often mentioned. Organizational survival and development is only possible, when ecological demands are met by organizations in addition to economic and social demands.

2. Organizational protection of the environment as an object of organizational design - foundation and concepts

Environmental protection has to be integrated on all levels and in all areas of management. The ecological dimension becomes part of the normative, strategic, and operational management. At the strategic and operational level, environmental protection has the character of a cross-cutting function. The strategic implementation of environmental protection consists of the following elements: (1) leadership including motivation and education, (2) organization, (3) management systems, especially information systems, communication, and controlling.

The integration of environmental protection within organizational action not only presumes an environmental consciousness of the decision makers, but also requires the institutionalization of the ecological concept regarding organizational control systems. The division of labor, communication, and coordination are elements of organizational design. They emphasize the view of the constituents. Space-time-regulations are structured within the context of organizational workflow. Due to their characteristics, these design tasks are part of the strategic management. They belong to the field of badly structured decision problems and are analyzed more detailed in the following pages.

In the middle of the discussion about the organizational design of environmental protection, you will find tasks associated with the perception of environmental protection. In Germany, the academic dispute of organizational requirements evolved around the creation and institutionalization of jobs specifically dealing with environmental protection programs. Examples of this stream of research can be found in Ullmann (1981) and Repenning (1988).

Over the last decade, structural implications of environmentally responsible behavior have become more and more important for organization theorists. Recent research focusses on the distribution of tasks related to environmental protection among the organizational units and on the creation of new units whose task is the scanning of the surrounding for new tasks regarding environmental protection. Furthermore, the coordination of activities related to environmental protection programs has found some academic attention. Empirical research by Antes, Steger, and Tiebler (1991) pointed to a broad spectrum of organizational change due to environmental protection programs. For most of those organizations, legal necessities, higher efficiency of managing environmental protection, and a better image among the constituents were crucial factors. Motivation and the identification of personnel with the organization were also shown to be stimuli in the reorganization process.

Designing organizational environmental protection consists of the integration of environmental protection programs into the existing structure of the organization, which implies questions of deciding where and on which level of the hierarchy managing environmental protection is located. The organizational design of environmental protection deals mainly with the question, how the area of environmental protection itself should be structured. The formal structure of organizational design tasks in the instrumental perspective of organizations can be aimed at elements or processes. The following considerations are based on the first view. Hence, objectives, conditions, and instruments are of interest for designing organizational environmental protection.

According to this instrumental perspective of organizations, tasks, which follow organizational rules concerning the constituency, time, and space, are known. They are defined by earlier decisions of the organization or by the external constituency regarding kind, scope, and time. Because of that, a list of tasks has to be made, before environmental protection can de designed. This list reflects the scope of understanding environmental protection. The following are examples of organizational tasks regarding environmental protection: (1) use, maintenance and repair of installations to protect the environment, (2) measuring and control systems, (3) research on, development of, and experimentation with direct or indirect installations, (4) administrative aspects of environmental protection, and (5) education and development of personnel dealing with environmental tasks. External tasks are a result of current legal developments regarding products and processes and of the fulfillment of legal duties.

Of course, such a list of environmental tasks may be broad or narrow in its scope. It is mainly determined by the principal environmental policy of the organization and its resulting base strategy. An active environmental policy of an organization is exacting higher demands of the organizational structure than a passive policy.

The conditions for the organizational design of environmental programs can be classified in terms of (1) origin and (2) validity. The contextual conditions are based on different sources and causes. Legislators at the national and the supra-national (EC) level who are represented by various boards of control and the jurisdiction already place high claims on organizations' environmental protection, at both the strategic and the operational level. Environmental groups who represent the public, as well as the media and pressure groups try to carry their point directly or by indirect means to the organizations.

The state and its policy, trade unions, trade associations, insurance companies, financial groups, customers, and suppliers are more or less interested in the environmental programs of organizations nowadays, especially those which affect the organization itself. In the concrete case of designing the organization, however, difficulties arise which center around operationalizing and forecasting the kind and intensity of influence which is exerted by the constituents. In addition, interests often contradict one another which suggests that organizations aim at specific forms of conflict management as well.

Exemplary with respect to legal design requirements are the functions of the environmental liaison according to Bundes-Immissionsschutzgesetz, Wasserhaushaltsgesetz, and Abfallgesetz: (1) internal control systems, (2) education of personnel, (3) annual reports, (4) development and implementation of environmentally friendly products and processes, and (5) comments about investment decisions. These laws represent the minimal standards for the organizational design of environmental protection.

The characteristics of internal conditions regarding the design take into account the location, the organization's mission, the objectives, the existing structure, and the technology, as well as the motivation and the qualification of the personnel for environmental protection programs.

The objectives of designing organizations with respect to environmental protection programs consist of two parts. The first part deals with directly resulting goals. Rules are supposed to avoid, to lessen, or to eliminate environmental harm. The second part is built by sub-goals, which are based on the subsystems [hierarchical order] of the organization. Goals have to be deduced from the organizational objectives. The choice among suggestions for the implementation of different rules is not only determined by factual, but also by economic and social goals. One might think of examples such as the reduction of complexity, the relief of high-level managers, higher quality of decisions concerning the environment, and the motivation of personnel.

General organizational instruments such as the division of labor and coordination can be used for the concrete design of environmental protection within an organization. This paper will look at the following instruments in more detail: (1) centralization and decentralization of environmental tasks horizontally and vertically and (2) coordination of activities within the organization as well as of those between the organization and its external constituency.

Two basic concepts of organizational design concerning environmental protection have to be differentiated: (1) integration of ecological tasks into the existing structure and (2) the additive-functional organization of environmental protection.

The integrative model connects environmental tasks directly with the existing organizational units. The job descriptions within those units are explicitly enriched and enlarged by the ecological tasks, no additional organizational units are created. Low specialization and high decentralization are the main characteristics of this model. This differs from the additive-functional solution. In the latter model new specific units are created, who become responsible for ecological tasks. High ecological specialization within those units and accordingly high centralization are determinants of this model. The concept of the ecological liaison directly follows this second model of an additive-functional design.

Once one has decided to use the additive or central solution, the hierarchical integration of the newly formed units has to be determined. Since environmental protection has become part of the higher management tasks, the organization should aim at locating the new units near the strategic apex. Currently newly created units are not only located among the staff, but also increasingly in the central areas of the organization. Interesting is the concept of an ecology center. Well proven solutions in other areas of management such as work teams and quality circles may also be successful design solutions.

The cross-cutting function of environmental protection creates a nigh need for coordination, which has to be met with organizational instruments. Panels, conferences, and committees represent efficient instruments concerning environmental protection. They can be located at different levels of the organizational hierarchy.

3. Organizing environmental protection in German firms

According to the situational paradigm, concrete goals and conditions determine the organizational solutions and its efficiency. From this perspective differing solutions in different organizations are easily understood. At this point, I want to draw your attention to the cases of Bayer AG and Siemens AG so that you can see how these companies organize environmental protection. Due to their specific enterprises they face distinct problems of environmental harm, which are reflected in the differences of their organizational structures.

Looking at Bayer AG you will find that ecological units are represented at all levels of hierarchy. At the top level, environmental protection is planned in a special executive committee which also plans occupational safety. In addition, central commissions exist. At the next level, each of the six areas employs one manager dealing with ecological questions, who is responsible for the coordination of environment protective activities in his or her division. Most of these divisions are organized as profit centers. Furthermore, one of the five central areas not only takes care of works administration and occupational safety, but also of central execution, control, and advice concerning environmental protection. This unit connects operations and information groups. Each works has an environmental liaison, who is vertically connected with the headquarters. The ecological unit of Bayer AG has more than 1000 employees with different rights to give orders.

Siemens AG has a very broad product line which offers a more differentiated structure with respect to environmental protection. The divisional structure of Siemens AG leads to a decentralized fulfillment of ecological duties. Contrary to Bayer AG, new tasks are delegated to already existing units. Responsibility and area of competence are strictly separated from each other. The ecological unit, which is located within the production and logistics function, mainly fulfills staff functions and gives advice to the executive board. Liaisons in all 15 divisions and the five central functions are coordinated and harmonized in this unit. The liaisons in these divisions have mostly support roles as well. The employment of more than 250 employees working in the area of environmental protection is more than 4 times bigger than legally required. In addition to these staff jobs, Siemens AG also has about 50 work teams which make suggestions regarding environmental protection programs and other organizational problems.

4. Perspectives for the further development of organizational environmental protection and organizational importance

The discussion about environmental protection, which has started in the 1970's, will continue and even increase in its importance in Germany. Recent events in the chemical industry have shown this point with all clearness. In the long run, concerns within organizations will increase rather than decrease. Examples of current consideration include: (1) draft of an environmental law code (2) introduction of environment liability. The standardization and summarization of rules and regulations concerning environmental protection which can be found in various laws led to the draft of an environmental law code. While the procedure itself is discussed controversially, some of its suggestions are very interesting. For example, the concept of an environment director is introduced and environment protecting organizing developed in detail. Recommendations for the design of organizations are given which will influence decision making in organizations heavily in the future. The introduction of environment liability will lead to similar situations as those concerning product liability. When organizations are required to show that they do not harm the environment, consequences in several areas can be expected. Accounting, insurance policies, and organizational structure have to be questioned with respect to these new conditions and partly to be changed as a consequence.

The relationship between management and environmental protection will remain tense. Structural and economic difficulties which German organizations face and are going to face in the future, influences the importance of organizational environmental protection. Looking at the concept of lean management, which is mainly reflected in rigid cost management, one will notice that the tension between economy and ecology will not decrease but increase. Organizational action might help to ease this tension, but will not be able to eliminate it.

References

Antes, R./Steger, U./Tiebler, P.: Umweltorientiertes Unternehmensverhalten - Ergebnisse aus einem Forschungsprojekt, in: *Steger, U.* (ed.): Handbuch des Umweltmanagements, München 1992, p. 375-393

Breuer, R.: Empfiehlt es sich, ein Umweltgesetzbuch zu schaffen, gegebenenfalls mit welchen Regelungsbereichen?, München 1992

Brink, H.-J.: Umweltschutz, Planung des, in: Handwörterbuch der Planung, Stuttgart 1989, col. 2044 - 2052

Dorn, D.: Betrieblicher Umweltschutz in einem Großunternehmen. Das Beispiel Siemens AG, in: zfo 1989, p. 89 - 93

Freimann, J. (ed.): Ökologische Herausforderungen der Betriebswirtschaftslehre, Wiesbaden 1990

Frese, E./Kloock, J.: Internes Rechnungswesen und Organisation aus der Sicht des Umweltschutzes, in: BFuP 1989, p. 1 - 29

Gorges, H.A.: Organisation im Umweltschutz, in: Handbuch des Umweltschutzes, München 1977, p. 1 - 13

Hopfenbeck, W.: Umweltorientiertes Management und Marketing, Landsberg/Lech 1990

Johann, H.P.: Umweltschutz in Klein- und Mittelbetrieben, in: Angewandte Arbeitswissenschaft 1991, p. 20 - 37

Klemmer, P.: Umweltschutz und Wirtschaftlichkeit. Grenzen der Belastbarkeit der Unternehmen, Berlin 1990

Malle, K.-G.: Organisation des Umweltschutzes bei der BASF AG, in: zfo 1989, p. 94 - 100

Meffert, H./Kirchgeorg, M.: Marktorientiertes Umweltmanagement, 2nd ed., Stuttgart 1993

Meuser, Th.: Umweltschutz und Unternehmensführung, Wiesbaden 1993

Michael, B.M.: Wenn der Rückschritt plötzlich zum Fortschritt wird, in: Horizont, 1990, No. 46, p. 38

Nitze, A.: Die organisatorische Umsetzung einer ökologisch bewußten Unternehmensführung, Bern-Stuttgart 1991

Repenning, K.: Der Umweltschutzbeauftragte - Umweltgewissen des Unternehmens, in: Umweltmagazin 1988, p. 68 - 71

Repenning, K.: Zur Stellung des Betriebsbeauftragten für Umweltschutz in der betrieblichen Organisation. Umweltschutz bei der Deutschen BP AG, in: zfo 1989, p. 118 - 122

Schulz, W./Wicke, L.: Organisation des Umweltschutzes im Betrieb, in: RKW-Handbuch Führungstechnik und Organisation, Berlin 1989, p. 1 - 80

Seidel, E.: Zur Organisation des betrieblichen Umweltschutzes, in: zfo 1990, p. 334 - 341

Seidel, E./Strebel, H. (ed.): Umwelt und Ökonomie, Wiesbaden 1991

Steger, U. (ed.): Handbuch des Umweltmanagements, München 1992

Ullmann, A.A.: Der Betriebsbeauftragte für Umweltschutz aus betriebswirtschaftlicher Perspektive: Umweltpolitische Notwendigkeit oder gesetzgeberischer Perfektionismus?, in zfbf 1981, p. 992 - 1013

Information Systems for Waste Disposal Management

Kirsten Meyer/Franz Schober/Marcus Siefert

1. Introduction

Few subjects are as controversially discussed as the (supposed) conflict between ecology and economy. Depending on the time horizon of a decision-maker ecological and economic goals are either conflicting or complementary. A reactive compliance with legal standards and the consideration of ecological measures as cost factors lead to the former, a strategic attitude that combines ecological achievements with long-term economic performance leads to the latter perception of these two goals[1].

An ecologically particularly sensitive field is the disposal of residuals from industrial production processes. Private enterprises as well as public research facilities face this problem under the advent of increasingly restrictive legal requirements and growing public concern in addition to the increasing scarcity of deposits and processing sites for chemical waste. Continuously rising costs for chemical waste disposal demand extended usability of the materials in the production or research process before final disposal, in other words recycling.

Reuse of chemical materials can be improved only through the application of efficient information systems and techniques. The potential users of such a system need reliable information about the volume and composition of the recycled materials as well as ready access to that information. This is a typical situation where the institution of an electronic market[2] for chemicals would be of use both to the supply (emergence of chemical residuals)

---

[1] *Hansen, U.:* Die ökologische Herausforderung als Prüfstein ethisch verantwortungsvollen Unternehmerhandelns (the ecological challenge as a touchstone for ethically responsible corporate decision-making). In: *Wagner, G.R.* (ed.): Ökonomische Risiken und Umweltschutz (economic risks and environment protection), München 1992, p. 114-118.

[2] *Schmid, B.* et.al.: Die elektronische Revolution der Märkte (the electronic revolution of the markets). In: IO-Management-Zeitschrift 60 (1991) No. 12, p. 96-98.

and the demand side (input of chemicals) of such materials (see Fig.1). Such a market could focus on transactions either within one single enterprise or even across enterprises.

This paper deals in chapter 2 with waste disposal management in more general terms, and defines the requirements an information system has to meet in order to support the efficient reuse of chemical waste. Chapter 3 specifically describes such an information system. It has been jointly designed by the department of information systems and several departments of the natural sciences at the university of Freiburg to support the recycling of chemical materials[3].

2. Waste disposal management

2.1. Goals and tasks of waste disposal management

An industrial enterprise may be interpreted as a unit that uses energy and material input from its environment and transforms it into energetic/material output.

Production of goods usually is managed with the classic logistic chain consisting of the three functions procurement, manufacturing and market distribution. However, this chain manages only part of the transformation process and its outcome includes energy and materials, which are not marketable in conventional terms (waste). According to thermodynamic laws, total energetic/material input of a production process always equals total energetic/material output[4]. If the waste part of this equation is not handled properly, the transformation process will lead to an unfavorable increase of entropy, i.e. in the level of not reusable energetic/material resources. Therefore, in order to meet nature's needs, waste disposal management has to be added to the logistic chain to strive for a reduction of emissions into the natural environment, i.e. reduce the rate of entropy increase.

---

[3] *Siefert, M.:* Konzeption eines Informationssystems für die Wertstoffbörse der Universität Freiburg (concept of an information system for the "Wertstoffbörse" at the university of Freiburg). Master thesis at the Faculty of Economics, University of Freiburg 1992.

[4] *Apitz, K./Gege, M.:* Was Manager von der Blattlaus lernen können (what managers could learn from the plant-louse), Wiesbaden 1990, p. 17; Matschke, M.J., Lemser, B.: Entsorgung als betriebliche Grundfunktion (waste disposal as a fundamental business function). In: BFuP 45 (1992) No. 2, p. 85ff.

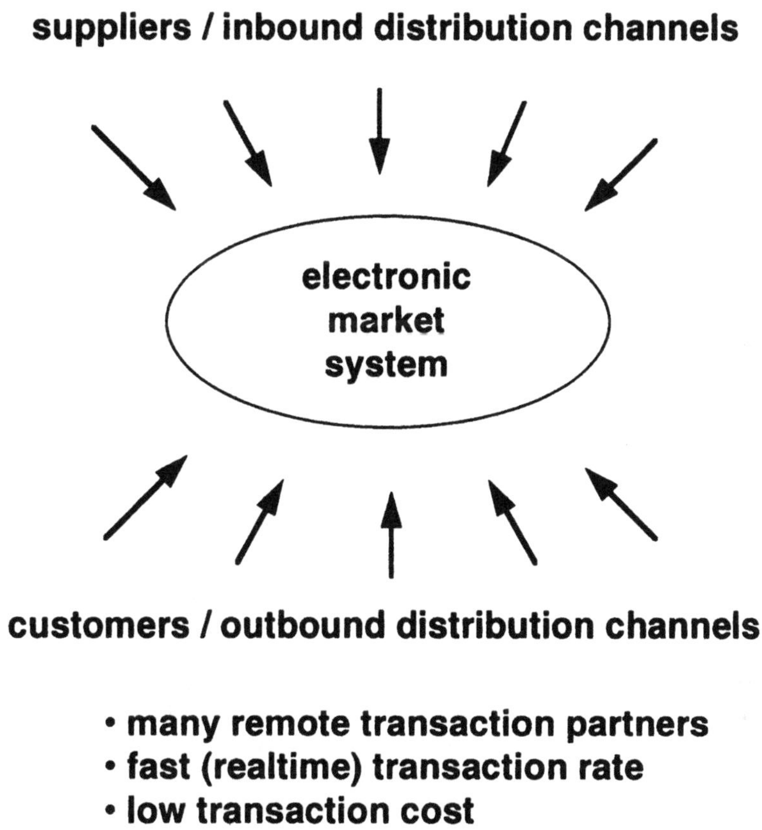

Fig. 1: Electronic market system

The main ecologically motivated objective of waste disposal management can therefore be seen to be a prolonged circulation of materials in the production process[5] in order to relieve the natural system from excessive anthropogenous immission. This objective has also been recently implemented in the amendment of German law for waste disposal that calls for avoidance or at least reuse of waste materials before final disposal [§1a AbfG][6].

This very long-term and general objective of lower entropy combines ecological and economic aspects. In the short-run, however, ecological and economic goals may conflict. Therefore trade-offs have to be made: too high a consideration of ecology (ecological "leader" strategy) may drastically increase cost, too little consideration ("laggard" strategy) may decrease market share. In both cases, the result is a loss of competitiveness. The right balance is a matter of business strategy (see Fig.2).

Accordingly the main tasks of waste disposal management include the treatment of "unwanted" by-products that emerge mainly in the manufacturing process, such as toxic or radioactive residuals (see Fig.3). But also non-toxic residuals are unwanted because they use up scarce land for deposit. The term "unwanted" by-products suggests that they are of no value. This is not always true, since production residuals can mostly be recycled into valuable materials and thus be reintroduced into the process or sold to other enterprises with profit. Or even better, materials with unwanted side effects can be substituted by better alternatives. If no longer recyclable, materials can be treated by thermic or other means to reduce the final volume for deposit.

In order to fulfill these tasks efficiently, waste disposal management needs permanent analysis and evaluation of all existing material flows under several aspects: amount, type, ecological relevance, time and place of occurrence, processing possibilities and capacities for reuse, disposal cost, potential revenues in case of sale, redesign of the production process[7].

---

[5] *Schreiner, M.:* Umweltmanagement in 22 Lektionen (environmental management in 22 lessons). 3rd ed., Wiesbaden 1993, p. 57ff.

[6] *Sondermann, W.D.:* Umweltgesetze und Umwelthaftung in der Praxis (environmental laws and environmental liability in practice). In: *Sietz, M.* (ed.): Umweltbewußtes Management (ecology-oriented management), Taunusstein 1992, p. 36ff.

[7] *Wehking, K.H./Sommer, M.:* Entsorgung: neues Logistik-Problemfeld (waste disposal management: new problem area in logistics). In: IO-Management-Zeitschrift 58 (1989) No. 7/8, p. 47ff.

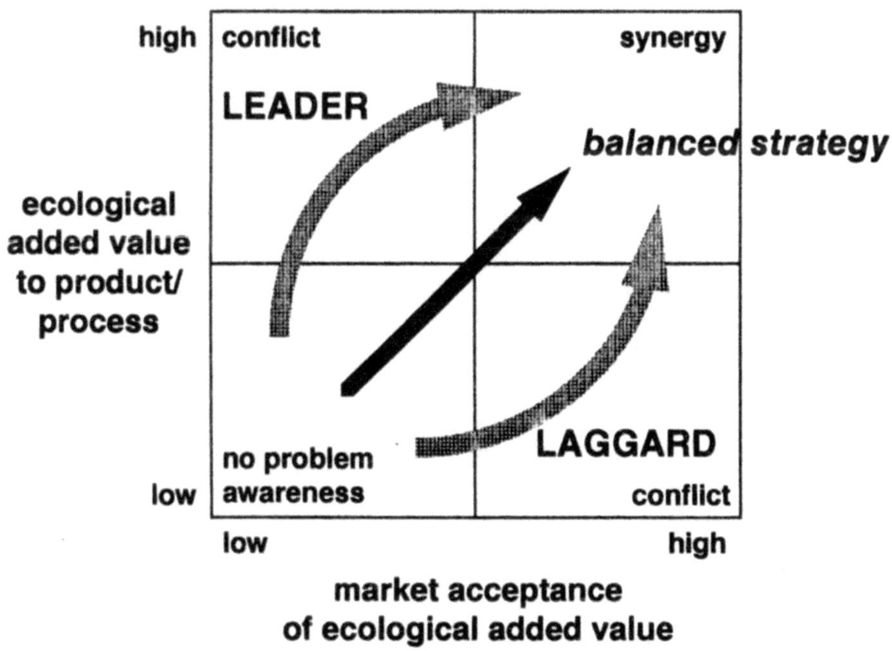

Fig. 2: Ecological versus economic goals

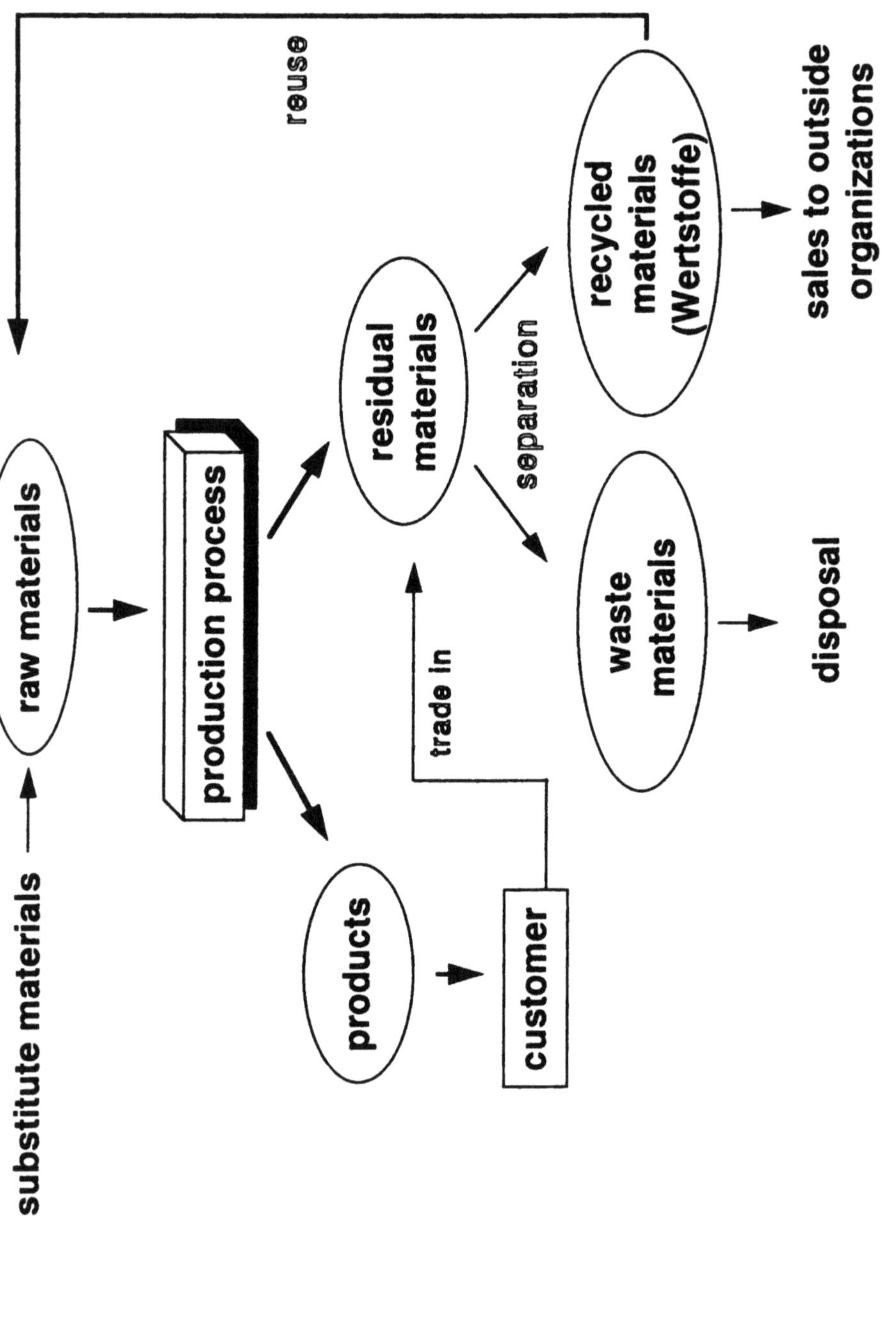

Fig. 3: Tasks of waste disposal management

2.2. Information systems requirements for waste disposal management

Information systems for waste disposal management show several characteristics that distinguish them from other information systems and make them hard to design and implement. Information on residual materials and their environmental compatibility are characterized by complex and dynamic factors as well as extremely long-term and uncertain impacts.

Problems start with the classification of residual materials, because these materials often appear in form of mixtures, which are difficult to describe and classify in informational terms without intensive preprocessing of the materials. Secondly, the ecological impact of many materials is not yet precisely known. The toxicity of a specific chemical depends not only on the chemical itself, but also on its concentration in the environment, along with the concentration of other chemicals and complicated systemic interactions. Furthermore, the dynamic aspects of emissions and immissions have to be considered. In some situations ecological problems will be coped with by nature in a self-regulating fashion, in other situations damage can be observed only after a long lead time. The number of impacting variables and data is often immense. Large, good explanatory models have yet to be developed, though progress in this area of scientific modelling and simulation is evident[8]. In the meantime auxiliary indicators and tolerance limits have to be used as rules of thumb.

In order to accomplish effective waste management additional internal and external information sources must be retrieved[9]. These include legal regulations for emission levels, storage, transport, disposal of chemicals, internal guidelines, etc.

Internal safety guidelines cover subjects such as storage and handling of dangerous materials and required behavior in fire emergencies and accidents. Since the guidelines can be quite long and numerous, good structuring and easy access within an integrated information system can enhance the compliance with guidelines which otherwise would have hardly be noticed. Other sources of vital information on potential waste materials are the bill of

---

[8] *Hälker, M./Jaeschke, A.* (ed.): Informatik für den Umweltschutz (computer science for environmental protection), Berlin u.a. 1992.

[9] *Pfohl, H.-C./Stölzle, W.:* Das Informationssystem der Entsorgungslogistik - Bericht aus einem Forschungsprojekt (the information system for waste disposal logistics - report from a research project). In: *Wagner, G.R.* (ed.): Ökonomische Risiken und Umweltschutz (economic risks and environment protection), München 1992, p. 194ff.

material and other data processed in computerized production planning and control systems.

External, publicly accessible information sources are databases such as AWIDAT, a commercial database provided by the Federal Environmental Office with information on waste suppliers, waste processing technologies, and waste processing companies[10]. Further valuable sources are publications of research institutes on new methods of waste treatment. The stock exchange market on chemical waste organized by the regional branches of the German Chamber of Industry and Commerce is another helpful source of information. Enterprises that cannot recycle their residuals themselves may advertise their materials free of charge in a monthly newsletter of the Chamber[11]. The Association of the German Chemical Industry offers a similar service. On the European level the introduction of an "European Waste Data Bank" is planned[12].

The concept of stock exchange markets for chemical residuals needs further consideration. This is an ideal instrument to enhance the interindustrial reuse of chemical materials. In this way the required circulation of materials can be drastically enhanced. The efficiency of transactions on this market can be even more improved by an electronic market system. With the implementation of intelligent search and retrieval routines supply and demand can thus be matched almost instantaneously. This results in a decrease in transaction costs due to the acceleration of market processes.

Such an electronic market system has to comply with certain requirements to ensure the high interactivity necessary for spontaneous market transactions[13]:

- common market terminology, i.e. standardized formats of market data exchange (analogous to EAN or EDIFACT in warehouse systems),
- compatible communication channels for data exchange,
- system services for the mediation of market partners,

---

[10] *Pfohl, H.-C./Stölzle, W.:* Das Informationssystem der Entsorgungslogistik - Bericht aus einem Forschungsprojekt (the information system for waste disposal logistics - report from a research project). In: *Wagner, G.R.* (ed.): Ökonomische Risiken und Umweltschutz (economic risks and environment protection), München 1992, p. 195.

[11] *Frank, W.:* Die Abfallwirtschaft als Teil der Rohstoffwirtschaft (waste management as part of materials management), Stuttgart 1990, p. 37.

[12] *Michels, B.:* Abfallmanagement (waste disposal management). In: *Sietz, M.* (ed.): Umweltbewußtes Management (ecology-oriented management), Taunusstein 1992, p. 177.

[13] *Schmid, B. et.al.:* Die elektronische Revolution der Märkte (the electronic revolution of the markets). In: IO-Management-Zeitschrift 60 (1991) No. 12, p. 97f.

- front-end software applications for the system users.

Electronic markets can also be set up within a single organization to substitute external market transactions. One obvious example is the support of material recycling by the system as an alternative to the purchase of new materials. Electronic markets are needed in situations where many members in the organization qualify as market actors. This is also the case in the application at the university of Freiburg described below.

3. An electronic market system for chemical materials at the University of Freiburg

Before discussing the system itself, a brief outline of the lifecycle of chemical materials at the university will be helpful (see Fig.4). Several independent research departments make use of chemical materials: chemistry, pharmacology, biology, geoscience, forestry, physics, medical sciences including the university hospitals. In the past some coordination of purchase order activities has been established to ensure favorable price conditions. However, little coordination was exerted for the disposal of materials no longer needed, resulting in a high volume of final deposit. Unlike in industrial production, where only a part of the input material turns into chemical by-products, in a research environment all chemical inputs ultimately become waste.

In recent years purchase order activities have been partly centralised, as well as first experiences made with waste recycling and disposal management. The latter responsibility has been assigned to the "Wertstoffbörse" (stock market for materials), an organization dedicated to the recycling of chemical materials across research institutes. The specific tasks of the "Wertstoffbörse" include:

a) the acceptance of residual materials no longer used in the current research process (sometimes even in unopened and unused containers)
b) the analysis of residual materials,
c) the classification and evaluation of residual materials in respect of purity, toxicity, radioactivity, etc.,
d) the processing of residuals before recycling (if required) and the storage of residuals,
e) the listing of offers in the same way as for order lists of outside suppliers in order to allow for direct comparison of quality, and distribution of the lists to potential users
f) the physical delivery of the ordered recycled materials,
g) the support of the users in the correct handling of chemical materials,

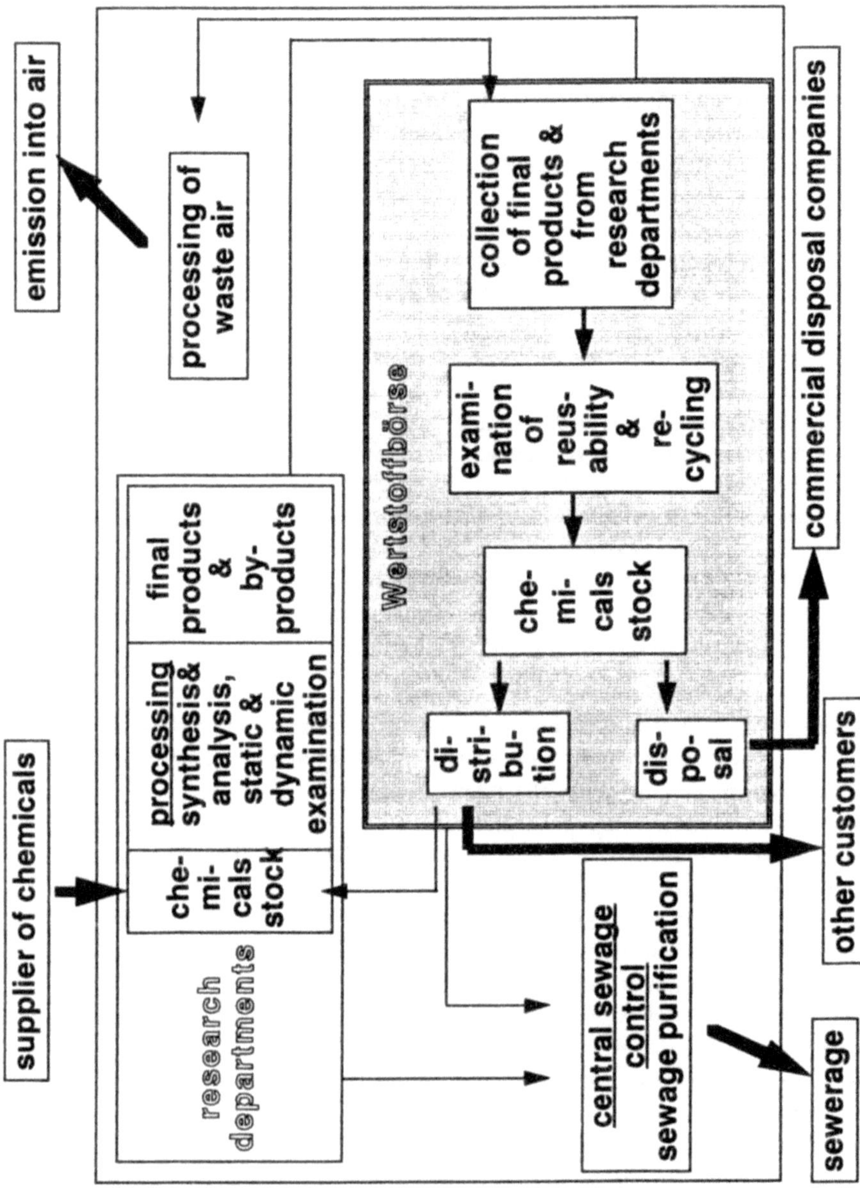

Fig. 4: Chemical materials life-cycle at the University of Freiburg

h) the disposal of materials according to legal requirements, that cannot be further recycled. This may include further preprocessing before disposal, e.g. phlegmatizing of highly reactive substances.

In order to support the numerous tasks of the "Wertstoffbörse" the design of an electronic market system has been decided.

Since the "Wertstoffbörse" is fairly new and still in flux the system design and implementation had to meet certain requirements such as being open and flexible enough to make later modifications easy. Furthermore, the currently installed computer and network infrastructure at the university had to be taken into consideration. This lead to the following system objectives:

- reintegration of some already existing, but less sophisticated applications for the management of chemical materials and the avoidance of isolated applications in the future,
- support of a multi-user environment in a technically heterogenous infrastructure,
- system expansibility,
- compliance with current and expected standards, especially in the field of communication (e.g. ISO/OSI standards).

The core of the system consists of a relational database (ORACLE) storing all required information. The database will be centrally installed on a dedicated workstation under UNIX, which acts as a database server for the user stations (clients). This client-server architecture offers the best solution facing the current computer and network infrastructure, which is mainly based on personal computers (PC) and smaller workstations (WS), either stand-alone or connected within a local area network (Ethernet or Token Ring). Front-end applications that make use of the data delivered by the server will be installed on the user's PC or WS. Some users are already linked to a fast 10MB/sec. local network currently under construction, others are connected to the slower X.25 network which still serves as the main communication vehicle on the campus.

Once this system is fully operational, it is expected that the circulation of chemical materials among the university research departments will be substantially increased due to better transparency of the internal chemicals market. This will lead to the environmentally desirable reduction of chemical disposal as well as to the economically desirable reduction in purchasing costs for new chemical materials.

4. Conclusion

Ecological activities in organizations are motivated by both public and private objectives. On the one hand, it can no longer be tolerated that the bulk of environmental cost be covered by the tax-payer; these should be charged to the producer. On the other hand, ecological leadership may also pay-off economically in the long run. This point is certainly valid in the case of waste disposal management. In the future, sensitive waste deposits will be challenged by increasingly sensitive public attention, increasingly restrictive legislation, and increasingly high costs. Therefore, organizations are well advised to invest in technology and systems for reduction or even better, avoid sensitive waste disposal. One example is investment in information systems for waste disposal management.

The ultimate judgement of the ecological benefits is certainly beyond the competence of economists and information engineers. However it is within their realm to propose and design systems which enhance organizational effectiveness in relation to any given objective. If the objective is the awareness of nature's needs, then waste disposal management systems and information systems such as the one presented should help.

References

Apitz, K./Gege, M.: Was Manager von der Blattlaus lernen können (what managers could learn from the plant-louse), Wiesbaden 1990

Frank, W.: Die Abfallwirtschaft als Teil der Rohstoffwirtschaft (waste management as part of materials management), Stuttgart 1990

Hälker, M./Jaeschke, A. (ed.): Informatik für den Umweltschutz (computer science for environmental protection), Berlin u.a. 1992

Hansen, U.: Die ökologische Herausforderung als Prüfstein ethisch verantwortungsvollen Unternehmerhandelns (the ecological challenge as a touchstone for ethically responsible corporate decision-making). In: *Wagner, G.R.* (ed.): Ökonomische Risiken und Umweltschutz (economic risks and environment protection), München 1992, p. 109-128

Matschke, M.J./Lemser, B.: Entsorgung als betriebliche Grundfunktion (waste disposal as a fundamental business function). In: BFuP 45 (1992) Nr.2, p. 85-101

Michels, B.: Abfallmanagement (waste disposal management). In: *Sietz, M.* (ed.): Umweltbewußtes Management (ecology-oriented management), Taunusstein 1992, p. 171-182

Pfohl, H.-C., Stölzle, W.: Das Informationssystem der Entsorgungslogistik - Bericht aus einem Forschungsprojekt (the information system for waste disposal logistics - report from a research project). In: *Wagner, G.R.* (ed.): Ökonomische Risiken und Umweltschutz (economic risks and environment protection), München 1992, p. 184-226

Schmid, B. et.al.: Die elektronische Revolution der Märkte (the electronic revolution of the markets). In: IO-Management-Zeitschrift 60 (1991) No. 12, p. 96-98

Schreiner, M.: Umweltmanagement in 22 Lektionen (environmental management in 22 lessons), 3rd ed., Wiesbaden 1993

Siefert, M.: Konzeption eines Informationssystems für die Wertstoffbörse der Universität Freiburg (concept of an information system for the "Wertstoffbörse" at the university of Freiburg). Master thesis at the Faculty of Economics, University of Freiburg 1992

Sietz, M. (ed.): Umweltbewußtes Management (ecology-oriented management), Taunusstein 1992

Sondermann, W.D.: Umweltgesetze und Umwelthaftung in der Praxis (environmental laws and environmental liability in practice). In: *Sietz, M.* (ed.): Umweltbewußtes Management (ecology-oriented management), Taunusstein 1992, p. 27-60

Wagner, G.R. (ed.): Ökonomische Risiken und Umweltschutz (economic risks and environment protection), München 1992

Wehking, K.H., Sommer, M.: Entsorgung: neues Logistik-Problemfeld (waste disposal management: new problem area in logistics). In: IO-Management-Zeitschrift 58 (1989) Nr.7/8, p. 45-48

Information Technology and Traffic Issues
- Shifting the Point of View -

Günter Müller/Thomas Hummel/Detlef Schoder/
Frank Stoll/Ralf Strauß

1. Introduction

Cultural and social tendencies such as the rising "leisure culture" have lead to an increasing amount of auto traffic, the increase in vacation travel, whether for fun or recuperation, and the international division of labor.

At the same time, it was recognized that the extension of traffic systems and the quality of traffic services have a considerable influence on the quality, functioning and efficiency of a modern economy. Increased auto traffic has lead to strong growth of traffic services, along with the emergence of ecologically related problems. The environmental burden of auto traffic has become an intensively discussed topic in the wake of increased sensitivity in society.

Although the ecological costs of traffic growth have been recognized, up to now solutions have rarely existed with regard to the reduction of environmental burden.

Information technology (abbreviated IT) is expected to provide potential solutions that avoid environmental problems caused by traffic. Experience with the use of technology has shown again and again the limitation of existing approaches in the reduction of ecological damage. Obviously it is not just enough to use technology. It is more important to use technology effectively.

In order to reach a noticeable reduction of traffic related environmental effects, a plea for a new point of view is given, which takes into account social and economic factors, i.e. mobility patterns and acceptance towards the use of IT.

2. Potential for solutions of traffic problems through IT and their conventional implementation

In the following, different approaches of IT are discussed that provide for the solution of traffic and environmental problems:
(a) substitution of physical traffic through telecommunications
(b) use of autonomous systems
(c) use of cooperative systems
(d) traffic system or network related innovations for the guidance and coordination of transport processes in and between different traffic networks.

2.1. The substitution hypothesis

Through use of the existing IT infrastructure, new services and new levels of freedom are coming into being, which seem to be suitable to form a potential substitution for physical traffic. Three important fields can be cited:

- *Teleshopping*: through interactive videotex systems (e.g. Minitel or Datex-J) advertisements of many different products are accessible. Orders can be placed directly with the same system. Teleshopping is very popular in the US, and through the availability of cabel TV it is growing rapidly in Europe. Shopping channels advertise products on talk shows, which can immediately be ordered by telephone. The trip to the grocery store or the supermarket becomes unnecessary.

- *Telebanking*: endowed with account number and password of a local bank account, transactions can be made free of geographic locations through the use of personal computers and networking software. Neither a letter nor a personal appearance is required.

- *Teleconferencing*: conferences can take place with considerable support of information technology in special video conferencing rooms. The participants can save the trip to the conference location which would otherwise be necessary. They would normally be forced to travel to a remote meeting place.

These examples show that potential solutions can be realized for substituting mobility and the corresponding traffic demands. This would reduce the environmental burden (substitution hypothesis).

2.2. Autonomous systems

Autonomous systems in the sector of traffic technology are systems which process only information from within the automobile, i.e. they do not communicate with other cars or elements of the infrastructure. These systems attempt to reduce pollution and the risk of accidents.

Accidents can be avoided through systems like the anti-blocking system (ABS), the airbag, and the anti-slip regulation (ASR). In the first place passengers are protected against injuries, moreover, traffic jams due to accidents are prevented and thus, the flow of traffic is indirectly maintained.

The deployment of digital motor electronics (motor management systems, electronic ignition control systems, etc.) is an attempt to optimize the efficiency of motors and thus to economize fuel consumption and maintain performance.

2.3. Cooperative systems

A possibility for the guidance of traffic emerges from the use of coperative systems, which provide communication between automobiles and the IT infrastructure. With travel guidance, safety and efficiency could be improved, and unnecessary environmental damage might be avoided.

In non-stationary systems traffic objects like automobiles are used as a moving transmitter, receiver, and processor of information. Control applications in the form of distance, lane changing, and traffic crossing control systems help to increase road safety. By provision of traffic information services, accident and general early warning information applications aim at the optimization of the traffic flow [Spaniol et al. 1992].

A special form of cooperative systems are traffic guidance systems. They provide a locally placed possibility for traffic control. Particularly problematic locations can be influenced by route guidance systems and speed limit modification in order to maintain the traffic flow.

2.4. Traffic system related innovations

Due to reciprocal interdependences of the components of the traffic system, there is not only a need for optimization in subsystems, but especially an absolute necessity for the integration and optimization of different traffic objects. IT can and should take on the task of data gathering, processing and evaluation. Many programs are subsidized by the European Community (EC), such as DRIVE (Dedicated Road Infrastructure for Vehicle safety in Europe). These programs analyse integration support aspects and measurements under the shorthand expression RTI (Road Transport Informatics).

An example of traffic system related IT innovations are parking management systems. Mainly used in urban areas, parking garages are linked through information technology and provide electronic information services on their used capacity. A central computer collects all data, evaluates it and transmits signals to traffic advisory boards, which are distributed over the appropriate traffic area. Thus, drivers in search of a parking space can be electronically guided to the next free parking garage.

A similar concept, which is non-cooperative, is the route guidance system, that provides guidance services on traffic advisory boards. They are operated through a traffic guidance center. The data is collected through electronic auto counting stations along the street. With their implementation a more efficient use of traffic and parking space is expected. According to statements of the American Office of Technology Assessment (OTA), the traffic reducing effects of conventional route guidance systems are about 10-20%.

Another IT innovation are freight traffic and distribution centers. These provide an interface between long and short distance traffic, as well as between different carrier types (rail, road, water, air). Logistic services can be optimized by use of IT.

3. Counterproductive results of conventional approaches in the field of information technology

3.1. De-emphasis of the substitution hypothesis

At first the substitution hypothesis is fascinating because of its plausibility. The deployment of videotex systems within *electronic banking* can reduce necessary trips to the bank-window. Personal shopping can be replaced by mail-order houses - reducing trips to specialized dealers in a substantially manner. Also telephone communications connections with the office computer and co-workers enable a reduction in office visits.

During a more detailed analysis of the *teleshopping* example it may be noticed that through the delivery of ordererd products a greater amount of traffic results. Finally, there is really no difference between the drive of a self-collecting customer to the department store and the drive of a delivery service agent. At best, the rise of traffic can be substantially reduced through route optimization within the organization of the professional delivery service.

The substitution factor of 'teleworking' at home can best be realized in the field of *teleconferencing*. The demand for video communications has risen dramatically since the beginning of the Persian Gulf War in the first quarter of 1991. A normalization of the demand went along with the settlement of the Gulf crisis. This demonstrates that IT very well may represent an enduring alternative to professionaly caused passenger traffic, especially air traffic. The potential for substitution can be estimated at a relatively modest rate of 10-20% according to a study by Ollmann [Ollmann 1990]. Furthermore, potentials are said to have occurred only in specific areas, such as in the field of information and communication.

Other unwanted effects must be mentioned besides those described above. Few workers arc allowed to work at home and make use of, or can make use of 'teleworking'. Commuter traffic cannot be substituted by IT for physically active workers with fixed working locations, and for sales and service agents.

In conclusion, acceptance of the substitution hypothesis can only be achieved with emotional reservations. Potentials for substitution - being stressed to a relatively low extent - are only relevant for *informational*, not for *material* exchange relationships.

3.2. Single-sided technical point of view at the development and deployment of autonomous systems

The understanding of innovations to autonomous systems can be realized with the help of programs like PROMETHEUS and DRIVE. Both programs examine the usage of electronics as well as IT for the improvement of system-immanent weaknesses of vehicles with regard to:

- a more efficient use of existing infrastructures
- a reduction of accidental risks
- an increase of driving comfort
- a reduction in the field of harmful exhaust emissions and noise pollution.

These goals partially compete with each other for their realisation and therefore limit expectations for improvements only to specific branches [Spaniol et al. 1992]. Moreover, Rothengatter [Rothengatter 1991] refers to the most serious conceptional deficits of these programs. The focus of the criticism points out that European research efforts are very oppressive in the technical sense. Topics concerning electronic driver support systems like tail gate warning systems, street condition recognition, and automatical track guidance reflect this standpoint.

The goal of protecting the environment through a reduction of traffic related negative effects can hardly justify the efforts. Vehicle related innovations do not reduce the degree of mobility; their attractiveness even enlarges the appeal for individually motorized mobility. The technically biased point of view therefore causes more traffic rather than the desireable effect of a traffic reduction.

The disadvantages of a technically biased point of view can easily be emphasized with the example of ABS (Anti-Blocking System). The German Association of Insurance Companies (HUK) recommended in 1984 to reward ABS owners with corresponding discounts. Actually the confidence in the ABS technique lead to an exponentially increasing willingness to take risks, promptly resulting in an increased number of street accidents. The discount has been abolished three years later [Spaniol et al. 1992]. Do not misunderstand, security techniques should not be argued against. On the contrary, the development and improvement of such systems is desirable, according to the authors. First, because they definitely save lives. Second, because not all drivers have been prompted to adopt a higher degree of risk.

The ABS example shows drastically that great significance must be attached to non-technical factors while designing complex systems.

3.3. Single-sided point of view during development and deployment of cooperative systems

On one hand the necessary travelling time to a destination could be generally reduced in a large-area experiment to examine the potential of the route guidance and information system LISB (Leit- und Informationssystem Berlin). On the other hand a higher level of danger was detected because of frequent glances to the display installed in the car, and to the actual situation on the road. This caused an information overload for the driver. Similar effects can be expected for warning signals, i.e. in the case of a short distance. Moreover, problems arise from another aspect. The driver may switch off the warning systems to continue driving without any disturbance.

Systems not fixed at a specific location may be concerned with another problem that has not yet been stressed in the actual discussion. No implementation strategy exists for cooperative systems until now. Cooperative systems only make sense if they are used by a large number of drivers.

Firstly, because the guidance of traffic is enabled when widely used. Secondly, because programs like tail gate warning reduce accidents when everyone uses it.

Truely, an area covering implementation of cooperative systems cannot be developed over night. The reduced functionality of the system would be accepted by a large number of drivers in the mean time and would not be a serious problem if the technology would be cheap or even free of costs. It may be worthless in an economic sense for the car driver to order and install such a described system if implementation lasts too long and only small market penetration is achieved. The investment may be considered worthless if an extremely long period is required to achieve full functionality.

The technology may not receive the necessary distribution for a successful deployment because of neglect to meaningful and supportive implementation strategies, and low product attractivity (the reader only has to take into consideration that the average human being is everything else but an altruist).

Moreover, it is doubtful whether such systems can be installed in older vehicles at justifiable costs. The maximum age of a car that allows a worthwhile investment appears to be another point. The way out of this dilemma may be seen in legislative measures. A '(cooperative) system commitment' might be introduced, that depend on the age of the car, similar to safety-belt regulations. As a consequence the influence of non-cooperative vehicles would diminish in their significance within a couple of years. Even in this case a standard (in form of a transmission protocol) should be available at least to generate the basis for the communication between objects in the traffic.

Furthermore, a consensus has to prevail about the necessary and possible characteristics of cooperative systems (especially in regard to the problem in the field of data protection). Considerations about the introduction of these systems in urban areas has to be made in addition. State and federal highways in general exhibit only motor vehicles. Who would equip pedestrians and bicyclists with tail gate warning systems within cities (in commercial areas, in the neighbourhood of freight centers, next to park-and-ride stations, etc.)?

The (unsolved) problem of product liability also has to be stressed. Who is responsible for accidents? The *system*, because it did not pass out warnings (or because it passed out false warnings - for example a full-stop breaking on an icy road curve) or the *human being* because he or she neglected the school zone warning signals? The functional (dis-)order can be easily proved in the case of minor damages to the bodywork of the car, but not in the case of more serious accidents that leave scattered car parts on the road, the driver in the hospital, and relatives who want to sue for damages. Are American product liability conditions threatening? Will every vehicle have to be equipped like a passenger air plane with a black box?

3.4. Traffic system related innovations and their inadequate IT transfer

The programming effort of many research projects do not attach the necessary status to the *integration* and *coordination* of different means of traffic with regard to optimization within the overall traffic system [Zoche/König 1990].

Technological developments being mentioned in the projects of PROMETHEUS and DRIVE almost only concentrate on specific sorts of traffic carriers (car, railroad, ship, plane) or on isolated regional sections and therefore on *partial sytems* of the overall traffic system [König/Harmsen 1991].

Measures promoting integration have been investigated within the program DRIVE of the european community, but dealing with the problem often closely sticks to technical details. As a matter of fact greater importance should also be allocated to social factors - like the usage habits. Park and traffic guidance systems for example often enlarge the attractiveness of roads as traffic carriers. According to a study by Apel and Lehmbrock [Apel/Lehmbrock 1990] a reduction in traffic looking for a parking space of 21% to 25% could be determined. Over time this effect has been evened out through a 10% increase in the number of persons searching for a parking place; also the passenger traffic on the access roads to the city center increased significantly.

4. Plea for a new point of view

The goal of all efforts is the improvement in todays' traffic situation, which encompasses the reduction in environmental burden caused by traffic. In principle, there are two possibilities: people will drive less, or economical traffic systems will be used to a greater extent.

The latter seems to be relatively utopian, in view of the huge amount of vehicles on the road. In the near future little emission savings due to the use of clean-exhaust vehicles will hardly be achieved, even with the reduced average consumption use of fuel. The reasons for that are an increasing number of vehicles, an increasing volume of traffic due to the wish to have more mobility, and the long exchange period of vehicles using a high amount of fuel in relation to those using a small amount. Thus, the reduction in environmental burden requires the efficient use of IT supported organizational measures.

4.1. Extension of the examination to non-technical factors

The analysis as described in the third chapter shows that IT alone does not prove to be a solution. Obviously the pure application of a technology is not sufficient - the main importance has to be seen in the concentration on the *'How'* of the technological usage. However, the well-directed use of IT suited to non-technical factors may help to support and purposefully to bring on organizational measures, e.g. by integrating different traffic systems.

Innovative technology shaping must satisfy the following common criteria in order to be societally acceptable, to conform with the constitution, and to be economically successful:

- *Shapeability*
  The technology as a part of the societal process must also be designable for the end user. Possible criteria for the design, like the possibility of corrections of certain (partial) functions as well as the complexity of usage have to be taken into account.

- *Informational Self-Determination*
  The jugdement of the constitutional court ('Verfassungsgericht') in 1983 concerning the census guarantees every individual the right of informational self-determination. The federal German law of privacy and data protection ('Bundesdatenschutzgesetz') insures the right of the person being concerned in regard to the saving of personal data (like the right of information, adjustment, deletion or blocking) and therefore counteracts the often emphasized methaphor of the "glassy" human being or the "barcode on the forehead".

- *Traceability*
  Every action concerning data worth of protection may be traced afterwards. Therefore all the actions may be easily controlled to discover any abuse of data. It must be proved in front of neutral instances - who - generated, changed, passed on and dispatched - at what time - what kind of - data.

- *Binding Effect*
  Agreements which are made through the use of information technology must be judicially effective and judicially enforceable.

The potential for solutions to traffic issues that was expected from information technology will only be exhausted, if economical and social factors are taken into account.

Please note that, for instance, road users want to have cost-efficient traffic links. While using public traffic services they want to change less, to have a starting point close to home, and to arrange their trip flexibly with regard to time. Moreover, they want to have the ease of luggage transport. The level of mobility must be maintained.

IT can make a contribution here. Up to now, IT was often used in the wrong way, which is reflected in the traffic inducing effect of road guidance systems and parking management systems. A more sensible approach seems to be the use of IT to integrate and coordinate different traffic systems. This will achieve better traffic links, demand dependent speed management, and extended decentralized transport services.

With the integration of modern communication systems, like Datex-J (a German interactive videotex system) and radio paging systems, information centers can be created that provide passengers with necessary information through onboard information systems and thus make a more favourable form of transport links possible for them.

Social usage and mobility patterns may also be changed by economic control processes. Since the increasing number of vehicles cannot be stopped by measures that limit and hinder traffic (labyrinthines of one-way streets, traffic islands, fewer parking places, expanded no-traffic zones, etc.), the introduction of road pricing is seen as a reasonable instrument for traffic control.

4.2. Road pricing - an instrument for traffic control

The introduction of road pricing shall guarantee the financing of the present and future road infrastructure. Furthermore, it is possible that the ecological cost of accidents, of congestion (in particular within city centers), and of environmental pollution will have an economic effect.

Traffic control, due to political desire or environmental conditions, may be tackled in such a way that the use of particular roads is subject to tolls. Particular traffic systems become more expensive due to additional fees.

Since an increase of oil taxes as well as the charging of a lump sum in the form of a vignette (a monthly or yearly pass) does not offer traffic guidance and ecologically meaningful differentiation in the amount of street usage, systems for automatic registration of usage and street dependent toll seem to offer adequate potential for solution. A guidance of traffic can be achieved by varying tolls for routes in the inner city regions on traffic burdened streets. The ecological differentiation could be realized with corresponding increase tolls for drives, for instance, in conservation areas.

4.3. Toll systems and social acceptance

Due to economic and practical reasons only automatic drive-through toll systems with automatic debiting are examined today [Mesqui et al. 1991]. To put it simply, each driver must install a magnetic card from which the toll is remotely debited. Vehicles without the magnetic card would be registered in an appropriate way.

Automatic toll systems should guarantee the confidentiality of data and a direct driver checking of transactions. A two-way communication system is provided to ensure the validation and verification of any payment. Moreover, it is considered important to offer integrated systems, which include toll pricing and information dissemination through the radio data system, and traffic guidance services. This will save investment by use of the existing technical infrastructure.

During such an implementation of toll systems, data security issues should be given attention in view of social sensitivity, like the examples ISDN and mobile communications have shown. Any technology that is not developed in a societally acceptable way will be subject to huge acceptance issues. Today's automatic toll systems, being focused on central design concepts, are technically over-sized and violate existing constitutional standards [Gliss 1993].

In using a post-payment approach only identification data is recorded from the vehicle-installed magnetic card. Afterwards this identification data is linked with a person and a bank account, respectively. In this case, there is the possibility to document the movement of any vehicle (or driver) during a certain period.

Due to the fact that data security could not be completely guaranteed using a post-payment scheme, an experiment with a technically sophisticated electronic toll system in Hong Kong was cancelled during the pilot phase [Hills/Thorpe 1991].

4.4. An alternative proposal for a toll system development

To label our concept of a straightforward, user-oriented road pricing system, which will be described in the following, we introduce the expression *L*ean *R*oad *P*ricing *S*ystem (LRPS) [Müller 1993]. The basis for the conceptualization of LRPS consists of two aspects. First, there has to be defined an order which forces people by law to pay the toll. Second, it is generally assumed that people will usually pay the required toll. Possible inequities in some cases will not be cleared up by any means. Thus, any measure that makes circumvention more difficult or avoids misuse is of minor priority.

For tracking down violations we apply the principle of 'de-coupling'. This means that the technical formation of road pricing system and the prosecution of violations by authorities are strictly seperated in accordance with their responsibilities. A security measure to discourage misuse might be a considerably high fine as well as a periodic inspection (i.e. in the German context performed by the TÜV) of the components installed in the car.

Considering the criteria mentioned above we can derive three fundamental and straightforward principles for the conceptualisation of our Lean Road Pricing System:
- Mobility
- Simplicity
- Anonymity.

Mobility: With mobile beacons one can easily react to variations in the infrastructure, or to changes in the flow of traffic. It is therefore possible to realise a politically motivated control of the flow and amount of traffic. It is not necessary to use or to install additional steel girders as they are already used for traffic signs.

Simplicity: Due to usage of already existing (informational) infrastructures it is realistic to establish a cheap and technically simple system. Simplicity is given priority over the complete covering of all exceptions. Storing or trakking any individual data will not be considered at all.

Anonymity: With the principle of anonymity, which is in accordance to the constitution, it is aimed to de-couple the system from prosecution by other autorities (principle of 'de-coupling'). Data security, user acceptability and efficiency comes first. Aspects of prosecution like storage of individual data for proof of violation comes second.

Essentially, the LRPS will be composed of [Stoll/Strauß 1993]:
- a pre-paid card
- a deduction box
- a roadside communications beacon.

The *pre-paid card* electronically stores a certain amount of credit units and can be purchased or renewed with credit units at specific vending-machines at petrol stations, services areas, etc. This pre-paid card has to be carried in the car while driving and to be put into the deduction box.

The *deduction box* is composed of a card reader, a microwave transponder and a processing unit each of which should not be susceptible to manipulation - which may include the application of cryptography in an appropriate manner. It is strictly assigned to a vehicle and contains the pre-paid card while driving. In choosing the deduction box for a specific vehicle the debiting value for different classes of vehicles (cars, lorries, etc.) is fixed. This may happen when the vehicle is registrated or during inspection (i.e. in the German context performed by the TÜV). Vehicles belonging to public services, public transport, or vehicles that should not be charged may be equipped with a special deduction box, which does not require a pre-paid card and whose signals are used for statistics only.

A semi-passive microwave communications approach will be used, whereby the transponder receives a microwave signal from the roadside beacon causing the debiting of one credit unit to the pre-paid card. As the result of the debiting, either the deducted value in the positive case or a specific error code in the negative case will be sent back to the roadside beacon as a status code (see Table 1).

Table 1: Relation between status code and result of debiting

	Normal Case	**Error Cases**
Debiting Status	debiting of a credit unit has succeeded and was correct	debiting failed due to: • disturbance • pre-paid card not in box or no more credits
Status Code	value of the deducted credit unit	specific error code

The deduction box contains a buzzer. Correct or faulty debitings are shown to the driver by different short acoustic signals. It is equipped with a display on which the currently available credit will be shown.

Foreign road-users can borrow a deduction box with a security deposit. They have to buy a pre-paid card. Vehicles without a pre-paid card, vehicles with a pre-paid card without credit, or vehicles without a deduction box may be registered in different ways. First, a random visual control may be applied by the authorities, for instance the police. Furthermore, in combining a vehicle recognition system with the roadside communication beacon it is possible to detect whether a vehicle has passed the beacon area, but the beacon has not received any signal about the debiting status. Using this information, the passing vehicle may be registered, e.g. by a flash unit, in analogy to speed checks. However, this prosecution is subject to the afore-mentioned principle of 'de-coupling', which means, that the registration of vehicles without deduction box is not part of the LRPS in any case, but has to be put into effect by regional or local authorities.

In contrast to other approaches of automatic toll collection systems, the *roadside communications beacon* is designed as a geographically flexible system with its own power supply. It continously sends a directed microwave signal causing the debiting of one credit unit to the pre-paid card when the deduction box with the pre-paid card has been put into the transmit range of the beacon. The beacon authenticates itself to the deduction box unequivocally through a code enclosed in the transmitted signal. That way, improper deductions made by 'false' beacons can be prevented. Multiple deductions, e.g. in case of traffic jams, can be avoided, because consecutive deductions of one beacon can easily be technically forestalled in the deduction box. Regarding transmission, a microwave system with a center frequency of around 6 GHz will be useful, with data rates of about 250 Kbit/s (down/up-link). Considering the more advanced infrared technology, an infrared based transmission system will also be suitable [Ongaro 1991].

The roadside communications beacon records a status code for each debiting (amount deducted or received specific error code). This results in a total storage requirement of e.g. 2 bytes for each debiting in the beacon. This data can regularly be transmitted to a regional or central data processing center. Either the individual transactions can be sent (quotas for different classes of cars can be processed for statistical use), or summary data for the roadside communications beacon can be sent (e.g. the total amount of toll collected, the relative quota of different classes of cars and the number of errors).

The transmission will be done automatically, e.g. every 60 minutes, or after reaching a given number of deductions, e.g. 500. In addition to the above mentioned values, the location and the beacon identifier (along with the date and time) will be transmitted. The data accumulating in the data processing center can be prepared and, among other things, used for traffic control. Due to mobile useability of the beacon there is the possibility for road usage statistics and dynamical road pricing.

Due to the mobile usage of the roadside communications beacon, the data transmission between the beacon and the data processing center can be provided only by a mobile communications service. A service suitable in Germany is the public mobile data communication service MODACOM, which will be introduced for nearly full area coverage in 1994. Data can be exchanged independent of location and of network access via the German packet-switched public data network (Datex-P). The data rate is 9600 bit/s. MODACOM is conceptualized for frequent, high quality and economical transmissions of small amounts of data and for control messages. The costs for using the MODACOM infrastructure can be estimated to be less than the costs for the integration of the beacons into a GSM infrastructure (Global System for Mobile communications). Such a GSM infrastructure is currently being built (D1 and D2 networks) in Germany and is planning to use a greater amount of radio cells for the future (E network).

5. Conclusions

In this paper we have outlined conventional approaches to the solution of traffic issues. We have analysed both the problems, and the lack of solutions to these problems. We have come to the realization that it is necessary to integrate economical and social factors.

Since the increase of vehicle usage cannot be controlled by measures that limit or hinder traffic, an approach based on the road pricing concept was proposed in order to influence social usage and mobility patterns. Innovative technology shaping must satisfy common criteria like shapeability, informational self-determination, traceability, and the binding effect, in order to be societally acceptable, to conform with the constitution and to be economically successful.

Our concept of a straightforward, user-oriented road pricing system, named *L*ean *R*oad *P*ricing *S*ystem, is based on the three essential principles of mobility, simplicity and anonymity. These principles are derived from the criteria mentioned above. In particular, this takes into account data security interests in order to guarantee the social acceptance of the proposed system.

References

Apel, D./Lehmbrock, M.: Stadtverträgliche Verkehrsplanung, DIFU Deutsches Institut für Urbanistik, Berlin 1990

Gliss, Hans: Autobahngebühren: "Permanente Volkszählung" durch die Hintertür. In: Datenschutz-Berater, No. 3, März 1993, p. 1-2

Hills, P./Thorpe, N.: Traffic-Demand Management in Urban Areas, the Role for Pricing. In: Proceedings of the DRIVE Conference 'Advanced Telematics in Road Transport', Brussels, February 4-6, 1991. Amsterdam: Elsevier, p. 658-676

König, R./Harmsen, D.-M.: Informationstechnik und Verkehr. In: FhG-ISI 1991, p. 198-204

Mesqui, J. et al.: Automatic Debiting Systems. A new Approach for Toll Roads. In: Proceedings of the DRIVE Conference 'Advanced Telematics in Road Transport'. Brussels, February 4-6, 1991. Amsterdam: Elsevier, p. 635-657

Müller, Günter: Leitgedanken zur Konzipierung eines Lean-Road-Pricing-Systems (LRPS). Diskussionspapier für die Arbeitsgruppe 8.1.2 ("Informationstechnik und Verkehr") der Informationstechnischen Gesellschaft (ITG) vom 13. März 1993

Ollmann, R.: Substitution von Personenverkehr durch Telekommunikation. In: *Henckel, D.* (ed.): Telematik und Umwelt, Deutsches Institut für Urbanistik, Berlin 1990, p. 166-197

Ongaro, D.: Vehicle/Roadside Communication for Route Guidance. In: Proceedings of the DRIVE Conference 'Advanced Telematics in Road Transport'. Brussels, February 4-6, 1991. Amsterdam: Elsevier, p. 294-312

Rothengatter, W.: Konzeptionelle Defizite im Verkehrssystem. In: *Albach, H.* et al. (Hrsg.), Technikfolgenforschung und Technikfolgenabschätzung, Berlin 1991, p. 237-260

Spaniol, O. et al.: Bedeutet die Informatisierung des Straßenverkehrs Fluch oder Segen? In: RWTH-Themen 5/92, p. 54-57

Stoll, F./Strauß, R.: Dezentralität versus Zentralität. Synthetischer Ansatz eines Lean-Road-Pricing-Systems (LRPS). In: InfoTech, No. 2, Mai 1993

Zoche, P./König, R.: Chancen des Einsatzes öffentlicher Datennetze bei der umweltverträglichen Steuerung des Personennahverkehrs. In: *Pillmann, W./Jaeschke, A.* (ed.), Informatik für den Umweltschutz, 5. Symposium, Wien, September 1990, Proceedings, Berlin 1990, p. 789-798

Contributors

Midori Aoyagi is working at the National Institute for Environmental Studies, 16-2 Onogawa, Tsukuba, Ibaraki 305

Yuko Arayama is professor of agricultural policy in the Faculty of Economics of Nagoya University

Knut Blind is assistant at the Institute of public finance in the Faculty of Economics of Freiburg University

Gerold Blümle is professor of mathematical economics in the Faculty of Economics of Freiburg University

Hans-Josef Brink is professor of business administration in the Faculty of Economics of Freiburg University

Theodor Dams is emeritus professor of economic policy in the Faculty of Economics of Freiburg University

Hans-Hermann Francke is professor of public finance in the Faculty of Economics of Freiburg University

Siegfried Hauser is professor of statistics and econometries in the Faculty of Economics of Freiburg University

Thomas Hummel is assistant at the Institute of Informatics and Society of Freiburg University

Tamiki Kishida is associate professor of business administration in the Faculty of Economics of Nagoya University

Takashi Matsugi is professor of agricultural policy in the Faculty of Economics of Nagoya University

Kirsten Meyer is assistant at the department of economic computer science in the Faculty of Economics of Freiburg University

Günter Müller is professor of telematics in the Institute of Informatics and Society of Freiburg University

Yoichi Nishijima is Senior advisor, Safety, Quality and Environmental Management Division at the Chiyoda Corporations, Yokohama

Ryuhei Okumura is associate professor of international economics in the Faculty of Economics of Nagoya University

Franz Schober is professor of economic computer science in the Faculty of Economics of Freiburg University

Detlef Schoder is assistant at the Institute of Informatics and Society of Freiburg University

Marcus Siefert wrote his diploma thesis at the Institute of economic computer science in the Faculty of Economics of Freiburg University

Frank Stoll is assistant at the Institute of Informatics and Society of Freiburg University

Ralf Strauß is assistant at the Institute of Informatics and Society of Freiburg University

Yoshida Takeshi is lecturer in the Faculty of Economics of Nagoya University

Hiroshi Yanagioka is Chief Engineer at the Chiyoda Corporation, Yokohama

MIX
Papier aus verantwortungsvollen Quellen
Paper from responsible sources
FSC® C105338

Printed by Libri Plureos GmbH
in Hamburg, Germany